Springer Series: FOCUS ON WOMEN

Violet Franks, Ph.D., Series Editor

Confronting the major psychological, medical, and social issues of today and tomorrow. *Focus on Women* provides a wide range of books on the changing concerns of women.

Joan C. Chrisler is Assistant Professor of Psychology at Connecticut College in New London. Her research has focused on issues of importance to women's health.

Doris Howard is a psychotherapist in private practice in San Francisco. She is also Assistant Director of an Acute Diversion Unit, which provides mental health services to the homeless.

NEW DIRECTIONS IN FEMINIST PSYCHOLOGY

Practice, Theory, and Research

Joan C. Chrisler
Doris Howard
Editors

SPRINGER PUBLISHING COMPANY
New York

Springer Publishing Company, Inc.
536 Broadway
New York, NY 10012-3955

92 93 94 95 96 / 5 4 3 2 1

Library of Congress Cataloging-in-Publication Data

New directions in feminist psychology : practice, theory, and research   / Joan C.
Chrisler & Doris Howard, editors.
     p. cm. — (Springer series, focus on women ; v. 13)
    Includes bibliographical references and index.
    ISBN 0-8261-7540-6
    1. Women — Psychology. 2. Feminist psychology. 3. Feminist
psychotherapy. I. Chrisler, Joan C. II. Howard, Doris.
III. Series.
HQ1206.N39   1992
150'.82 — dc20   91-5168
                                                      CIP

Printed in the United States of America

Contents

    Gloria Cowan and Geraldine Butts Stahly

18 Courtship in the 1980s: Female and Male Responses to a
    Personals Ad   215
    Karen Keljo Tracy

19 The Effects of Gender-Role Salience on Women's Causal
    Attributions for Success and Failure   226
    Beverly Ayers-Nachamkin

20 Stereotypes and Desirability Ratings for Female and Male Roles   239
    Michele F. Larrow and Morton Wiener

    Conclusion   250

    Index   253

Preface

Twenty-five years of examining the real meaning of gender in contemporary Western culture has produced a large body of literature. Feminist scholarship has been invigorating the field of psychology since the late 1960s and has led to the development of feminist therapy and feminist research methodologies. Collections of previously unpublished papers, such as those contained in this volume, are frequently organized in order to gather together and draw attention to new ways of thinking about gender issues.

Some social scientists seem to consider gender research and feminist theory pertinent only to women, as though men's behavior is uninfluenced by gender-role socialization. The chapters we have selected for this collection reflect gender as it actually affects our daily lives, our theory, our research, and our practice of psychotherapy. This volume is organized in three sections—practice, theory, and research—although the areas sometimes overlap within individual chapters because new research strategies and new theory about the development of personality and human behavior inevitably lead to new techniques in the practice of psychotherapy.

Many of these chapters were presented at the thirteenth national conference of the Association for Women in Psychology in March 1988, in Bethesda, Maryland. They have been revised and updated for this volume and make a significant contribution to the evolving body of feminist literature. The title of this collection was taken from the title of that conference. The editors are grateful to the conference coordinators, Judith Sprei and Bonnie Katz, for their helpful comments on the preparation of this book. We also thank Jennifer Archibald for her help in preparing the index.

We have selected chapters that we think are particularly interesting and that represent recent and current approaches to the study of the psychology of women. Each chapter presents new findings, new scholarly approaches, or new extensions of theories of feminist therapy. This collection is intended to be educational and of practical use to mental health professionals, scholars, and students who seek to further their knowledge of the study of gender and to discover new directions in feminist psychology.

Contributors

Rosalie J. Ackerman is a clinical neuropsychologist at the Rehabilitation Neuropsychology Unit and the Center for Biofeedback at the Mount Carmel Medical Center in Columbus, Ohio. For the past 12 years she has been doing therapy with families of brain-injured people.

Beverly Ayers-Nachamkin is Associate Professor of Psychology, Director of Women's Studies, and Head of the Division of Social Sciences at Wilson College, Chambersburg, Pennsylvania.

Martha E. Banks is Associate Professor of Psychology at the College of Wooster in Wooster, Ohio. She has 15 years of clinical experience with brain-injured patients and their families.

Carole Baroody Corcoran is Assistant Professor of Psychology at Mary Washington College in Fredericksburg, Virginia. She has conducted research in the area of sexual assault.

Gloria Cowan is Professor of Psychology at California State University, San Bernardino. She has conducted several studies of gender differences in power strategies and has examined the images of women in pornography and slasher films.

Paula S. Derry is an independent scholar in Baltimore.

Lesley A. Diehl is Vice President for Academic Affairs at Columbia College, Columbia, South Carolina. Her recent research has focused on women in the history of psychology and sexual harassment on college campuses.

Lisa Forrester recently received her bachelor's degree in psychology from Wheeling Jesuit College, Wheeling, West Virginia.

Marni-Lynne Gaines recently received her bachelor's degree in psychology from Bethany College, Bethany, West Virginia.

Gwendolyn L. Gerber is Associate Professor of Psychology at John Jay College of Criminal Justice in New York and is also actively engaged in the practice of psychotherapy. Her research has focused on gender stereotypes and how they affect relationships between the sexes.

Eugenia Proctor Gerdes is Associate Professor of Psychology and Dean of the Faculty of the College of Arts and Sciences at Bucknell University, Lewisburg, Pennsylvania. Her research focuses on race and sex discrimination and on stress for women in traditionally male work roles.

Judith M. Glassgold is a psychotherapist in private practice in central New Jersey. She has taught psychology and women's studies at Rutgers University and is especially interested in psychoanalysis and feminist theory.

Beverly Greene is Associate Clinical Professor of Psychology, St. John's University, Jamaica, N.Y. She also maintains a private practice in Brooklyn, New York.

Mykol C. Hamilton is Assistant Professor of Psychology at Centre College, Danville, Kentucky. She is a social psychologist and has done many studies on sex bias in language.

Debra B. Hull is Associate Professor of Psychology and Chair of the Psychology Department at Wheeling Jesuit College, Wheeling, West Virginia.

John H. Hull is Associate Professor of Psychology and Chair of the Psychology Department at Bethany College, Bethany, West Virginia.

Barbara Hunter is a doctoral candidate in social psychology at Pennsylvania State University. She is engaged in research on gender issues and legal issues.

Marianne Jackson is a clinical psychologist at the 125th Street Clinic of the Manhattan Psychiatric Center, New York. She also maintains a private practice and teaches psychology at New York University.

Rosa Joshi received her undergraduate degree from Bucknell University, Lewisburg, Pennsylvania. She is on the stage managerial staff for the theater program of the Juilliard School, New York.

Michele F. Larrow is a graduate student in clinical psychology at Frances L. Hiatt School of Psychology, Clark University, Worcester, Massachusetts. Her research interests include gender issues, communication in marital interactions, and language and children's play.

Marguerite A. Maynard Norchi received her undergraduate degree from Bucknell University, Lewisburg, Pennsylvania. She is now studying drama in a masters of education program at Xavier University.

Rebecca S. Miner received her undergraduate degree from Bucknell University, Lewisburg, Pennsylvania. She is a real estate investment analyst for Massachusetts Mutual Life Insurance Company.

William E. Mitchell is a postdoctoral fellow in clinical child psychology at the University of Rochester School of Medicine and Dentistry in Rochester, New York.

Mary C. Dominguez Ranallo received her undergraduate degree from Bucknell University, Lewisburg, Pennsylvania. She is currently a case manager, supervising services for refugees and migrant workers; she plans to enter a graduate program in school psychology.

Mary Ricketts is presently teaching psychology in the First Year University Program at Central Newfoundland Community College, Grand Falls, Newfoundland, Canada.

Geraldine Butts Stahly is Assistant Professor of Psychology at California State University, San Bernardino. She is engaged in research on domestic violence and victimology.

Shannon Stuart-Smith is a graduate of the University of Kentucky School of Law. She practices law in the Lexington, Kentucky area.

Leonore Tiefer is Clinical Associate Professor of Urology and Psychiatry at the Montefiore Medical Center/Albert Einstein College of Medicine, Bronx, New York. Trained in both experimental and clinical psychology, she has specialized in animal and human sexuality.

Karen Keljo Tracy is Assistant Professor of Psychology at Marygrove College in Detroit. Her research interests center on intimate relationships between women and men.

Morton Wiener is Professor of Psychology at Frances L. Hiatt School of Psychology, Clark University, Worcester, Massachusetts. He has conducted research on psychosocial transactions, verbal and nonverbal communication, and behaviors that are labeled pathological.

Part I
Practice

INTRODUCTION: NEW DIRECTIONS IN
FEMINIST PRACTICE

The modern development of feminist therapy has opened many doors for those with particular problems that had been previously ignored, misunderstood, or underestimated. The feminist practice of psychotherapy has led to increasing clarification and reversal of the negative impact of sexism on women's mental health. In recent years, exciting new directions in psychotherapy have emerged for women. Some are variations of traditional techniques; more are entirely new.

To understand the psychology of women, it is necessary to understand the importance of gender-role socialization and stereotyping. Women's changing roles have introduced new interpersonal problems and challenges. New directions in feminist theory and practice are evolving to meet these contemporary demands. The chapters in this section address several of those problems and challenges.

The first two chapters are concerned with separate issues that have devastating effects on women. William Mitchell presents an analysis of the social pressures that lead to eating disorders because of the negative and distorted self-image many women develop. He presents a feminist perspective on the ways in which therapists can redirect eating-disordered clients.

Racial differences and similarities in the therapeutic relationship are reexamined by Beverly Greene in a cogent analysis of the issues that arise in the therapy situation because of the differences in socialization between women of color and white women. Greene de-

1

scribes the negative impact on the practice of therapy resulting from the race and gender stereotypes that may have been internalized by both the therapist and the client.

Paula Slomin Derry discusses changes in the perspective of the woman psychotherapist after she has become a mother. Derry contrasts the perceptions of clinician/mothers before and after they become parents, and shows how the changes affect their perceptions of their clients who are mothers.

The following chapter presents evidence to demonstrate the value of feminist goals and behavior in improving the quality of couples' relationships. Doris Howard presents case examples to show how interpersonal conflicts can be reduced when each partner learns to practice understanding, sensitivity, and other so-called feminine characteristics.

In another chapter about psychotherapy with couples, Gwendolyn Gerber describes the ways in which gender stereotyping disrupts relationships. In a further development of her paradigm of balance within relationships, Gerber shows how a feminist perspective can improve interpersonal relating.

Marianne Jackson and Doris Howard discuss the results of their survey of psychotherapists who have worked in private practice with severely disturbed clients. They conclude that feminist therapy with such clients, though difficult, can be rewarding for both client and therapist.

In the final chapter in this section, Rosalie Ackerman and Martha Banks describe techniques in the practice of family therapy as a component of neuropsychological rehabilitation of brain-injured persons. The focus is on women as primary caregivers and the ways in which cultural expectations may overburden them. Ackerman and Banks use a feminist analysis to define alternatives that support women in the roles of caregivers.

Despite the great progress women have made in recent years, we are still under pressure to occupy traditional roles that fit outmoded sociocultural expectations. Ageism, racism, and sexism are historically interconnected in the stereotypes of women. The goal of contemporary feminist theory and practice of therapy is to reverse those expectations and stereotypes. The authors of these chapters hope to advance the process of that reversal and to suggest new directions in feminist practice.

■ 1
Psychotherapy for Bulimia from a Feminist Perspective

William E. Mitchell

In the last decade, bulimia[1] has become the subject of considerable discussion in psychological and medical journals as well as in the popular press. The discussions have centered on prevalence, etiology, and treatment. Although the prevalence of bulimia has been relatively well established at approximately 8% to 10% of the female population,[2] theories concerning etiology abound, as do theories about effective therapeutic interventions. A potential theoretical and therapeutic approach to the etiology and treatment of bulimia, one that appears to have been underdeveloped in the literature, is a sociocultural framework of etiology and a feminist approach to therapy. Although most investigators agree that bulimia is multidetermined, the importance of societal pressures in the development of the syndrome seems to have been downplayed while the intrapsychic theories and "victim blaming" theories of etiology and treatment have prevailed.

This author posits that a closer examination of these sociocultural influences is warranted and that therapeutic interventions that remain cognizant of the power of these influences are definitely needed. This chapter addresses some of the sociocultural influences and suggests that psychotherapists can better help their bulimic clients by remaining aware of such factors. The focus is on considerations and entry points to the syndrome of bulimia from a feminist perspective. The goal is to offer a framework and guiding principles to facilitate the understanding of bulimia in light of the values and the expectations that permeate our society. It will be left to individual clinicians to utilize their own therapeutic styles and techniques within the context presented here. The intent is not to presume to tell others how to do therapy but to encourage new thinking along feminist lines.

HISTORY/THEORY

Because it is clear that the vast majority of bulimics are female, it would appear that something about being female in today's society puts one at risk for bulimia. Many investigators have documented the emphasis that our culture places on attractiveness in general and on thinness in particular (e.g., Boskind-White & White, 1983; Garner, Rockert, Olmstead, Johnson, & Coscina, 1985). This emphasis places women in the position of believing that they are what they weigh. Being thin and attractive (these are often synonymous) becomes highly valued. This makes being average an undesirable status and being overweight a highly stigmatized one.

Women have, throughout history, been identified with the natural, the physical, and the corporeal. Greenspan (1983) refers to this phenomenon when she speaks of "woman as body." Women have for centuries been judged by their bodies, and for centuries they have attempted to make their bodies conform to what was seen as desirable at the time. Chernin (1981) reminds us of the ever-changing definition of feminine beauty:

> If we were admired for having fat around the neck, as women were in 1911, and were permitted to have large abdomens and well-padded hips, tens of thousands of women would not kneel down next to the toilet tonight and put our fingers down our throat, and vomit. (p. 87)

As women began to enter the workplace in increasing numbers during the past 25 years, conflicts regarding assertion and competition became more salient. The feminist movement encouraged women to be more assertive, a stance that dovetailed with the requirements of traditional masculine jobs. It is clear, however, that despite the "new freedoms" the past several decades have brought, many of the old rules are still in effect, and women are now expected to obey both the old and the new.

The demands of the '80s and '90s are evident in the images of the superwoman that are splashed across the movie and television screens, billboards, and popular magazines. The message is "You can have it all; you can be it all!" If a woman is really functioning fully, she can be a mother and a wife (the traditional roles) and can also be a sexy, intelligent, dynamic, and powerful career person. Cauwel (1983) captured these assertions when she said, "The proper figure seems to represent reserves of tremendous energy that transform the average woman with a bit of ambition into a superwoman." Women receive a number of mixed messages about how to achieve happiness, approval, and success, but the point is made painfully clear that everything will be better once they are thin (Orbach, 1978).

With the emphasis on beauty and thinness in our society, it should come as no surprise that many women are on diets, are considering starting one, or are practicing restrained eating much of the time. This self-denial sets the stage for a binge in several ways. First, the dieter is trying to overcome the physiological defenses of the body to maintain a certain body weight. The body may well be "playing catch-up" to defend the physiological setpoint (Bennett & Gurin, 1982; Polivy, Herman, Olmstead, & Jazwinski, 1984).

Second, various researchers have documented an increase in food and eating fantasies and food-related thoughts while dieting (Bruch, 1978; Franklin, Schiele, Brozek, & Keys, 1948). This sets up dichotomous thinking styles in which food is either good (nonfattening) or bad (fattening) (Garner, Garfinkel, & Bemis, 1982). This then leads to an all-or-none eating pattern based almost exclusively on cognitive controls because physiological signals are being ignored (see Marlatt & Gordon, 1985). In addition, as the media portrays weight loss and gain as a matter of willpower, a woman can very quickly begin to define herself in terms of her eating behavior. She can be good and strong and not eat "bad" foods, or she can be weak and eat what she wants.

Third, women are denying themselves a basic need that also happens to be pleasurable, as most people enjoy eating. It seems quite possible that a woman may binge as a reward for having done something of which she is proud. Women are socialized to believe that the food that they prepare for their families represents their love for them (Orbach, 1978). It isn't a large leap to postulate that women may feed themselves as a form of self-love and nurturance. The woman diets in order to be the slim, trim object of beauty that she is told to be, she ignores and/or fights her body's natural messages to eat, she eventually succumbs to her body's needs, and then she binges. Society clearly stigmatizes women for being other than thin, and there is a firm injunction against women stating, and meeting, their own needs. Then, because a binge is experienced as self-indulgent, the woman must find a way to atone for her "sins." She purges both as a way to avoid gaining the dreaded pounds that a binge would add and as a cathartic effort.

Bulimic women often report feelings of depersonalization, irritability, self-doubt, weakness, helplessness, inadequacy, and feelings of uncontrollable hunger or irresistible cravings for certain foods prior to a binge (Gandour, 1984). Many of these feelings might be engendered by the conflicting messages and misogynist notions that women face every day. Binges most frequently occur around mealtime, in the late afternoon, and after school or work (Johnson & Larson, 1982; Pyle, Mitchell, & Eckert, 1981). The binge is intensely personal. The woman is feeding her own wants and needs exclusively and is unconcerned with the needs of others. Unfortunately, this pleasuring exercise is not without cost.

THERAPY

This leads us to the issue of therapy for bulimic women. Therapies range from behavior therapy to psychoanalysis and from individual to group, family, and couples therapy. Many of these approaches seem to have something to offer in the struggle to help bulimic clients. Rather than attempting to lay out a comprehensive treatment plan, the remainder of this chapter will be concerned with issues to keep in mind when working with bulimics. Clinicians can utilize the skills and techniques with which they are comfortable in their individualized treatment approaches. The overarching principles that bind these ideas together, however, will be the philosophical tenets of feminism.

Feminist therapy is not so much a collection of techniques as it is an attitude. It addresses the tremendous impact that society's gender expectations have on the behavior of men and women alike. Feminist therapy attempts to free men and women from the constraints and handicaps that traditional gender–role stereotypes have on their well-being. It is a therapy rooted in health, rather than illness. The client and the therapist are encouraged to separate the client's disorder from what is disordered in society.

An essential part of working with a bulimic woman is helping her to understand the pressures and contradictory expectations that a woman faces. The focus is on helping the bulimic to identify and understand feelings that are associated with these contradictions. The therapist should emphasize the fact that these feelings are quite appropriate and understandable and are not signs of failure on her part. This is a difficult and delicate task for therapists. Awareness of these contradictions and their concomitant feelings may come more easily to a female therapist, but it is not impossible for a male therapist to understand many of the experiences of a woman in today's society (Greenspan, 1983). In addition, the female therapist must also be cognizant of sexist premises that she may have inadvertently accepted while being trained in male-dominated educational institutions.

Male and female therapists alike may find that some clients are reluctant to acknowledge their experience of these binds. It is essential that the therapist respect the client's experience and not introduce premature interpretations or explanations into the client's perceptions of her world before she is ready to acknowledge them. A large part of feminist therapy is accepting and affirming the client's thoughts and feelings about her predicament. One focus is on encouraging the client to trust her own feelings and to have increasing faith in her ability to decide what is right for her (Bruch, 1973).

It is also important that the therapist encourage empowerment of the client. The client must learn that she is going to be primarily responsible for her progress. This is important in many situations but is of critical importance in working with bulimics. Vognsen (1985) points out that food surrounds us daily and that for a woman to feel confident that she is in control of her behavior she must believe that therapeutic progress is due to her efforts and has not been brought about by the therapist. Vognsen states:

> Control must be experienced as emanating from inner sources if the bulimic is to encounter food with pleasure and confidence. The bulimic client should not be overwhelmed by the treatment regimes or therapist prowess. We recommend that the therapist take a low posture and act in such a way that the client herself constantly feels the need for change and the courage to maintain that change. (p. 79)

Despite the widespread coverage that eating disorders have received over the past 10 years, there is still a tremendous sense of isolation that accompanies the bulimic's experience. This stems, in part, from the solitary nature of the activities associated with bulimia. Women usually binge and purge alone (Abraham & Beumont, 1982; Fairburn & Cooper, 1982; Pyle et al, 1981). A bulimic woman may also feel isolated as a result of the "other focus" she often adopts (Inbody & Ellis, 1985). Because her role is defined by her service to others, to have close relations with men or other women in which she is something other than caregiver may seem selfish and self-serving and thus unacceptable.

A feminist therapist can help a client realize that she is not alone in the bulimic behavior or, even more important, in the feelings she has about her role in society and the contradictory expectations she experiences. Group therapy is particularly useful in this respect. In a therapy group for bulimic women, the members can see others who share the same pain. The group can serve as a sounding board in which feelings are shared. In addition, a thin group member can attest to the fact that thinness did not solve all of her problems (White & Boskind-White, 1981). The group can also be a place where distorted body images can be realistically examined in a warm and nurturing atmosphere. A male–female therapy team can be of particular value. The female therapist may have an easier time gaining the trust of the women in the group, and she may abe able to convey more quickly some feminist ideals. The male therapist can provide insight into men's attitudes about weight and femininity. He should be a nonsexist male in whose behavior women can note differences from the behavior of other men in their lives. He can also serve as a generic male in role-plays. Most important, the therapist team can model an appropriate, nonsexist relationship between two adults (Boskind-White & White, 1983).

There are five general tasks that the client and therapist must accomplish before the client will be able to express herself and attempt to meet her needs. First is the examination of the proscriptions women face with respect to meeting their own needs. It is important to identify why women may often think that their needs are unimportant and/or selfish. Lemkau and Landau (1986) have referred to the self-sacrificing behaviors and the pressures that cause them as "the selfless syndrome." They characterize the syndrome as one where the women "have in common a set of entrenched ideological beliefs prescribing self-denial and striving for satisfaction through vicarious means. For such a woman, the sense of self is perilously predicated upon meeting the needs of others, even when these conflict with her own" (p. 227). Women are supposed to be nurturant, loving, self-sacrificing, attractive, and pleasant to look at. Because this message is so often and so forcefully stated, it is easy to understand why women may feel that they are shirking their duties when they become aware of and act on their own needs.

Second, once the myriad contradictory demands and expectations are discussed and their implications examined, the next step is the acceptance and potential expression of these needs. Before these needs can be pinpointed, it is necessary to lay the intrapsychic groundwork for them. It is important to acknowledge the inevitability of having wants and needs. Women are highly socialized to believe that it isn't feminine to act directly on behalf of themselves and that acts on behalf of the self are often seen as selfish by society. The client must come to terms with the acceptability of her own needs as genuine, natural, and proper. The goal is for the client to say to herself, and eventually to others, "I have needs and I know they are legitimate." This is quite likely to be the most difficult part of the therapy and in all probability will be an ongoing process because the roles the woman is leaving behind are so strongly prescribed and are, in all likelihood, continuously reinforced (Lemkau & Landau, 1986).

Third, the needs themselves must be delineated. Obviously, these needs will vary somewhat from person to person, but there are some general themes that may surface. The need to feel good about oneself without having served someone else and apart from the role of caretaker is one recurring theme. The need to feel pleasure and self-worth resulting from one's own strengths and capabilities rather than stemming from the approval of others is another natural and healthy desire (Sturdivant, 1980). There are, of course, innumerable other needs that exist and that are entirely appropriate, but the bulimic women may have a great deal of trouble in identifying them as a result of the intense pressure to put them aside to better serve the needs of others.

The fourth step is the development of the skills and procedures involved in the possibility of asking others to meet some of their needs and the process of meeting their own needs themselves. Lemkau and Landau (1986) suggest that once a client becomes aware that she can stop ignoring her needs, she quickly realizes that she doesn't know how to start attending to them. The acceptance that such needs exist will be problematic, and thus it is important to have thoroughly covered that ground earlier. The first step, in light of the socialized passivity that defines the role of women, may be to ask others to meet her needs. This may be somewhat easier than the idea of meeting the needs herself and can serve as a stepping-stone to meeting her own needs later (Osborne & Harris, 1975; Stere, 1985). Assertiveness skills training should be an essential part of the therapy. It is a component, however, that requires that the therapist and the client be cognizant of the binds that define the role of women, as well as aware of the potential ramifications of these newly acquired skills. This must be accomplished before the client begins to develop her skills and to assert her needs to others.

Fifth, the potential rejection of the woman's desire to meet her own needs or to have them met by others must be addressed. Although the woman may have a better understanding of the legitimacy and primacy of her needs, others may not share her enlightened view. The client must be prepared for these rebuffs (Rosewater, 1984). These rejections are certainly not surprising, given the climate in which the woman lives, and should not be taken as signs that her wants and needs are unreasonable, undeserved, or unthinkable. This potential problem, that of a healthier person in a largely unchanged world, haunts much of feminist therapy, where so often an improved understanding and state of mind brings with it increased realization of the struggles left to fight.

This brings us to another issue in therapy for bulimics from a feminist perspective. Unlike many or most therapy styles, feminist therapy does not view the optimal state as one without conflict (Sturdivant, 1980). That would be unrealistic. To suggest that a state of nonconflict is possible would be unfair to clients and would set them up for disappointment and despair. The goal of therapy is to point out the problems that society has and to help clients see how these shortcomings affect them and their well-being. Therapy then becomes a process of developing skills that better equip the individual to handle the pressures, conflicts, and contradictions in society once they have become apparent.

CONCLUSION

In summary, bulimia is a multidetermined syndrome that can be understood from a number of perspectives. One way of framing the etiology and treatment of bulimia and one that seems to have both important explanatory power and therapeutic implications is the feminist position. Western cultures socialize men and women to think, feel, and behave in different ways with respect to themselves and to each other. These socializing pressures put a number of contradictory demands and expectations on women. These pressures may culminate in a number of binds that cause a great deal of physical and psychological pain. One way that these binds are manifested and subsequently dealt with by women is through the syndrome of bulimia, a physically destructive and psychically traumatic set of behaviors that wreak havoc on the woman's life and self-esteem. A feminist perspective on this syndrome offers the clinician and client an entry point to the syndrome that does not "blame the victim" and allows for understanding and treatment in such a way as to empower the client. In addition to the therapeutic efficacy that such an approach might have, it also sets the stage for additional growth in other areas and thereby may prevent future problems.

ACKNOWLEDGMENTS

I would like to thank Drs. Glenace Edwall and Susanne Haskell. Without their untiring help, this chapter would never have been written.

NOTES

1. In this chapter, we will utilize the DSM-III (1980) definition and criteria for bulimia because the newer DSM-III-R (1987) criteria have not been in use long enough for an adequate research base to have been established. It seems unlikely that the views presented here would require substantial modification in light of the newer criteria.

2. With range of 1% to 19% of the female population (Halmi, Falk, & Schwartz, 1981; Hart & Ollendick, 1985). Please see Cooper & Fairburn (1983); Katzman, Wolchick, & Braver (1984); Pope, Hudson, & Yurgelun-Todd (1984); and Stangler & Printz (1980) for additional information on prevalence. Although there are bulimic males, their numbers are so small as to be negligible (Pope, Hudson, Yurgelun-Todd, & Hudson, 1984; Stangler & Printz, 1980).

REFERENCES

Abraham, S., & Beumont, P. J. V. (1982). How patients describe bulimia or binge eating. *Psychological Medicine, 12*, 625–635.

American Psychiatric Association. (1980). *Diagnostic and statistical manual of mental disorders*, (3rd ed.). Washington, DC: Author.

American Psychiatric Association. (1987). *Diagnostic and statistical manual of mental disorders*, (3rd ed. rev.). Washington, DC: Author.

Bennett, W., & Gurin, J. (1982). *The dieter's dilemma*. New York: Basic Books.

Boskind-White, M., & White, W. C., Jr. (1983). *Bulimarexia: The binge/purge cycle.* New York: Norton.

Bruch, H. (1973). *Eating disorders: Anorexia, obesity, and the person within.* New York: Basic Books.

Bruch, H. (1978). *The golden cage.* Cambridge, MA: Harvard University Press.

Cauwels, J. M. (1983). *Bulimia: The binge-purge compulsion.* Garden City, NY: Doubleday.

Chernin, K. (1981). *The obsession: Reflections on the tyranny of slenderness.* New York: Harper & Row.

Cooper, P. J., & Fairburn, C. G. (1983). Binge eating and self-induced vomiting in the community. *British Journal of Psychiatry, 142,* 139–144.

Fairburn, C. G., & Cooper, P. J. (1982). Self-induced vomiting and bulimia nervosa: An undetected problem. *British Medical Journal, 284,* 1153–1155.

Franklin, J. S., Schiele, B. C., Brozek, J., & Keys, A. (1948). Observations on human behavior in experimental starvation and rehabilitation. *Journal of Clinical Psychology, 4,* 28–45.

Gandour, M. J. (1984). Bulimia: Clinical description, assessment, etiology, and treatment. *International Journal of Eating Disorders, 3(3),* 3–13.

Garner, D. M., Garfinkel, P. E., & Bemis, K. M. (1982). A multidimensional psychotherapy for anorexia nervosa. *International Journal of Eating Disorders, 1(2),* 3–64.

Garner, D. M., Rockert, W., Olmstead, M. P., Johnson, C., & Coscina, D. V. (1985). Psychoeducational principles in the treatment of bulimia and anorexia nervosa. In D. M. Garner & P. E. Garfinkel (Eds), *Handbook of psychotherapy for anorexia nervosa and bulimia* (pp. 513–562). New York: Guilford.

Greenspan, M. (1983). *A new approach to women and therapy.* New York: McGraw-Hill.

Halmi, K. A., Falk, J. R., & Schwartz, E. (1981). Binge eating and vomiting in a college population. *Psychological Medicine, 11,* 697–706.

Hart, K. J., & Ollendick, T. H. (1985). Prevalence of bulimia in working and university women. *American Journal of Psychiatry, 142,* 851–854.

Inbody, D. R., & Ellis, J. J. (1985). Group therapy with anorexic and bulimic patients: Implications for therapeutic intervention. *American Journal of Psychotherapy, 34,* 411–420.

Johnson, C. L., & Larson, R. (1982). Bulimia: An analysis of moods and behavior. *Psychosomatic Medicine, 44,* 341–353.

Katzman, M. A., Wolchick, S. A., & Braver, S. L. (1984). The prevalence of frequent binge eating and bulimia in a nonclinical sample. *International Journal of Eating Disorders, 3(3),* 53–62.

Lemkau, J. P., & Landau, C. (1986). The self-less syndrome: Assessment and treatment considerations. *Psychotherapy, 23,* 227–233.

Marlatt, G. A., & Gordon, J. R. (1985). *Relapse prevention: Maintenance strategies for addictive behavior change.* New York: Guilford.

Orbach, S. (1978). *Fat is a feminist issue.* New York: Berkeley Books.

Osborne, S. M., & Harris, G. G. (1975). *Assertive training for women.* Springfield, IL: Charles C. Thomas.

Polivy, J., Herman, C. P., Olmstead, M. P., & Jazwinski, C. (1984). Restraint and binge eating. In R. C. Fremouw & P. F. Clement (Eds.), *The binge/purge syndrome: Diagnosis, treatment and research* (pp. 104–122). New York: Springer Publishing Co.

Pope, H. G., Jr., Hudson, J. I., & Yurgelun-Todd, D. (1984). Anorexia nervosa and bulimia among 300 suburban women shoppers. *American Journal of Psychiatry, 141*, 292–294.

Pope, H. G., Jr., Hudson, J. I., Yurgelun-Todd, D., & Hudson, M. S. (1984). Prevalence of anorexia nervosa and bulimia in three student populations. *International Journal of Eating Disorders, 3*(3), 45–51.

Pyle, R. L., Mitchell, J. E., & Eckert, E. D. (1981). Bulimia: A report of 34 cases. *Journal of Clinical Psychiatry, 42*, 60–64.

Rosewater, L. B. (1984). Feminist therapy: Implications for practitioners. In L. A. Walker (Ed.), *Women and mental health policy* (pp. 267–279). Beverly Hills, CA: Sage.

Stangler, R. S., & Printz, A. M. (1980). DSM III: Psychiatric diagnosis in a university population. *American Journal of Psychiatry, 137*, 937–940.

Stere, L. K. (1985). Feminist assertiveness training: Self-esteem groups as skill training for women. In L. B. Rosewater & L. A. Walker (Eds.) *Handbook of feminist therapy: Women's issues in psychotherapy* (pp. 51–61). New York: Springer Publishing Co.

Sturdivant, S. (1980). *Therapy with women: A feminist philosophy of treatment.* New York: Springer Publishing Co.

Vognsen, J. (1985). Individual therapy: Brief, strategic treatment of bulimia. *Transactional Analysis Journal, 15*(1), 79–84.

White, W. C., & Boskind-White, M. (1981). An experiential-behavioral approach to the treatment of bulimarexia. *Psychotherapy: Theory, Research and Practice, 18*, 501–507.

■ 2
Still Here: A Perspective on Psychotherapy with African-American Women

Beverly Greene

I've been scarred and battered.
My hopes the wind done scattered.
Snow has friz me, sun has baked me.
  Looks like between 'em
  They done tried to make me
Stop laughin', stop lovin', stop livin'—
  But I don't care!
  I'm still here!

—Langston Hughes, Still Here (1959)

Therapists who treat African-American women may be influenced by the racial differences and similarities between them and the interaction between those variables and the personal history of the therapist. The ways in which those issues may be manifested in the therapeutic process, a brief view of the racial and cultural context in which psychotherapy occurs, and its influence on the perceptions therapists hold of African-American women constitute the focus of this chapter.

The term "black" will be used to refer to American women whose ancestors came primarily from the tribes of West Africa and were the primary objects of the U.S. slave trade. Although many clinical observations of black women apply to other women of color as well, the focus here will be on the treatment of black women.

Black women live and develop in the context of a culture that is not only different from African culture but also antagonistic to it. That context contains variables reflecting cultural differences between black and white Americans and differences between black Americans of African versus Caribbean origin, as well as a history of sexism and racism that institutionalizes the idealization of white women as it devalues and disparages black women (Davis, 1981; Epstein, 1973; Hooks, 1981; Joseph & Lewis, 1981; Lewis, 1977). The pervasive and institutionalized devaluation of black persons is an important factor to understand in the individual development of a black client.

It is fair to suggest that black women occupy a structural, social, and economic position subordinate to that of white men, white women, and black men, with less access to positions of power and authority (Davis, 1981; Epstein, 1973; Hooks, 1981; Joseph & Lewis, 1981; Myers, 1980; Robinson, 1983; Rollins, 1985). It would follow that black women experience the combined effects of racism, sexism, and, for black lesbians, homophobia. The interrelationship between these three dimensions must be appreciated for its complexity in the therapeutic process.

The social problems that accompany racial and sexual differences are ubiquitous in the cultural fabric of the United States. Consequently, tensions between black and white persons may be exacerbated by racial incidents that are prominent in the media and may evoke dormant racial conflicts in both the client and the therapist. They are rarely, however, a formal focus of attention in the training of clinicians who work with black women. In reviews of texts on psychology of women, mention of black women is quite sparse if not conspicuously omitted. This tendency to exclude or to include only token references to black women in these discussions may leave readers with seemingly benign but nonetheless destructive inferences (Brown, Goodwin, Hall, & Jackson-Lowman, 1985).

One inference is that results of investigations into lives of women of European descent are generalizable to all women, no matter what their circumstances or history. Another, more malignant inference is that women of European descent are more worthy of scholarly consideration than women of color (Brown et al., 1985). This kind of invisibility is no less damaging than the existing abundance of stigmatizing psychological folklore that depicts black women in a negative light.

Although black women share in and suffer from the ill effects of a sexist culture as white women do, Ladner (1971) notes that race can operate as a more powerful social variable than others and can transcend and intensify the effects of class, education, and occupation. As a result, it is suggested that race may transcend and intensify the effect of gender for black women, who may not share similar status, roles, values, or sets of life expectations with white women. Black women are not seen simply as women but rather as black women. The parameters of their roles as women are influenced by race and racism. It therefore becomes difficult, if not impossible, to disentangle completely the effects of sex and race in black women's lives.

Traditionally, black women have not received the customary courtesies of femininity and are held accountable to standards based on the white female ideal (Cade-Bambara, 1970; Epstein, 1973; Freudiger & Almquist, 1980; Harley, Terborg, & Penn, 1978; Hooks, 1981; Lerner, 1972; Myers, 1980; Neal & Wilson, 1989; Robinson, 1983). For many of the above reasons, black women may prioritize their feminism differently from white women. Black women share their status as a disadvantaged group with black men and often view white women as more privileged than either black women or men (Lewis, 1977).

Many of the goals of the feminist movement were articulated by middle class white women and have not meaningfully addressed the issues that affected the realities of black women's lives. Furthermore, it was not unusual historically for black women to be employed by white women whose behavior was no less oppressive than that of white men. As a result, many black women remain distrustful of an alliance with white women and do not see themselves reflected in feminist struggles. This does not mean that black women are oblivious to their oppressed status as women, rather that it is tied to other struggles as well and is not as circumscribed as it may be for white women. The effects and understanding of the aforementioned factors in black women's lives and their impact on the development of coping strategies must be explored.

PSYCHOLOGICAL REALITIES OF BLACK WOMEN AND BLACK LIFE

Black women face a range of interacting personal and environmental realities that may differentially affect certain aspects of their development and behavior. For black lesbians there is the additional stress of managing the dominant culture's homophobia and the gay and lesbian community's racism, in conjunction with the aforementioned realities. All of these factors converge in some form in the presenting problem. The extent to which they converge and the relative importance of each factor will vary from one client to another.

An important consideration in understanding contemporary black women involves an understanding of their ethnic heritage. In the United States, black women have always been required to be bicultural in an environment that is both racist and sexist. The development of a positive racial identity among black Americans has been complicated by many factors. One is the Western historian's obfuscation and blatant distortion of African culture to make it appear inferior to European culture and therefore lacking in legitimacy. This was reflected in the omission of an accurate portrayal of the exploitive nature of the relationship between Africans and other nations that were mineral-, land-, and people-poor. Africa and Africans were consistently characterized in pejorative ways (Akbar, 1985; Chestang, 1973; Friedman, 1966; Greene, 1990b; Nobles, 1974, 1975).

It is suggested that the distorted and degraded image of Africa and Africans, reinforced by mainstream media portrayals of Africans as cannibals, savages, and subordinate to white authority figures, left many black Americans with the notion that they had either no culture at all before slavery or one that was degrading to them. The need to deny or experience shame about one's history and hence one's culture of origin has implications for the development of group identity, a sense of belonging and self-esteem, and access to sources of group support (Gibbs & Huang, 1989; Pinderhughes, 1989; Ross & Widen, 1973).

There is great diversity among black women as a group; however, they share constellations of distinct characteristics that have many of their origins in the values and practices unique to African culture. The therapist must be aware of these cultural imperatives in order to appropriately interpret and understand the values and behavior of black women. A detailed exploration of the unique aspects of African cultural derivatives in black American families is beyond the scope of this chapter. Therapists who wish to familiarize themselves with such material may refer to Akbar (1985), Billingsley (1968), Boyd-Franklin (1989), Greene (1990b), Hale-Benson (1982), Hill (1972), Ladner (1971), and Nobles (1974, 1975). These cultural derivatives may be accurately understood as examples of cultural distinctiveness that have served many adaptive purposes.

Family Endowments and Resources

Traditionally, black women have been blamed for the family ills and stresses that are, in fact, caused by institutional racism. A deficit-oriented social science literature has measured black women and their family structures against an idealized view of white families and labeled them defective or deprived (Moynihan, 1965). This deficit research model fails to take into account special stressors confronting black women that are not shared by their white counterparts. A ubiquitous stressor for black women is the pressure of racism and the concomitant need to develop mechanisms to minimize its damaging effects on themselves and their children. It is reflected in the amount of energy consumed in the ongoing requirement of coping with the dominant culture's prejudices and barriers.

Hill (1972) identifies what he considers to be five major characteristics and strengths of black families that reflect the derivatives of their African cultural roots as well as their need to adapt to a racist and sexist society. Strong kinship bonds are observed between nuclear family members and extended family. The adaptability and flexibility of family members in family roles are characteristics reflecting the African principles of cooperative work and collective responsibility. A strong religious and spiritual orientation has long been an important aspect of black life as well.

Finally, Hill (1972) cites a strong work orientation and achievement motivation as black family traits. This is reflected in the conspicuous presence of working black persons throughout history and the clear emphasis on the value of education.

Developing Coping Mechanisms in Response to Racism

For most black persons, racism is a living expectation, representing a continuous rather than a transient, episodic, or discrete phenomenon. It requires adaptation to ongoing levels of stress. Furthermore, it is associated with an unalterable physical characteristic that is always visible. The factor of visibility may intensify the experience of racism for black women in ways that may not be shared by women of other, less visible ethnic groups.

The influence of the dominant culture can be problematic for black women when it is accompanied by the dominant culture's negative view of them. These negative views are transmitted in subtle to overt ways to both black and white persons. If internalized by black women, these views may be manifested in a variety of behaviors. This means internalizing, unconsciously and without censor, both the negative stereotypes about black women and black culture and idealization of white women and their cultural values (Butts, 1971; Friedman, 1966, 1969; Gardiner, 1971).

Clinical manifestations of internalized racism may appear in psychotherapy in many forms. Among them is a black woman's need to act against or act out common racial stereotypes. The origins of these behaviors may be multiply determined. A few examples will be briefly discussed. Acting against stereotypes may have its origins in the fear that behavior resembling any stereotype of black women proves that all stereotypes of black women are true. This confirms the woman's worst internal fear. It should be clear that the client who displays this behavior unconsciously rejects parts of herself just as she appears to reject black persons as a group. The compulsion to act out stereotypes of black women may reflect the need to expose a feared part of oneself, the caricature of what is expected by others. This may leave the individual with a sense of control over being "found out." The therapist observes in such clients an inability to comfortably choose behaviors or characteristics that are most personally compatible. For a more detailed discussion of internalized racism in psychotherapy with black women, the reader is referred to Greene (in press).

Internalized racism and sexism in black women may be reflected in the Impostor Phenomenon. Clance and Imes (1978) conceptualize this as an internal sense of intellectual phoniness or of feeling like a failure despite repeated successes. It is frequently observed in women and may be the result of certain early family dynamics as well as the introjection of society's gender-role stereotyping. This concept can be carried one step further to include racial gender-role stereotyping. Trotman (1984) comments on this phenomenon in the treatment of black women. One may observe the woman's inability to appreciate the magnitude of her accomplishments or activities and a preoccupation with feeling like a fraud.

Despite the internalizing of racism as a maladaptive coping response, black women do not react passively to racism and its sequelae or blindly accept the dominant culture's values and views of them. There is ample evidence of a variety of resourceful strategies of adaptation throughout their history. A convergence of environmental and individual factors may be seen as major elements in an individual's coping strategies. Different strategies will be utilized by individuals at different stages of their emotional and social development as well as their racial stage of awareness.

Cultural paranoia (Grier & Cobbs, 1968) may be viewed, despite the pejorative terminology, as an adaptive coping mechanism. It may be observed in a sensitivity to the potential for maltreatment and exploitation in interactions with white persons and a heightened level of reserve or suspiciousness.

Many mechanisms developed for coping with racism are less than obvious. One strategy involves a black woman's protecting white persons from racial discomfort by engaging in behaviors presumed to make white persons more comfortable and inappropriately blaming themselves for the discomfort present in interracial interactions. This type of defensive maneuver may be utilized by the black woman who perceives or assumes that she elicits fear in whites, or to maintain a false sense of control in a situation where there is potential for victimization.

Both black and white therapists in these encounters must be careful not to encourage these behaviors by inadvertently communicating their anxiety about race to the client. White therapists in particular must be careful not to accept overly compliant behavior from black clients too readily. This compliance can often conceal the client's anger, fear, or other unacceptable feelings for the therapist. Another attempt at coping with racism is manifested in the denial of racism and/or one's racial identity. Denial of racial identity allows one to maintain distance from feelings of powerlessness and the pain associated with membership in a disparaged group. It also leaves one vulnerable to loneliness, personal isolation, and political powerlessness, and lacking the opportunity to correct distorted perceptions of the group and, of course, themselves (Hale-Benson, 1982; Kupers, 1981; Pinderhughes, 1989; Ross & Wyden, 1973; Spencer, 1983).

Physical Attractiveness and the Caucasian Beauty Standard

Physical attractiveness for women continues to serve a functional role analogous to social power among men. It is important to understand the messages communicated to black women about the adequacy of their physical characteristics and what steps must be taken to alter them. This is particularly true in a culture that idealizes Caucasian features, devalues African features, and rewards black women for approaching the Caucasian beauty standard (Boyd-Franklin, 1989; Greene, 1985, 1990b; Lewis, 1977; Miller, 1969; Neal & Wilson, 1989; Okazawa-Rey, Robinson, & Ward, 1987; Spurlock, 1985). If a black woman has accepted the dominant culture's standard of beauty, that standard and its surrounding conflicts may be passed on to her child without awareness. Derivatives of these conflicts may be observed in therapy with black women. To be womanly and feminine, in American culture, is to be white.

In this context it is predictable that skin color variations within black families can be a source of conflict between family members. Skin colors within the same family may vary from extremely dark to extremely light, or "fair." It is important, in therapy, to inquire about the skin color of family members, particularly those about whom there are intense feelings. Skin color differences and the conflicts associated with them may intensify a normal range of sibling and intrafamilial rivalries. This may help to expose some of the dynamics in clients who have been idealized or scapegoated within their families and to reveal how they may reenact those dynamics with other persons in their lives, including the therapist.

Concerns about skin color, hair texture, body size and shape, and facial features are commonly reported by black women in both individual and group therapies (Boyd-Franklin, 1987; Greene, 1990a, 1990b; Mays, 1986; Neal & Wilson, 1989; Trotman, 1984). All black women are not negatively affected by this legacy; however, many women with light and dark skin, both heterosexual and lesbian, report concerns about these matters in conjunction with feelings of shame, guilt, anger, and resentment.

It is important for the therapist to be sensitive to the emergence of cues that suggest the presence of such concerns and to situations in which they might be expected to occur. They must be explored with delicacy, as they are often the repositories of pain and shame and constitute a taboo topic that black persons are not to discuss or acknowledge to white persons.

The client may also harbor fears of disclosing such concerns to a black therapist out of fear of disapproval or of alienating the therapist.

Black women tend to have been stereotyped either as angry, volatile, castrating bitches, as nurturing, pious, caring mammy figures, or as morally loose and sexually promiscuous "whores." Many persons, both black and white, believe these stereotypes are true. Therapists are no exception. Factors leading to the predisposition to act out or assiduously avoid acting out any of these behaviors have been reviewed (Davis, 1981; Greene, 1990a, 1990b; Hooks, 1981; Lewis, 1977). This may create a perceived need to maintain a constant state of vigilance against expressing certain feelings that have been deemed unacceptable, with a concomitant loss of spontaneity in interpersonal relationships.

The implicit message to black women from the dominant culture is that they have a narrow choice of roles and images acceptable to and created by the dominant culture, despite circumstances that force them to assume a wide range of roles and functions. They are then criticized and accused of undermining the function of black men when they assume those roles and functions out of necessity.

Therapists must understand that black women bring many deep and painful wounds to therapy that are related to the legacy of racism and its psychological demands. The therapist must be able to tolerate hearing about and sometimes being the target of intense feelings of rage, anger, and shame. These feelings must be understood as a cry of pain. If the therapist misperceives the client's rage or despair as some kind of personal attack on the therapist or if the therapist is too comfortable in the absence of such feelings, this may further discourage the client from airing and exploring them. Failure to explore these feelings will preclude the development of strategies required to negotiate them and may reinforce the primitive fear, in some clients, that their feelings are dangerous or offensive to the therapist.

RACIAL COUNTERTRANSFERENCE DILEMMAS

As the cultural milieu continues to facilitate distorted and stereotypic attitudes toward images of black women, therapists may harbor those attitudes because they have developed as a part of the culture, not apart from it. It is suggested that the concepts of transference and countertransference can be applied in understanding how a client and therapist, with their own racial identities, may collude with one another to act out culturally conditioned patterns of interaction among black and/or white persons. Pinderhughes (1989) notes that a therapist with a distorted sense of self, who needs another person to project onto, will be unable to help clients feel good about themselves.

A detailed review of the potential racial countertransferential dilemmas is beyond the scope of this discussion, but they have been reviewed elsewhere in detail (Butts, 1980; Butts & Harrison, 1970; Gardiner, 1971; Greene, 1985, in press; Kupers, 1981; Pinderhughes, 1989). Generally, they suggest that therapists who work with black clients must be aware of their own racial and ethnic identities—how they feel about them and how those identities predispose them to view the world—and their attitudes, motivations, and feelings about working with black clients.

THERAPEUTIC INTERVENTIONS TO ASSIST THE DEVELOPMENT OF COPING STRATEGIES

In psychotherapy with black women it may be helpful to identify the conscious and unconscious methods they employ in confronting and responding to racial and other personal difficulties. One may then compare the client's strategies with a range of available options, helping her to make conscious and active choices, compatible with her own personal and cultural values and goals. This cannot take place if the therapist believes that problems resulting from racism are of minimal importance or that they are limited to black women in the lower economic and/or educational strata.

Therapy may also be useful in helping the client prioritize what she feels are important conflicts and issues, when it is most important to respond to them, and how to do so. In a racist, sexist, and homophobic culture, a black woman who feels compelled to actively respond to every suggestion, incident, or episode of racist behavior will have little energy available to address other life issues.

Introducing or responding to the issue of race within the treatment situation presents therapists with a dilemma that training often ignores. It is not unusual for a client to assume that she will offend, make anxious, or alienate the therapist if she initiates an inquiry into such matters. It is important that therapists communicate to the black client that they recognize the extent to which race and racism may play significant roles in her life and that she does not have to protect the therapist from her experiences or feelings about them.

It may be difficult for therapists to make distinctions between legitimate racial anger, race used in the service of resistance, and race as a metaphor for intrapsychic conflict. Certain aspects of a black woman's racial heritage and experiences with racism may be superimposed on or interact with structural and characterological dynamics and defenses in particular ways.

It is therefore important that the therapist observe the intensification of characterological conflicts that may be triggered by racial realities. It may be helpful if the therapist is sensitive to what precedes the initiation of a focus on race and whether or not there is a pattern to this. The purpose is to determine whether or not race becomes easier for the client to discuss than issues that may be even more painful and whether or not race is used to avoid exploration of other issues.

The therapist must avoid the temptation of using racial oppression to explain all of a client's problems. To do so deprives the client of understanding any role she may have in her own dilemma and the option of making changes. Therapists must also be careful not to romanticize successful struggles to overcome oppression without an awareness of the hidden costs.

SUMMARY

The mental health professions have not developed apart from this culture; rather, they are a part of it. Both black and white therapists have been trained and acculturated in institutions that are part of and represent the dominant culture's values, and they often support, rather than explore or challenge, the status quo.

For black women, racial issues may be the least important aspect of treatment or the most painful issue in their lives. Their importance will vary from client to client and will be a function of multiple factors that help to shape the psyche of black women just as they do for everyone else. Many environmental factors help to shape the psyche of black women on many levels; however, those factors always interact with salient aspects of who that person is. Early life experiences, familial relationships, and biological and constitutional factors are among the components that contribute to the shaping of the core self in most people. These individual factors, societal stressors, and cultural contexts all help to determine what resources or liabilities an individual brings to any situation.

Although black persons share many group characteristics, an individual black woman will attempt to cope with racial life stressors with the same characterological and defensive structures used to respond to other life stressors. This does not mean that black women are to blame for the scars that result from their victimization. Rather, it is suggested that for black women, particularly in the context of a racist society, race is an additional dimension, a complication, a source of support, and an enrichment integral to their lives. It therefore presents an additional dimension for treatment consideration.

REFERENCES

Akbar, N. (1985). Our destiny, authors of a scientific revolution. In H. McAdoo & J. McAdoo (Eds.), *Black children* (pp. 17–31). Beverly Hills, CA: Sage Publications.

Billingsley, A. (1968). *Black families in white America.* Englewood Cliffs, NJ: Prentice-Hall.

Boyd-Franklin, N. (1987). Group therapy for black women: A therapeutic support model. *American Journal of Orthopsychiatry, 57*(3), 394–401.

Boyd-Franklin, N. (1989). *Black families in therapy: A multisystems approach.* New York: Guilford.

Brown, A., Goodwin, B., Hall, B., & Jackson-Lowman, H. (1985). A review of psychology of women textbooks: Focus on the Afro-American woman. *Psychology of Women Quarterly, 9*, 29–38.

Butts, H. F. (1971). Psychoanalysis and unconscious racism. *Journal of Contemporary Psychotherapy, 3*(2), 67–81.

Butts, H. F. (1980). Racial issues in psychotherapy. In L. Bellak & B. Karasu (Eds.), *Specialized techniques in individual psychotherapy* (pp. 352–381). New York: Brunner Mazel.

Butts, H. F., & Harrison, P. (1970, July). White psychiatrists' racism in referral practices to black psychiatrists. *Journal of the National Medical Association,* pp. 278–282.

Cade-Bambara, T. (1970). *The black woman: An anthology.* New York: New American Library.

Chestang, L. (1973). Character development in a hostile environment. *Occasional Paper No. 3.* Chicago: University of Chicago, Social Services Administration.

Clance, P. R., & Imes, S. A. (1978). The impostor phenomenon in high achieving women: Dynamics and therapeutic intervention. *Psychotherapy: Theory, Research and Practice, 15*, 241–247.

Davis, A. (1981). *Women, race and class.* New York: Vintage Books.

Epstein, C. F. (1973). Positive effects of the multiple negative: Explaining the success of black professional women. *American Journal of Sociology, 78*, 912–935.

Freudiger, P., & Almquist, E. M. (1980). *Sources of life satisfaction: The different worlds of black and white women.* Paper presented at the annual meeting of the Southwestern Sociological Association, Houston.

Friedman, N. (1966). James Baldwin and psychotherapy. *Psychotherapy, 3*(4), 177–183.

Friedman, N. (1969). Africa and the Afro-American: The changing Negro identity. *Psychiatry, 32*(2), 127–136.

Gardiner, L. K. (1971). The therapeutic relationship under varying conditions of race. *Psychotherapy, 8*, 78–87.

Gibbs, J. T., & Huang, L. N. (Eds.). (1989). *Children of color: Psychological interventions with minority youth.* San Francisco: Jossey Bass.

Greene, B. (1985). Considerations in the treatment of black patients by white therapists. *Psychotherapy, 22*, 389–393.

Greene, B. (1990a). Sturdy bridges: The role of African American mothers in the socialization of African American children. *Women & Therapy, 10*(1), 205–225.

Greene, B. (1990b). What has gone before: The legacy of racism and sexism in the lives of black mothers and daughters. In L. Brown & M. P. Root (Eds.), *Diversity and complexity in feminist therapy* (pp. 207–230). New York: Haworth Press.

Greene, B. (in press). African American women. In L. Comas-Diaz & B. Greene (Eds.), *Women of color and mental health.* New York: Guilford.

Grier, W., & Cobbs, P. (1968). *Black rage.* New York: Basic Books.

Hale-Benson, J. (1982). *Black children: Their roots, culture, and learning styles* (rev. ed.). Baltimore: Johns Hopkins University Press.

Harley, S., & Terborg-Penn, R. (Eds.). (1978). *The Afro-American woman: Struggles and images.* Port Washington, NY: Kennikat Press.

Hill, R. (1972). *The strengths of black families.* New York: National Urban League.

Hooks, B. (1981). *Black women and feminism.* Boston: South End Press.

Hughes, L. (1959). Still here. In L. Hughes (Ed.), *Selected poems of Langston Hughes* (p. 123). New York: Vintage Books.

Joseph, G., & Lewis, J. (1981). *Common differences: Conflicts in black and white feminist perspectives.* New York: Doubleday.

Kupers, T. (1981). *Public therapy: The practice of psychotherapy in the public mental health clinic.* New York: Macmillan.

Ladner, J. (1971). *Tomorrow's tomorrow: The black woman.* Garden City, NY: Doubleday.

Lerner, G. (Ed.). (1972). *Black women in white America: A documentary history.* New York: Vintage Books.

Lewis, D. K. (1977). A response to inequality: Black women, racism and sexism. *Signs, 3*(2), 339–361.

Mays, V. (1986). Black women and stress: Utilization of self help groups for stress reduction. *Women & Therapy, 4*(4), 67–79.

Miller, E. (1969). Body image, physical beauty and color among Jamaican adolescents. *Social and Economic Studies, 18*(1), 72–89.

Moynihan, D. P. (1965). *The Negro family: The case for national action.* Washington DC: U. S. Department of Labor.

Myers, L. (1980). *Black women—do they cope better?* Englewood Cliffs, NJ: Prentice-Hall.

Neal, A., & Wilson, M. (1989). The role of skin color and features in the black community: Implications for black women and therapy. *Clinical Psychology Review, 9*(3), 323–333.

Nobles, W. (1974). African root and American fruit: The black family. *Journal of Social and Behavioral Sciences, 20*(2), 52–64.

Nobles, W. (1975). *The black family and its children: The survival of humaneness.* Unpublished manuscript.

Okazawa-Rey, M., Robinson, T., & Ward, J. V. (1987). Black women and the politics of skin color and hair. *Women & Therapy, 6*(1/2), 89–102.

Pinderhughes, E. (1989). *Understanding race, ethnicity and power: The key to efficacy in clinical practice.* New York: Free Press.

Robinson, C. R. (1983). Black women: A tradition of self reliant strength. *Women & Therapy, 2*, 135–144.

Rollins, J. (1985). *Between women: Domestics and their employers.* Philadelphia: Temple University Press.

Ross, P. H., & Wyden, B. (1973). *The black child: A parents' guide.* New York: Wyden.

Spencer, M. B. (1983). Children's cultural values and parental child rearing strategies. *Developmental Review, 3*(4), 351–370.

Spurlock, J. (1985). Survival guilt and the Afro-American of achievement. *Journal of the National Medical Association, 77*(1), 29–32.

Trotman, F. (1984). Psychotherapy with black women and the dual effects of racism and sexism. In C. Brody (Ed.), *Women therapists working with women* (pp. 96–108). New York: Springer Publishing Co.

■ 3
Motherhood and the Clinician/Mother's View of Parent and Child

Paula S. Derry

Researchers have explored many factors that might influence how psycho-therapists think of or behave with their clients. Individual characteristics of the clinician, such as theoretical orientation, personality characteristics, sex role biases, or liking of the client have been studied most often (Hersen, Michelson, & Bellack, 1984). A second, less common, research area has been that of exploring how the clinical situation affects the practitioner. For example, burned-out clinicians might conceptualize their clients in a more critical manner (Farber, 1983). A third possible area that might influence the behavior and experiences of therapists has been relatively under-studied, namely, whether the clinician's experiences outside the clinical situation systematically affect what happens within it.

The emphasis in the psychotherapy literature follows from implicit assumptions about how personal and professional life interrelate. The two areas of experience are assumed to be distinct. Personal and professional roles do not generally interpenetrate or influence each other. If the areas do interpenetrate, this is most often because there is a problem. Thus, research that has addressed how personal roles might influence therapy has tended to focus on episodic occurrences—that is, events that intrude on an ongoing therapy and create a potential or real problem. Pregnancy, for example, has

Research support was provided by a grant-in-aid from Sigma Xi.

been one of the more studied of the events in a clinician's personal life that might influence therapy, as when researchers have explored the range of client responses to this violation of therapist anonymity (Guy, 1987). When the effects of other typical experiences associated with adult development have been studied, they are also most often treated as problems, intrusions on therapy that might warrant examination.

This chapter describes the results of research in which women report that two of their social roles — namely, maternity and the professional role — do interpenetrate. Experience as a mother results in personal change that is brought to the clinical situation. It is not that maternity creates a problem in conducting therapy or intrudes as an episode on the professional role in a way that must be dealt with. Rather, how the clinician experiences conducting therapy is altered in an ongoing, rather than an episodic, manner.

This research was conducted from the perspective of "transformational research" (Crawford & Marecek, 1989). To avoid interpreting the experiences of the clinician/mothers in terms of preconceived categories, especially those derived from research on largely male samples, the clinicians were asked to describe their experiences from their own point of view and were regarded as informants. Such preconceived categories may include the ideas that work and personal roles do not interpenetrate; if these two areas of experience do affect each other, it is because there is a conflict or problem: personal life is inferior to professional experience and knowledge; motherhood is devalued. The research method was phenomenological. A representative sample of clinicians[1] met once with the author for a face-to-face interview. They were asked to discuss each of a set of topic areas. For example, they were asked whether being a mother had influenced their experience of conducting therapy in any way; if so, they were asked for specific examples. The interviews were tape-recorded and transcribed. The results can be best thought of as a composite case study of the range of experiences of the women interviewed.[2]

Why might maternity be expected to influence clinical experience? Paradoxically, although not emphasized in the literature, anecdotally it is common for clinicians to say that they bring the fruits of their own experience to therapy. Clinicians, for example, who have worked through how to deal with their anger might say they feel greater empathic understanding of the dynamics involved in this issue. Parenthood might be expected to have similar effects because it is a major life experience, involving pervasive changes in the clinician's emotional and social life. The clinician becomes a member of the group of "parents," experiencing events from the parental, rather than from the child's, point of view. Further, in a society such as ours, in which most adults have little experience interacting with young children until they become parents themselves, parenthood involves a profound shift in one's knowledge base about parenting and about early childhood.

In addition, maternity might be expected to exert enduring, as opposed to episodic, effects if maternity is a stage of adult development. The concept of "adult development" involves the hypothesis that adults, no less than children, experience periods of developmental change (Levinson, 1978). The stages of the adult life cycle consist not only of events such as the development of long-term relationships but psychological changes as well. Theoreticians and researchers from a broad range of backgrounds have with increasing frequency been asking whether becoming a parent has an effect on the parents themselves (e.g., Benedek, 1952; Erikson, 1963; Koumans, 1987; Partridge, 1988). If motherhood does involve psychological changes, it is plausible to think that these changes might influence how the psychotherapy situation is perceived.

This chapter explores the phenomenology of how becoming a mother influenced clinicians' perceptions of clients and the experience of conducting therapy. The clinicians in this study lived in two-parent households, and 72% of them had at least one preschool-age child. The mothers were primary caretakers of their children. In only one case did the father provide child care while the mother worked, and the mothers rated themselves as providing the majority of routine care. As reported elsewhere (Derry, 1990), this sample of mothers overwhelmingly elected part-time employment while their children were preschoolers, but they did not differ from a comparison group of nonmothers when basic job attitudes such as commitment, satisfaction, and professional aspirations were evaluated statistically.

Seventy-two percent of the clinicians worked in private practice (rather than institutional) settings, and 64% worked fewer than 30 hours per week. Ninety-six percent of the clinicians rated their theoretical orientation as psychodynamic, either entirely (36%) or as part of an eclectic style (64%). The eclectic therapists most commonly combined dynamic with cognitive/behavioral or family-oriented techniques. Ninety-six percent of the clinicians reported that they treated adults; 44%, children; and 88%, couples or families.

INCREASED EMPATHY: AN EXPERIENTIAL SHIFT

An almost universal effect of having children, as reported by the mothers, was a subtle but pervasive effect on attitudes in interactions with clients: 88% of the mothers stated that they felt greater empathy, understanding, or emotional knowledge about parents. The clinicians thought differently about the early memories of adult clients reconstructing the past; they thought differently about individual adult clients or couples who were parents; and they thought differently about the parents of a child in treatment.

Almost every clinician, whether she became a mother when finishing graduate school or after 10 years of clinical experience, felt a sense of having gained experiential knowledge:

> Respondent 17: Having a child, in terms of helpfulness as a psychologist, is very much like having been through therapy. Theory is one thing; intimately experiencing it is another.

The most general and common change reported by the mothers was a felt difference when doing therapy. It felt different to hear clients discuss parents or parenthood when the clinician could relate to this material experientially. This shift could enrich the experience of conducting clinical work:

> Respondent 11: (in response to interviewer's asking whether "increased empathy" meant the increased detail in her understanding of issues that she had described): No, it's also the level of passion, it's the level of intensity, it's knowing and feeling the emotional impact of what it's like to have children.
>
> Respondent 21: I was not concerned . . . with whether [becoming a mother] would enhance my work life. It turns out that it has. . . . I think [if I were not a mother] the work would be much drier.

The clinicians varied in interpreting how this experiential knowledge was integrated into their overall style. Some clinicians believed that their conceptualizations and interventions (as opposed to how it felt to conduct therapy) were affected a great deal by increased empathy; others believed there was little effect. In general, changes in general theoretical orientation, such as adapting or discarding a psychoanalytic viewpoint, were rare. Some clinicians did believe that their development in a chosen theoretical direction was furthered when observations of their children confirmed their beliefs. However, many clinicians believed that although their understanding of parents' experience changed, they were not aware of doing anything very different in the therapy situation.

Yet what was striking to the interviewer was that even when clinicians stated that they were not doing anything different they typically could give a concrete example of how they were thinking differently. In one striking example, a clinician discussed a female client who had decided to give up custody of her son to her ex-husband. The clinician believed that before having had a child herself she would have felt critical of this client for abandoning her son. Instead, she was more accepting. She better understood the client's experience in dealing with a very difficult situation, and she focused on the possible advantages for all concerned in the new arrangement. Yet this therapist believed that her changed perspective was not reflected in her interactions with this client!

DIFFERENTIATION OF VIEWPOINTS OF PARENT AND CHILD

Whether clinicians believed that their conceptualizations and interventions were affected a great deal or very little by increased empathy, almost every clinician could give an example of how her thinking about a specific client was different. These specific examples of "increased empathy" varied but reflected similar themes. The similarity of themes was a second uniformity in the data. Whether clinicians believed that their increased empathy had a broad effect on their interactions with clients or that their attitude change had little effect, when the range of responses of the clinicians was inspected (for what clinicians mean when they say they feel increased empathy), the responses fell into a general pattern: Clinicians were more identified with the position of parent than that of child, and/or the clinicians better differentiated between the two positions. These results will be presented as a composite case study: No one clinician exemplified the entire pattern, but the responses of each clinician were facets of these themes.

The old view, stated in an extreme form, was an expectation that parents should be "good parents" (understanding, sympathetic, patient) who gratify their child's needs. If the child's needs, as defined by the child, are not met, the parent has in some way failed and is judged in a critical manner. If a parent experiences feelings such as anger that interfere with being sympathetic and understanding, the parent is judged critically, and attributions of pathology might be made to account for the parent's lapse in performance. On the other hand, after having children themselves, the clinicians are more likely to perceive the behavior of parents from the parent's point of view, rather than from the point of view of how the behavior affected the child. The child's perspective on what motivates the parent is better separated from the parent's viewpoint. Parents are judged less harshly; the clinician is less likely to feel critical of the parent or attribute pathology. The parents' feelings are comprehensible, and the pressures on the parent are perceived more clearly. The clinician might also perceive more clearly how the child is contributing to the interaction or that certain conflicts reflect normal, inevitable processes between parent and child.

One component, then, of the shift in attitude that clinicians experience when they become mothers is that idealism about parenthood is deflated:

> Respondent 23: After you have children, it is very humbling, and suddenly you realize that it's much more difficult, how much phenomenally more difficult, it is to be a parent than you can ever conceive of.

The clinician who sees in herself less than perfect parenting might be more willing to accept that imperfection as part of the normal course of things.

> Respondent 8: I can see that parents can be caring and still make mistakes, as I can already see the kinds of mistakes I'm making that I don't really want to be making. So I'm not as hard on parents.

> Respondent 7: I see in myself the conflict between knowing probably the doctrinaire, appropriate thing to do or the right kind of discipline to use . . . and then the fact is that I've run out of energy or patience at the time, so I do something that I know is probably not wise. . . . If I weren't on the inside of it and I saw a parent do that, I might think, "They know better, why don't they stop and think." . . . Theoretically, I knew that it was true, but there's nothing like being there a few times to be reminded what that's like.

Even when parents are well-motivated, the clinician might also believe that child rearing is not the science that she previously considered it:

> Respondent 23: Kids aren't going to respond all the time, whereas, before, I thought there was some kind of magic answer. If the parents were doing the right thing, the child would respond appropriately.

The clinician has intimate knowledge of the range of emotions associated with parenting, and having experienced them in herself, she is more likely to perceive these feelings as being basically normal, for example, the strength of the attachment bond to the child and the central importance of children to their parents:

> Respondent 11: The main thing I've learned that's surprised me in having a kid is how passionate an experience it is, how intense it is, and how high the highs are and how low the lows are and how incredibly strong the bond is. I think it's really hard, I think you almost have to take it on faith, if you don't have a child, how incredibly strong those feelings are.

Parents also experience other feelings, such as the desire to protect one's child, rage when children are frustrating, sadness when children separate:

> Respondent 25 (speaking about child abusers that she works with): [After having a child I was] more empathetic and less angry. . . . I understood more about the reaction, about the intensity of their anger toward their child. I still didn't understand how they acted on it. . . . Before, I would have denied that that feeling [of anger] was very universal because I would never have those feelings. That's what I thought.

The clinician who has experienced parental feelings from the inside might be more likely to view these feelings as understandable or comprehensible in clients. The clinician might perceive how even behavior that appears pathological can start out in a motive or feeling that is natural for a parent to have. By identifying with this starting point, the clinician may feel less need to attribute pathology or to judge the parent. This does not mean that the clinicians do not perceive that the behavior might have a negative effect on a child or that they do not encourage introspection or behavior change.

One clinician, for example, who worked on an adolescent inpatient unit, found that when clients were restricted for misbehavior their parents would sometimes intercede for them, requesting that the restriction be lifted instead of supporting the clinical staff in setting limits. Before becoming a parent herself, the clinician would typically be angered by these requests. She would wonder why the parents were colluding with their children in sabotaging treatment. After becoming a parent, the clinician was no longer angered. She would understand how a parent could be motivated by a desire to protect a child. The clinician still made the same intervention — namely, increasing the parents' understanding of and cooperation with limit setting. What had changed was her anger and her need to attribute pathology to the parents.

Even when the clinician believes that the parent is experiencing significant pathology, this identification with the starting point of the process — the feeling of the parent — can result in less anger:

> Respondent 21: I certainly understand that you can get very, very frustrated with a child and wish to be punitive and *be* punitive. So I feel much less judgmental. I address the issues and what they mean to the patient. And sometimes end up by saying "I think it might be better if you did not do that behavior." I am talking about someone who is very disturbed. For example, I have one patient now who, when she gets very withdrawn and absorbed, hits her child and makes the child go away.

In addition to identifying with the feelings of parents, a second aspect of increased empathy is a more detailed understanding of the situation of parents. The clinician now knows that parenting is a difficult, stressful job:

> Respondent 11: I have a client now who has a one-year-old who hasn't started sleeping through the night yet. . . . Before I had [my son] I would have thought, "My god, that's awful, this guy must be tired," but I wouldn't have the hands-on knowledge of what it feels like to never have eight uninterrupted hours of sleep and how tired you are and the stresses on your marriage and how angry you get at the kid and how guilty you feel.

This appreciation of the stresses of parenting can sometimes bring the clinicians to a focus on here-and-now problems, rather than on how a client's family history has produced psychopathology:

Respondent 19: Rather than just imagining that a lot of [the client's] difficulties, or almost all of them, stem from her own impoverished family, I'm now fusing that with the legitimate difficulties of parenting.

The clinician might better appreciate the stresses of multiple roles, a mother's need for nurturance, or the stresses of being at home with the kids:

Respondent 23: School vacations. I notice a difference in the women I see [during] the week the kids are home. They're much more stressed.

Respondent 22: I have empathy for what mothers are going through, who are working and have to manage and don't have enough time for themselves.

Respondent 1: I give couples assignments to have time alone together. I know from my own experience that this is important.

Respondent 14: I respect women who stay home with their kids more than I did before.

The increased empathy with the feelings and situations of parents can result in a clinician hearing in a different manner the adult client's memories of his or her past. The clinician might recognize that she had previously identified with the child's point of view:

Respondent 7: Before I had children, it was much easier for me to identify with the kid's point of view . . . and sometimes to have trouble understanding why parents did what they did or where they were coming from or why it made sense to them.

Respondent 16: I feel that I have more of an empathic understanding of the difficulties of being a parent. And I guess, in my work, I had a tendency to identify with the child more, and to see the parents as the people with the problem.

In being less identified with the child, the clinician might be more likely to separate out the perspective of the parent from that of the child:

Respondent 2: I probably am better able to figure out what parental motivation, or parental activity, might mean. I may be less likely to hear the patient's concerns about parents as, "Gee, aren't they awful," but rather as the patient's perception of the parents. And recognize that there's another side of the story. And how to recognize those differences. And also make room for the differences in perceptions.

Respondent 4: If patients are disappointed or angry with their parents, I hear it from a point of view of wondering what it would be like to be that person's parent, and what the parent's pressures are, or why the parent might not be sympathetic or listen. I can still see how [it] feels to be the patient, but I also might wonder more if there's a reason for the mother being this way in how [the patient] presents this to her. In their relationship has there been so much conflict that it's hard for the mother to be sympathetic, or what are her pressures or problems?

Separating out the points of view of parent and child, rather than being identified with the child's perspective, can result in a different sense of the dynamics of relationships. The clinician might feel that she has a more systemic view of relationships. She might move away from a simple causal model in which parents act and children react:

> Respondent 4: I feel [being a parent] has added to my appreciation of the complexities of the relationship over time.
> Respondent 21: [Having my own children] modified some of my views about rebellion. . . . I used to have more of an attitude that parents "do things" to children . . . like sometimes they withhold certain things . . . and it was very important for the children to speak up . . . and sometimes I would feel like I was fighting along with the kids.

For some clinicians, this altered sense of causality involved an altered philosophical stance. The clinician might no longer believe that there always is a right and a wrong way to do things. In diagnosis, this might involve a less doctrinaire stance toward using theory or diagnostic categories. In child rearing, this might involve a sense that there isn't always a right answer to every situation:

> Respondent 14: I'm not sure I'm doing anything different than I would have if I had seen these [clients] a few years ago [before having her child], but I think it's just harder for me to think in pat sorts of ways. I think I just have a better appreciation for, you know, that there aren't any easy answers and it's an incredibly complex relationship and intense relationship.

INCREASED UNDERSTANDING OF CHILD DEVELOPMENT

Another way the clinicians were alike was in a common belief that their basic understanding of child development deepened (65% explicitly stated this). As was found in their understanding of parental psychology, clinicians very rarely made an observation that challenged the theories that they held, with the same exception that was seen with parents: their idealism was deflated. As discussed above, this was manifested in a greater tendency to perceive children as actively contributing to relationships rather than as passively suffering the effects of parental behavior. Children can be willful and misbehave, their behavior can help to shape the behavior of parents, and they might be born with constitutional factors that shape relationships.

Increased understanding of child development could inform the recommendations clinicians make to parents. Clinicians often felt that their recommendations were more practical or that their recommendations had greater credibility with parents who were patients:

> Respondent 15: Before, I would rely on just what I read in books in terms of giving feedback to parents, in terms of things that they could do. Now, I can choose from information that I give, information that I feel would be useful, versus information that I feel would be impractical.

The greater understanding of child development also could inform the clinician's understanding of adult clients reconstructing the past:

> Respondent 13: I work with a number of patients with borderline personality disorders and I have a much richer appreciation of what it must have been like to have parents unavailable during those early developmental stages around rapprochement time. . . . What I try to do with some of the healthier folks is to create a picture of what it might be like to try to separate and to discover there isn't that steady or supportive person there.

Whether working with adult clients reconstructing the past or with children, the clinician might vary from what she had been taught by developing a less idealized view of childhood. In part, this was related to increased empathy with parents. The clinician might be less likely to identify with the client as having been victimized by the parent. The clinician might now believe that children can be demanding and willful, to want things not in their own interests, and to misinterpret the motivations of parents:

> Respondent 8: I think it's always been hard for me to see the parts of patients that are willful or stubborn or just downright demanding, that I've always taken their side, quite a bit. And as I see in my children, whom I can still love, an awful lot of demanding, willful, stubborn stuff, it helps me to gently point those things out to my patients.
> Respondent 4: I guess I can see the perspective that the [patient's] demands are very unreasonable or unrealistic. And maybe what the patient needs to do or can do in therapy is separating better so they don't expect those kinds of things from their parents.

The clinicians also might give greater credence to the idea that the parent's control of the relationship is constrained by the child's constitutional factors:

> Respondent 12: One thing I think I took very literally was that parents create their children. . . . I see now that [my daughter] came to us with some real constitutional factors. . . . I think that, before, I felt the parent must have been doing something bad. And now I see that kids are born with certain predispositions. And it isn't anybody's fault.

IMPLICATIONS

The psychotherapy literature has emphasized the independence of personal and professional life. When interrelationships between the two areas have been explored, the emphasis has been on carryover from professional to personal life (as when burned-out clinicians are emotionally distant from their families) or, at most, on episodes in which personal life intrudes on professional life (as when pregnancy intrudes on the therapy situation). In this study, however, an experience in personal life produced an enduring change in the phenomenology of clinicians conducting psychotherapy.

Whether clinicians had children while in graduate school or after 10 years of clinical experience, almost every clinician (88%) reported an experiential shift. It felt different to hear clients discuss their parents or their parenting because the clinician could now relate to this material experientially. This increased empathy for the position of parents enriched how it felt to do therapy, in the sense that the clinicians felt more affectively connected to the material or understood the material in greater detail.

Some clinicians believed that the effect of their increased empathy was confined to a few clinical situations, whereas other clinicians believed that their thinking about clients had been affected a great deal. The clinicians thus differed in how the shift was integrated into their overall style, but a second uniformity in the data was that most of the examples they gave of increased empathy were aspects of the same themes: the clinicians were more identified with the position of parent than that of child, and/or the clinicians better discriminated between the two positions.

Elaine Heffner (1978) has written: "It certainly is not new or startling to find that women feel the desire to take care of their children. What is new is the number of women who are startled by such feelings" (p. 11). Even among these psychotherapists, whose professional competence is in the area of family relationships, the emotional realities of mothering are something to be learned. Perhaps this is in part because, in this culture, very few women have experience with young children before become mothers themselves. As parents, the clinicians were exposed to nuts-and-bolts information about childhood and parenting not previously understood. Perhaps this also reflects the cultural devaluation of mothering: although motherhood is held up to women as their most important role, paradoxically, it is not culturally defined as a powerfully significant experience.

Motherhood is also inadequately defined culturally as a major life transition. In the workplace, maternity is often thought of as an episode or intrusion. When a woman becomes a mother, the issue most discussed might be maternity leave or how long employment must be interrupted before normal duties are resumed. However, when a woman becomes a mother, her responsibilities and situation are permanently altered. In this research, maternity is perceived to be a life transition psychologically, a permanent change in perspective.

Maternity resulted in an enduring change in how the clinicians experienced conducting psychotherapy. The pattern of changes observed is most consistent with the hypotheses that (1) the clinicians had experienced developmental change that affected how they viewed the therapy situation, and/or (2) the clinicians experienced a change in reference group.

Developmental change is suggested by the clinicians' better discrimination between the positions of parent and child, rather than solely identifying with the child's perspective. Further, the clinicians might develop a perspective that integrates both points of view. Change in reference group is suggested by the clinicians' change in basic viewpoint to that of a parent. In being less idealistic about parents, the clinicians are more forgiving of the parents' limitations; in being less idealistic about children, they are clearer-eyed about the negatives in children.

The change in perspective associated with maternity is one of increasing psychological differentiation, not one of increasing psychological fusion. That is, the stereotypic mother is understanding, sympathetic, patient, someone who gratifies her child's needs, someone who perceives her child's needs as opposed to her own point of view. What these clinicians describe, on the other hand, are experiences of separating out the perspectives of parent and child and seeing both in a more realistic manner. This is, after all, as it should be. Interconnectedness, or intimacy, requires a sense of oneself and the other as separate but related. (If children really do lack a sense of this separation, that is no reason why their parents, who are adults, should identify with their perspective.)

In perceiving the experiences of parents from their own perspective, some clinicians report that they attribute less pathology or feel less anger. The clinician might perceive how motivation begins with a universal feeling or motive or understand the parents' own constraints and pressures. This has implications for understanding the sources of "mother-blaming." For these clinicians, blaming the mother was associated with an overidentification with the child's perspective and a lack of differentiation of the perspective of the mother.

Some of the changes that the clinicians report are changes that, one would hope, occur developmentally for all individuals and for all clinicians: gaining more maturity in seeing and accepting parents realistically and becoming less dependent on doctrinaire theoretical formulations. It should be stressed that no implications should be drawn from this study about the maturation of nonparents or fathers. We don't know whether these groups develop in similar ways, drawing on different experiences, or develop in different ways. We also have no data about whether mothers and nonmothers differ in their clinical interventions and style, much less their effectiveness.

The conclusions that we can draw are phenomenological. The experience of the clinician/mothers is enriched by increased empathy, and in the structure of their lives, parenthood is intertwined with the experience of developmental change.

NOTES

1. Twenty-five mothers who were actively practicing psychotherapists were randomly selected from lists of all licensed psychologists and all members of a clinical social work group listing three North Carolina towns as their address. To be included in the study, participants had to be currently employed, with a minimum of 3 years of clinical experience, and had to be living in two-parent households containing at least one child under the age of 14.

2. The interview method was similar to that used in other studies exploring the phenomenology of respondents (e.g., Cherniss, 1980; Piotrkowski, 1979). Each clinician met once with the author for a face-to-face interview. She was asked to address each of a set of topic areas, and was asked further questions as needed to clarify or amplify responses. The range of themes that were present in the data was described and organized into a coherent set of categories. Information about interactions with clients that occurred at any point in the interview was studied. The results reported are not quantitative; they describe the range, not the frequency, of responses. To ascertain reliability in the few cases in which it was desirable to report response frequencies, the author and a research assistant independently coded a subset of cases from the codebook developed by the author, with an interrater agreement of at least 90%.

REFERENCES

Benedek, T. (1952). Parenthood as a developmental phase. *Journal of the American Psychoanalytic Association, 7*, 389–417.

Cherniss, C. (1980). *Professional burnout in human service organizations*. New York: Praeger.

Crawford, M., & Marecek, J. (1989). Psychology reconstructs the female: 1968–1988. *Psychology of Women Quarterly, 13*, 147–165.

Derry, P. (1990). *Motherhood and the professional life: The case of female psychotherapists*. Bristol, IN: Wyndham Hall.

Erikson, E. (1963). *Childhood and society*. New York: Norton.

Farber, B. (1983). Dysfunctional aspects of the psychotherapeutic role. In B. Farber (Ed.), *Stress and burnout in the human service professions* (pp. 97–118). New York: Pergamon.

Guy, J. (1987). *The personal life of the psychotherapist*. New York: Wiley.

Heffner, E. (1978). *Mothering*. New York: Doubleday.

Hersen, M., Michelson, L., & Bellack, A. (1984). *Issues in psychotherapy research.* New York: Plenum.

Koumans, A. (1987). The effect of children on adult development. *International Journal of Family Psychiatry, 8,* 417–428.

Levinson, D. (1978). *The seasons of a man's life.* New York: Knopf.

Partridge, S. (1988). The parental self-concept: A theoretical exploration and practical application. *American Journal of Orthopsychiatry, 58,* 281–287.

Piotrkowski, C. (1979). *Work and the family system.* New York: Free Press.

■ 4
Couples in Psychotherapy: The Positive Effects of a Feminist Perspective on Interpersonal Satisfactions

Doris Howard

Over the past 25 years, women's movement toward greater social, political, and economic equity in society has led to new research in gender and personality issues. In addition, it inevitably led to new psychotherapies that evolved in response to women's changing needs. This chapter demonstrates a connection between gender-role research and feminist therapy.

By the early 1970s, a wide range of research began to explore new definitions of femininity and masculinity (e.g., Bem, 1974; Broverman, Vogel, Broverman, Clarkson, & Rosenkrantz, 1972; Constantinople, 1973). Scales were constructed to assess the presence or absence of gender-related personality characteristics and their relation to the behaviors of women and men (Bem, 1974; Spence, Helmreich, & Stapp, 1974). Bem (1974) arrived at the conclusion that the androgynous personality, high in both feminine/expressive and masculine/instrumental characteristics, was the most flexible and represented a new model for positive mental health.

As social learning theorists began to map out the destructive effects of gender-role socialization, feminist theories of therapy underwent development and definition. Increasingly, gender-role socialization was cited as the source of many, if not most, of the problems women experience, including marital difficulties (Bernard, 1981; Brodsky & Hare-Mustin, 1980; Franks & Rothblum, 1983; Miller, 1976).

In a study examining compatibility in male–female relationships, Ickes and Barnes (1978) found evidence of greater interpersonal incompatibility in traditional dyads of feminine women and masculine men than in dyads in which one or both partners were androgynous. Fischer and Narus (1981) used the Bem Sex-Role Inventory (BSRI) to study gender-role effects on intimacy in couples. They defined intimacy in terms of shared concerns and shared experience of need satisfaction. They found that femininity was independently related to intimacy, whereas masculinity was not. They also found the highest intimacy scores in relationships in which both partners rated high on the BSRI in femininity, and the lowest intimacy scores in relationships in which both partners rated high in masculinity.

In another important study, Antill (1983) interviewed 108 married couples in Sydney, Australia, using the BSRI to measure gender-role orientation and the Spanier Dyadic Adjustment Scale (Spanier, 1976) to measure marital happiness. He found that both men and women were significantly happier when paired with a feminine or an androgynous partner than when paired with a masculine or an undifferentiated partner. Happiness was positively correlated with femininity in the opposite partner. Couples in which both partners were high in femininity or androgyny were happier than any other combination. This study did not devalue masculine characteristics. Antill merely observed that highly valued masculine characteristics did not contribute much to happy, long-term relationships. Traits such as compassion, warmth, and sensitivity to the needs of others were most highly correlated with happiness in both partners and have obvious implications for maintaining successful intimate relationships.

Gerber (1986) conceptualized success in female–male relationships through three principles: the positivity balance, the leadership balance, and the satisfaction balance. Ideally, both partners achieve equal measures of positivity, leadership, and satisfaction in a successful relationship. Gerber postulated that satisfaction depends upon the sum of feminine traits in both partners being greater than the sum of masculine traits. The higher the sum of the feminine traits, the greater is the shared level of marital happiness.

These reports corroborate the experience of the author as a feminist therapist working with couples. The author was originally trained in the interpersonal theory of therapy (Sullivan, 1953). Some of the basic concepts of interpersonal psychotherapy are similar to feminist concepts: both share the basic belief that personality is shaped by environment and culture. In feminist terms, this translates into gender-role stereotyping. Girls are taught to be feminine, and boys are taught to be masculine. In previous years, women were expected to remain primarily in the home attending to child care and homemaking. If they did work outside the home, it was usually in low-paying employment that they did in addition to child care and home care. Men were expected to be the major income earners and to participate little in home and child care. These roles reflected the traits labeled feminine and masculine, respectively.

In recent years, women's greater participation in the work force has permitted men to participate more in home and child care. The world "permit" is chosen deliberately, in the belief that men benefit from sharing more with their families, just as women benefit from greater participation in career roles. Currently, there is the largest female paid work force in history, in contrast to past generations when women worked at home or on farms, with little or no personal financial recompense. The fact that women now work outside the home creates a need for greater cooperation between partners in sharing parenting and home care responsibilities.

Some parents experience stress and conflict not only from the demands of multiple roles but also because of the interference of gender-role socialization. For example, many women resist learning how to mow lawns or take care of cars, and men resist learning how to use a vacuum or do grocery shopping. Other couples fare better because they are less gender-role-oriented and sometimes because they are open to therapeutic interventions.

A successful intervention was made with a married couple who began therapy in their 30s. They had one small child. They had demanding careers and long commutes to work. The wife was feeling severely overburdened; she complained that her husband was not assuming sufficient responsibility for home and child care. She criticized him for not doing more but later revealed in therapy that, by doing most of the housework while continuing to berate him, she felt she had more control over him by manipulating his guilt feelings. He had been brought up to think of home and child care as the wife's responsibility and, further, that it was part of a normal relationship that his wife would scold him for not doing what she never expected him to do in the first place. In the course of therapy, he gradually came to understand that her complaints about his lack of participation were valid. He found that he received more satisfactions at home relative to his greater participation. As he put more caring, effort, and sensitivity into his family and home and as she gave up her efforts to control him, relations improved between them and between him and their child. They both eventually realized that their power struggle severely undermined the possibility of real happiness for them.

Another example is a couple who had conflicting expectations of marriage because of their different backgrounds. The husband had been brought up by parents in a dual-career family. His expectation was that he would share home care. He was, in fact, a competent cook and housekeeper. The wife had lost her mother at age 11 and had developed an intense dependency upon her rather inadequate father. Her father had continually reassured her—even through his unpleasant second marriage—that he would always be there to care for her. In addition, she had been taught nothing about the management of either a home or finances. She transferred to her husband the expectation that a man would take care of her. In this case, therapy helped the woman to learn about increasing her sensitivity to the needs of others and to give up her romantic and unrealistic expectations.

In another case, conflict in gender-role socialization was brought to therapy by a young woman client. She was the second of three children and had been the academic star in the family. Her mother had directed her toward a successful professional career that duplicated her father's. Her drive and ambition led her to a career track in a prestigious firm that guaranteed a minimum annual income of $250,000 within a few years. She had also been taught, however, that her husband must always earn more than she so that she would have the option of not working should she so desire. Her husband chose a career in a field that does not provide the same large income. Thus, there was a conflict between the wife's demands of her husband and his capacity to earn a larger income than she could.

Through feminist therapy, they gradually resolved these issues. They worked out plans for each to have the desired career and planned how to use time and money to share home and child care. The wife eventually understood her conflict and realized the difference between her real needs and the goals of her parents. This woman and her husband now find satisfaction in the knowledge that each has the career of choice, regardless of who earns the greater income.

A development that sometimes occurs in working with couples is that therapists may find themselves in the position of giving more attention to the male partner. This usually occurs when the husband is new to the therapeutic process and is hearing for the first time that feminine/expressive characteristics are what he is being asked to call forth in himself. Siegel (1982, p. 10) describes this as "breaking the taboo against uncovering male vulnerability."

The therapist must keep in mind the feelings of the woman whenever more attention is given to the man, however briefly. Robbins (1983) noted that whenever she gave more attention to the man, she feared that the woman might interpret it to mean that a woman's concerns were less important. Robbins also thought that it was sometimes difficult for a female therapist to be a good role model for another woman in the presence of a man. Presumably, this refers to the internalized submissiveness and deference that women, even women therapists, often show to men. It is nevertheless true that the therapy session can provide an excellent opportunity for a female therapist to be a good role model for a female client in the presence of a male partner by demonstrating assertiveness and impartiality.

The issues presented here have been concerned with gender-role socialization. Other issues such as anxiety, depression, and low self-esteem, deriving from negative or inadequate parenting, have not been addressed. These are not to be considered unimportant issues. This chapter addresses only gender stereotyping and its negative impact on intimate relationships. It seems clear that with hard work and compromise, couples can achieve greater sharing, mutual support, and understanding. In couples' therapy, it is evident that both partners benefit when they demonstrate high levels of feminine/expressive qualities such as warmth, understanding, tenderness, and sensitivity to each other's needs.

Although this chapter has addressed therapy with female–male couples, it should be noted that the author's experience with male–male and female–female couples differs little from that described here. Men and women alike integrate and internalize gender-role stereotypes, even though they may not be same-sex characteristics. It is the therapist's responsibility to help women and men to reeducate themselves about relationships and roles.

Warmth, sensitivity, and understanding have been associated with women in the past. They are not, however, innate female behaviors or characteristics. Men can be warm, tender, sensitive, and understanding as well. These are human characteristics that both women and men can bring to intimate relationships. It is the work of therapy to help clients to realize this in order to facilitate the greatest levels of satisfaction in couples' relationships.

REFERENCES

Antill, J. K. (1983). Sex role complementarity versus similarity in married couples. *Journal of Personality and Social Psychology, 45,* 145–155.

Bem, S. L. (1974). The measurement of psychological androgyny. *Journal of Consulting and Clinical Psychology, 42,* 155–162.

Bernard, J. (1981). *The female world.* New York: Free Press.

Brodsky, A. M., & Hare-Mustin, R. (Eds.). (1980). *Women and psychotherapy.* New York: Guilford.

Broverman, I., Vogel, S., Broverman, D., Clarkson, F., & Rosenkrantz, P. (1972). Sex-role stereotypes; A current appraisal. *Journal of Social Issues, 28,* 58–78.

Constantinople, A. (1973). Masculinity–femininity: An exception to a famous dictum? *Psychological Bulletin, 80,* 389–407.

Fischer, J. L., & Narus, L. R. (1981). Sex roles and intimacy in same sex and other sex relationships. *Psychology of Women Quarterly, 5,* 444–455.

Franks, V., & Rothblum, E. (Eds.). (1983). *The stereotyping of women: Its effects on mental health.* New York: Springer Publishing Co.

Gerber, G. L. (1986). The relationship balance model and its implications for individual and couples therapy. In D. Howard (Ed.), *The dynamics of feminist therapy* (pp. 19–27). New York: Haworth Press.

Ickes, W., & Barnes, R. D. (1978). Boys and girls together — and alienated: On enacting stereotyped sex roles in mixed-sex dyads. *Journal of Personality and Social Psychology, 36,* 669–683.

Miller, J. B. (1976). *Toward a new psychology of women.* Boston: Beacon.

Robbins, J. H. (1983). Complex triangles: Uncovering sexist bias in relationship counseling. *Women & Therapy, 2,* 159–170.

Siegel, R. J. (1982). The long-term marriage: Implications for therapy. *Women & Therapy, 1,* 3–12.

Spanier, G. B. (1976). Measuring dyadic adjustment: New scales for assessing the quality of marriage and similar dyads. *Journal of Marriage and the Family, 38,* 15–28.

Spence, J. T., Helmreich, R. L., & Stapp, J. (1974). The personal attributes questionnaire: A measure of sex-role stereotypes and masculinity and femininity. *JSAS Catalog of Selected Documents in Psychology, 4,* 43.

Sullivan, H. S. (1953). *The interpersonal theory of psychiatry.* New York: Norton.

■ 5
Gender Stereotypes and the Change toward Greater Personal Maturity in Psychotherapy

Gwendolyn L. Gerber

During the course of psychotherapy, it becomes apparent that some clients experience problems because of the need to see their own personalities as similar to the cultural expectations for their gender. To do this, they have to suppress important aspects of themselves: women have to suppress their urge toward self-assertion; men have to suppress their urge to show concern and accommodation toward others.

Not only do these cultural stereotypes determine the way clients see themselves; they also affect the way they see the other sex (Gerber, 1986, 1989). For example, when a woman thinks of herself as being highly accommodating in her relationships with men, she also thinks of most men as being highly assertive. In other words, the woman would see her own personality traits as being complementary to those of most men. To maintain this stereotypic image of herself and the other sex, the woman needs to avoid seeing herself and men as having any personality characteristics that conflict with cultural expectations. She would have to inhibit any impulses toward self-assertion in herself. She would also have to discount any expressions of warmth or accommodation on the part of men. Thus, the woman's

I would like to express my appreciation to Joan Einwohner, Marianne Jackson, Rascha Levinson, and Ruth Shapiro for their thoughtful comments on an earlier version of the paper.

image of herself as well as her image of the other sex would be based, in part, on a misperception and misinterpretation of reality.

When people change toward greater personal maturity in psychotherapy, they generally become better able to integrate the qualities of self-assertion and accommodation within their own personalities (Bakan, 1966; Hefner, Rebecca, & Oleshansky, 1975). This means that the image they have of themselves changes in very basic ways so that it no longer corresponds with cultural stereotypes. As a person's self-image changes, the image that person has of the other sex generally changes as well. Because people usually perceive themselves and the other sex as having complementary personality attributes, the other sex would then be seen in a more integrated way — as having the qualities of self-assertion in addition to those of concern and accommodation.

Unfortunately, the process of change in psychotherapy is often very painful and associated with intense anxiety. This can occur even when the enactment of stereotyped personal characteristics in intimate relationships has led to considerable personal distress. Part of the difficulty stems from people's need to maintain a sense of connection with others, particularly in their intimate relationships with members of the other sex. Without being aware of their underlying motives, clients often resist change because of their concern that their own personality characteristics will no longer be complementary to those of the other sex. They fear that their intimate relationships will then become disrupted and conflicted.

Sometimes these concerns are realistic; when clients change their own personalities in fundamental ways, their relationships with members of the other sex frequently do become increasingly unsatisfying. However, sometimes these fears are unrealistic and are based on ways of thinking about relationships that do not necessarily correspond with external reality (Fensterheim & Baer, 1988).

Recent research on gender stereotyping helps to explain some of the factors underlying clients' resistance to change (Gerber, 1987, 1988). This research has shown that people think in predictable ways about relationships. Sometimes their stereotypic expectations correspond with actual experience; sometimes they do not. The research helps to further our understanding of why the process of change toward increased personal maturity in psychotherapy is so difficult and is often fraught with so much anxiety.

GENDER STEREOTYPES AND RELATIONSHIPS

Most people believe that the two sexes have extremely dissimilar personality traits (Bem, 1974; Rosenkrantz, Vogel, Bee, Broverman, & Broverman,

1968; Spence, Helmreigh, & Stapp, 1975).[1] However, this is *not* due to some basic difference in men's and women's personalities. Instead, it is due to their enactment of roles that vary in power. Because women and men usually play differing roles when they interact with one another, people observe them acting in dissimilar ways and assume that they must have different personality traits (Secord & Backman, 1961).

In traditional relationships between the sexes, the man acts as the leader, and the woman acts as the follower. As a consequence, people believe that the man's personality is high in the agency that characterizes the role of leader and the woman's personality is high in the communion that characterizes the role of follower (Gerber, 1988). *Agency* refers to the personality traits that enhance one's individual self and involves the capacity to be self-assertive and to take charge and master. *Communion* refers to the personality traits that enhance relationships with others and involves the capacity to be empathic and accommodating toward other people (Bakan, 1966).

Research has found that when the traditional roles are reversed, and the woman is described as the leader in a relationship, the gender stereotypes are also reversed: the woman is seen as strong in agency, and the man is viewed as strong in communion (Gerber, 1988). In an egalitarian relationship with shared leadership, people do not perceive any personality differences between the sexes—both the woman and the man are seen as possessing the personality traits of communion as well as those of agency.

At first glance, the two types of dominant–subordinate relationships (traditional and woman-led) appear to be similar to one another, whereas the egalitarian relationship seems to be different. In dominant–subordinate relationships, one person is high in agency and the other person is high in communion; in an egalitarian relationship, by contrast, both persons are characterized by agency as well as communion. However, research shows that all of these relationships are based on the same underlying principle: the strength of one person's agency is matched by the strength of the other person's communion (Gerber, 1988).

The purpose of the match is to maintain stability within the relationship (Gerber, 1987). When an individual expresses needs and finds that the other person responds to these needs, he or she feels satisfied and motivated to continue the relationship. However, if an individual repeatedly tries to be self-assertive but finds that the other person refuses to accommodate, he or she feels frustrated and angry. If the other person continues to be resistant over a period of time, this generally leads to conflict and dissension, and the relationship might even break up (Gerber, 1986, 1989).

In dominant–subordinate relationships (traditional and woman-led), the leader takes most of the initiative and makes most of the decisions in the interaction, and the follower is highly accommodating to these acts of self-assertion. In other words, the strength of the leader's agency and the follower's communion are matched so that the two individuals have complementary personality traits. The follower is viewed as being low in agency, and the leader is seen as being correspondingly low in communion, thereby creating a match between the strength of these personality attributes as well. Even though the leader and follower express different amounts of agency, such a relationship meets both people's expectations. This establishes a stable interaction that is free of conflict.

On the surface, the egalitarian relationship appears to be conceptualized in a very different way. This is because the two sexes are perceived as having identical rather than complementary personality attributes. Again, however, the underlying principle is that the strength of one person's agency is matched by the strength of the other person's communion. Both sexes share equally in the leadership, so they are equally self-assertive (or agentic); both sexes support one another's assertions, so they are equally accommodating (or communal). Each individual would feel that her or his needs were being met by the other person, and consequently, the relationship would be stable.

These findings from the gender-stereotyping research are important for understanding why clients find it hard to change their image of themselves in psychotherapy. In order to modify their self-image, clients also have to alter their image of the kinds of relationships they have with the other sex (Gerber, 1986, 1989). For example, a man who needs to see himself in a typically masculine way, as being high in agency, would have to maintain traditional relationships with women. He would always have to enact the role of leader, and the woman would have to play the role of follower. If such a man were able to change so as to see himself as less masculine-typed and more communal, he would need to establish different kinds of relationships with women. His relationships with women would have to be altered so that they were more egalitarian.

Clients generally find it extremely difficult to modify the nature of their relationships with the other sex. This is *not* because these two types of relationships, traditional and egalitarian, are structured in fundamentally different ways. As we have seen, they are both based on the same underlying principle.

Furthermore, clients do not find it difficult to change to more egalitarian relationships because of an inability to imagine what such relationships would be like. The research on gender stereotyping shows that most people can readily describe the characteristics of a woman-led or an egalitarian relationship (Gerber, 1988). When they are given information about the leadership roles in a heterosexual relationship and are asked to describe the woman and man on the communal and agentic personality traits, most people do so with a strikingly high degree of consistency.

This does not imply that people are aware of the underlying principle that they use in conceptualizing various types of relationships. On the contrary, they generally employ this principle without being consciously aware of what they are doing and cannot articulate what it is, even when asked.[2] Sometimes, clients are aware that their capacity to be self-assertive affects the power that they can exercise with others. However, they often do not realize that the power they exert in a particular relationship is also dependent on their partner's response; in order for their self-assertions to be effective, the partner has to be accommodating to an equal degree.

IMAGES OF THE SELF AND THE SENSE OF CONNECTEDNESS

Even though they may be able to describe intellectually what an egalitarian interaction would be like for other people, clients who see themselves as highly gender-stereotyped rarely describe their own relationships in that way. Most of the interactions that they experience with members of the other sex are traditional ones in which their partners appear to have stereotypic personalities. However, they occasionally experience interactions in which the traditionally stereotyped roles are reversed. For example, a self-centered, controlling man will generally choose to form relationships with women who appear submissive and totally accommodating to him. He will try to discount any experiences with women that do not fit the expected pattern. Whenever it becomes apparent to him that a particular woman's behavior does not fit his expectations, he will avoid interacting with her if at all possible.

When situational pressures force him into interacting with a woman who is dominant, he will usually perceive her as an extremely unpleasant person and see her as trying to coerce him into playing a submissive role. If he happens to interact with a woman who acts in an egalitarian way toward him, he will usually misperceive her motives. Instead of feeling that she is treating him as an equal, he will see her as trying to dominate him.

What is evident from this example is that the man who tries to define himself in rigidly gender-stereotyped ways does *not* always experience himself as dominant. Even though a subordinate role is unacceptable to him, he sometimes feels submissive in his relationships with women. Whenever this occurs, he perceives the woman as "castrating" and as trying to force him into an "unnatural" role. By blaming the woman for his feeling of powerlessness, he can disown the experience and tell himself that she, rather than he, is responsible for his feelings. Whenever he experiences himself in a subordinate position, he usually directs all of his energies to reversing the roles so that he feels in charge. To do this, he can often engage in increasingly competitive and sometimes even abusive behavior.

This example also illustrates the way in which the man's evaluations of himself and the woman are dependent on the way he perceives their relationship. When he sees himself as dominant and the woman as subordinate, he feels good about himself and the woman. When the roles are reversed so that he sees himself as subordinate and the woman as dominant, he feels bad about himself and the woman.

According to Harry Stack Sullivan (1953), people learn to evaluate the self and the interactive partner as either "good" or "bad" in their early experiences with their parents. The relationship with the parent of the other sex is particularly important for learning gender-typed patterns of behavior — hence, the girl's relationship with her father and the boy's relationship with his mother are extremely influential.[3] If the parent holds to very rigid, traditional standards of behavior, the child learns to evaluate his or her behavior according to these standards. When the child enacts a culturally acceptable role, the parent approves and enacts the complementary culturally accepted role. The child feels relaxed and comfortable and perceives the parent and the self as "good." When the child acts in a culturally *un*acceptable way, the parent disapproves. The parent experiences the child as trying to force him or her to enact a culturally *un*acceptable role as well. The child experiences anxiety and discomfort and perceives the parent and the self as "bad." Thus, a child who has a strongly gender-stereotyped parent learns to suppress any feelings and impulses that go counter to these stereotypes. The little girl learns to inhibit her natural assertiveness; the little boy learns to dissociate his feelings of warmth and concern for others.

Regardless of the way in which the two persons are evaluated, the relationship between the parent and child is perceived as stable. When they both are "good," the parent and child manifest stereotypically gender-typed personality characteristics and have a traditional relationship. When they both are "bad," the parent and child manifest personality characteristics that go counter to gender stereotypes and have a nontraditional relationship. Both of these types of relationships follow a dominant–subordinate model in which one person is high in agency and the other person is high in communion. The strength of one person's agency is matched with the strength of the other person's communion, and as a consequence, the relationship is stable. Even when the parent and child interact in culturally *un*acceptable ways and the child experiences the parent and the self as "bad," the sense of having a stable bond with the parent remains.

A problem arises, however, when the child tries to integrate the qualities of agency and communion within his or her personality. To establish a stable bond with the child, the parent has to reciprocate by expressing the qualities of agency and communion as well. A rigidly gender-stereotyped parent would be incapable of doing this and so would be unable to enact a complementary role with the child. Such a parent would probably not even be capable of imagining what an egalitarian relationship with the child would be like. The parent would not be able to see that both persons could maintain a strong sense of self and could also feel connected and responsive to one another. In addition, the idea that a parent and child who were of different sexes could have similar personality characteristics would be extremely threatening. As a consequence, whenever the child tried to act in an integrated way, by expressing both communion *and* agency, the child would experience the loss of any sort of connection to the parent and would feel overwhelming anxiety.[4] The image of the parent would no longer provide an anchor for the sense of self, so there would be a feeling of disintegration of the self as well (Sullivan, 1953). To cope with these overwhelming feelings of anxiety, the child would learn to dissociate any experience of the self as acting in an integrated way.

THE PROCESS OF CHANGE IN PSYCHOTHERAPY

Clients' recollections of their early experiences with the parent of the other sex can help to clarify how they learned to define themselves in gender-stereotyped terms. These experiences can also help to illuminate why it is so difficult for clients to begin to experience themselves in nonstereotypic ways, even though they might wish to do so. The following case example illustrates the importance of these early experiences and what happens as the client changes during the course of psychotherapy.

Anne initially came for treatment because of chronic feelings of depression.[5] In her relationships with others, she generally felt inferior and acted in an extremely accommodating way. Because she played a submissive role in her relationships, she was extremely high in communion and low in agency. Thus, she manifested the personality traits that are stereotypically associated with women in our culture.

During the course of psychotherapy it became clear that her sense of inferiority and excessive acquiescence stemmed, in large part, from her relationship with her father. He was a very domineering person who expected to receive admiration and adulation from his daughter, as well as from the other members of the family. Anne had learned to please him by enacting a subordinate, admiring, inferior role with him. Her father would then approve of her and treat her as "special." She came to define her self in these terms and to see herself as a "good person" when she acted that way. Thus, the role that Anne had learned to enact complemented the narcissistic, controlling role that her father played (Kiesler, 1983).

The father's sense of self was very unstable, and he frequently perceived other people, including at times his daughter, as trying to put him down and make him feel inferior. On those few occasions when Anne tried to express some healthy self-assertiveness, her father would perceive her as being the domineering, superior person that he generally was with her. He would tell her that she was nasty and bad-tempered and would regain his superior position by putting her down.

Anne described one incident involving her father that had taken place when she was in fifth grade. She had received an A on a paper she had written and proudly showed it to her father. Anne very much valued her father's approval and hoped that he would share her sense of accomplishment. Unfortunately, the paper happened to be on a subject with which her father was not familiar. He had always been very threatened when Anne knew something that he did not. He responded by telling her that she did not have to act in such a superior way toward him because he was the one who had cleaned up her messes when she had toilet training accidents as a child. Anne recounted feeling startled and upset by her father's reaction because she had not intended to be threatening to him in any way.

On this occasion, Anne had been mildly self-assertive in bringing home her paper to show her father. She was trying to relate to her father in a more egalitarian way by expressing some agency as well as the communion that she usually expressed. She hoped that he would respond to her sense of pride and accomplishment with warmth and appreciation. Because the father's sense of self was rigidly anchored in the domineering role that he usually played, he could not perceive his daughter as trying to relate to him as more of an equal. Instead, he saw her as trying to reverse their roles, feel superior to him, and put him down. He reacted by trying to humiliate her in referring to her toilet training accidents. Anne responded to the event by feeling that she must have done something "bad" and must have deserved the put-down she had received from her father.

As a result of this early training, Anne had come to choose domineering men as friends and dating partners. She defined herself as a "good person" when she enacted an admiring, self-effacing role in her relationships with men. When she expressed any assertiveness with men, even when this was appropriate, she feared that she was being "bitchy" and that the man would dislike her. When men did put her down, she felt humiliated but also experienced a kind of comfort, which came from the familiar feeling of connectedness associated with that role.

In the incident involving her school paper, Anne had been only indirectly self-assertive and had primarily hoped that her father would react by being responsive (and communal) with her. The one occasion on which she remembered making a direct request of her father had been far more traumatic.

She had wanted to learn to play a musical instrument and had been given a flute for her eighth birthday. As soon as she unwrapped her present, her father asked to see it. He had played the flute himself as a child, so he wanted to try out the new instrument. He started playing the flute and continued for over half an hour while Anne waited patiently. Finally, she reached the point of total frustration and insisted that her father give the flute to her. He handed it over in angry silence and refused to talk to her for two days thereafter. This experience had been far more terrifying to Anne than being criticized, because she had felt totally isolated and alone. Her father was the central figure in her world, and the loss of this relationship meant that Anne felt she was without human connection of any kind. At the time, she had feared that she might never regain a sense of connection with her father again.

These two incidents had the potential of being positive growth experiences for Anne. If her father had been able to be responsive (or communal) when Anne began to experiment with being more self-assertive (or agentic), she could have learned that it was possible to relate to another person with respect and accommodation while still maintaining a strong sense of self.[6] In other words, she would have learned how to integrate her own agency and communion in an egalitarian relationship with another person. Unfortunately, her father had such a rigidly defined self-concept that he could not tolerate Anne's positive moves toward integration. When she asserted her rights as an equal with her father, he withdrew totally from her and acted as though she no longer existed.

During the treatment, Ann reenacted some of the old patterns that she had learned in interactions with her father. Initially, she acted like the "good" child and was very self-effacing and accommodating with the therapist. Whenever she expressed any needs or made any sort of request, she thought that the therapist would think that she was aggressive, inappropriate, and "bad." She then expected that the therapist would try to humiliate her and put her down. This was her way of reexperiencing with the therapist the only forms of connection that she knew.

Most of the time, she could not perceive the possibility of having an equal relationship with anyone, including the therapist. During the course of psychotherapy, she occasionally experienced herself as an equal for brief periods of time. However, she quickly became anxious and would then reinterpret her experience in terms of the old dominant–subordinate pattern.

At one point, the therapist asked what she imagined would happen if she felt adequate and capable of interacting as an equal. The image that came into Anne's mind was of an "explosion" in which the entire relationship was destroyed. The meaning of this image became clarified in subsequent sessions. It expressed Anne's newly found ability to be in touch with her healthy self-assertiveness, which included the capacity to feel anger. It was also a metaphor for what Anne sensed was happening to the dominant–subordinate pattern of relating with which she was so familiar. It reflected her sense that her old pattern of relating was breaking down, so she no longer felt locked into playing either a submissive or dominant role. She could begin to feel free to experience herself as an integrated person — someone who was capable of expressing agency as well as communion in her relationships with others.

Following this session, Anne's relationships with other people began to change in significant ways. She began to report interactions with friends in which she felt adequate and experienced the relationship as one of mutual respect. In addition, her father no longer seemed to be the overwhelming, domineering, and frightening figure that he had been in the past.

This case illustrates the way in which gender-stereotyped personality characteristics stem from the dominant–subordinate pattern of relating that a client has experienced as a child. Anne had learned to define herself as "good" only when she acted inferior and powerless in relation to others. Being dominant was an unacceptable role for her because it had meant that she was "bad."

Because of the traumas she had experienced with her father in the past, it had been impossible for Anne to see herself as an equal in a relationship with another person at the beginning of treatment. Consequently, it had also been impossible for her to see herself as an agentic as well as a communal person. The experience of being an integrated individual had become dissociated from her awareness because it was associated with terrifying experiences of being rejected and isolated as a child.

During psychotherapy, Anne was able to experience a new way of relating after the old, rigidly defined, dominant–subordinate pattern had "exploded." This led to a new and more integrated view of her self — of being self-assertive as well as accommodating. In addition, she discovered a new capacity to interact with other people in relationships of equality and mutual respect, relationships in which both partners could express the qualities of self-assertion as well as warmth and concern.

SUMMARY AND CONCLUSION

When clients need to define themselves in rigidly gender-stereotyped ways, part of the problem can often be traced back to the relationship with the parent of the other sex. Frequently, the child learned to enact stereotypic gender roles in the interactions with this parent. The girl learned to act in a subordinate manner with the father; the boy learned to act in a dominant way with the mother. Whenever the child enacted these roles, the parent would approve, and the child would learn to think of herself or himself as "good." If the child reversed the roles and acted in a way that went counter to the parent's expectations, the child would learn that he or she was "bad."

A highly gender-stereotyped parent is unable to integrate the qualities of communion and agency within his or her own personality. Attempts by the child to express both of these qualities are very threatening to such a parent and will generally be met with disapproval and rejection. Because of the need to maintain a stable bond with the parent, the child gives up the attempt at integration and learns to define his or her self in ways that met with the parent's approval.

The process of change toward greater personal maturity in psychotherapy is frequently very difficult. As the client begins to act in ways that were stifled in the past, all of the terror and sense of isolation that was experienced as a child is reinvoked. These anxieties can then be worked through in psychotherapy. As the power of the old images and fears diminishes, the client becomes freer to define his or herself in a new, more integrated way and is able to have more egalitarian relationships with others. In interactions with members of the other sex, the client becomes capable of expressing the agency that is necessary for a strong sense of self as well as the communion that fosters a sense of connection to the other person.

NOTES

1. Actually, however, women and men have been found to describe their own personalities in very similar ways (see Gerber, 1989, pp. 47–48).

2. Even after research participants had completed their ratings of a heterosexual couple, they were unable to describe the principle that they had used in doing the ratings. They usually responded by saying that they had thought of an imaginary couple with the same type of relationship as the one described in the experimental instructions, or else they thought of a couple they knew personally (Gerber, 1987, 1988).

3. The relationship with the parent of the same sex also contributes to gender stereotyping. However, we are focusing here on the relationship with the parent of the other sex.

4. Sullivan (1953) calls this personification of the self the "not-me," because it includes experiences that are dissociated.

5. This case is offered for purposes of illustration and, to preserve confidentiality, is a disguised composite of several cases I have treated.

6. As Kohut (1977) has emphasized, the parent's "mirroring" or empathic response is crucial for the development of autonomy in the child.

REFERENCES

Bakan, D. (1966). *The duality of human existence*. Chicago: Rand McNally.
Bem, S. L. (1974). The measurement of psychological androgyny. *Journal of Consulting and Clinical Psychology, 42*, 155–162.

Fensterheim, H., & Baer, J. (1988). *Making life right when it feels all wrong.* New York: Rawson Associates.

Gerber, G. L. (1986). The relationship balance model and its implications for individual and couples therapy. In D. Howard (Ed.), *The dynamics of feminist therapy* (pp. 19–27). New York: Haworth Press.

Gerber, G. L. (1987). Sex stereotypes among American college students: Implications for marital happiness, social desirability, and marital power. *Genetic, Social, and General Psychology Monographs, 113,* 413–431.

Gerber, G. L. (1988). Leadership roles and the gender stereotype traits. *Sex Roles, 18,* 649–668.

Gerber, G. L. (1989). Gender stereotypes: A new egalitarian couple emerges. In J. Offerman-Zuckerberg (Ed.), *Gender in transition: A new frontier* (pp. 47–66). New York: Plenum.

Hefner, R., Rebecca, M., & Oleshansky, B. (1975). The development of sex-role transcendence. *Human Development, 18,* 143–158.

Kiesler, D. J. (1983). The 1982 interpersonal circle: A taxonomy for complementarity in human transactions. *Psychological Review, 90,* 185–214.

Kohut, H. (1977). *The restoration of the self.* New York: International Universities Press.

Rosenkrantz, P., Vogel, S., Bee, H., Broverman, I., & Broverman, D. M. (1968). Sex-role stereotypes and self-concepts in college students. *Journal of Consulting and Clinical Psychology, 32,* 287–295.

Secord, P. F., & Backman, C. W. (1961). Personality theory and the problem of stability and change in individual behavior: An interpersonal approach. *Psychological Bulletin, 68,* 21–32.

Spence, T. J., Helmreich, R. L., & Stapp, J. (1975). Ratings of self and peers on sex-role attributes and their relation to self-esteem and conceptions of masculinity and femininity. *Journal of Personality and Social Psychology, 32,* 29–39.

Sullivan, H. S. (1953). *The interpersonal theory of psychiatry.* New York: Norton.

■ 6
Working with the Severely Disturbed Client in a Private Practice Setting: A Special Challenge for the Woman Therapist

Marianne Jackson and
Doris Howard

There is a population of severely disturbed people who seek treatment in psychotherapy with private practitioners rather than at outpatient clinics. One reason for this choice is that most of them are from a middle-class background and are historically accustomed to one-to-one professional services. Another reason they avoid public health clinics is that they dislike the use of psychotropic medication, either because of unpleasant past experience with side effects or because of the fear of loss of control over their bodies. Functioning marginally, these people have frequent problems with employment, financial instability, isolation, and loneliness. They are often very angry, demanding, and argumentative. They may be delusional and have auditory and/or visual hallucinations. They may have difficulty in keeping appointments, arriving on time, and leaving at the end of the allotted time. Although these are not uncommon treatment issues, they can be particularly difficult to manage with severely disturbed clients.

Therefore, treatment is often dominated by survival issues. Time may be consumed by repetitive discussions of the client's delusional perceptions, so the delusions seem to take over the therapy itself. The therapist, however experienced, may feel frustration and an erosion of self-confidence from working alone with such a client. In addition, it is often difficult to distinguish between reality and distorted perception in what the client reports. These client and therapist issues can be particularly intense and hard to manage when either party is a woman. The client may have extreme traits indicating gender-role socialization, such as dependency, lack of assertiveness, and low self-esteem. The woman therapist may be more available emotionally to a particularly needy client and therefore more vulnerable than a male therapist. Because of gender-role socialization, women therapists may be likely to blame themselves for lack of success or slow progress in treatment, rather than being aware of the limitations inherent in the therapeutic relationship.

The authors of this chapter became interested in this issue while working with severely disturbed clients in private practice. It seemed that many therapists were working with these clients but rarely discussed them at conferences or in published papers. It became an issue of interest to investigate the frequency of work with very disturbed clients and how a feminist analysis could help in understanding the problems women therapists have in this work.

Phyllis Chesler (1972) interviewed 60 women about their experiences as clients in private therapy and in the mental health system (24 had been in psychiatric hospitals). She concluded: "Most women who are psychiatrically hospitalized are not mad." In a romantic and inspiring passage, she wrote:

> Perhaps the angry and weeping women in mental asylums are Amazons returned to earth these many centuries later, each conducting a private and half-remembered search for her Mother-land — a search we call madness. Or perhaps they are failed Goddess-Mothers, Demeters, eternally and miserably unable to find their daughters or their powers. (p. 4)

Chesler's book set the tone for the next 15 years of feminist writing about women and mental health. Following Chesler's line of thinking, we have seen an impressive body of work developed by feminist researchers and therapists, in which a feminist interpretation has clarified the real nature of women's suffering.

Despite the promise of Chesler's work and other theoretical approaches to mental illness (e.g., Sturdivant, 1980), there is surprisingly little to be found about more disturbed clients in the feminist literature or in conferences on feminist therapy.

A FEMINIST ANALYSIS

Several articles have been written by feminists from the point of view of social policy. Test and Berlin (1981) pointed out that the special needs of chronically mentally ill women are not addressed by the mental health system. In their survey of psychiatric hospitals, they found that the women who are diagnosed as schizophrenic are quite different from the men. Women are hospitalized later in life; they are more likely to be married, to be sexually active, and to have children. Their primary difficulties are with housing, personal safety, and the side effects of medication. A feminist position paper sponsored by the National Institute of Mental Health, *Women's Mental Health: Agenda for Research* (Eichler & Parron, 1986) calls for research into the ways in which mental illness affects women differently from men and how women's special needs in this area should be studied and treated.

From a feminist perspective, we recognize severely disturbed women as the victims of chronic stress and trauma, and there is growing evidence for this view. Warner's (1985) review of the research on schizophrenia is a cogent demonstration of how much its prevalence is determined by environmental stressors. Rosewater (1985) compared the MMPI profiles of 18 battered women with a comparable group of 133 schizophrenic women (who were the basis for a standardization of the MMPI profile of schizophrenia). She found that the profiles were alike on two out of three scales (paranoia and schizophrenia) and concluded that battered women should be distinguished from the group of more disturbed women and treated for their actual problems (i.e., battering and abuse). The implication of Rosewater's research is that large numbers of battered women are unrecognized and hidden behind diagnoses such as schizophrenia.

There is also accumulating evidence that a large percentage of chronically mentally ill women have suffered from physical or sexual abuse in childhood or later. Carmen, Rieker, and Mills (1984) found that 53% of female clients in a psychiatric hospital had a history of physical and/or sexual abuse. Craine, Henson, Colliver, and McLean (1988) found that 51% of women they interviewed in 10 psychiatric hospitals had been sexually abused as children or adolescents. Of these, 56% had never been identified previously as victims of abuse. Moreover, 66% of the abused women met the criteria of the DSM-III diagnosis of posttraumatic stress disorder (APA, 1980). Their symptoms included compulsive sexual behavior, chemical dependency, sadomasochistic sexual fantasies, sexual identity issues, low energy or loss of interest in (and lack of enjoyment of) sex, and chronic fatigue.

Despite its obvious applicability, there have been very few papers on the practice of feminist therapy with very disturbed women, except in the literature addressing the problems of battered women. Ballou and Gabalac (1985) point out this lack and take the position that because feminist therapy requires "a level of reciprocal relationship," some women are too chronically mentally ill or retarded for feminist therapy. In their view, feminist therapy requires a rather high level of intellectual capacity in the client. The authors of this chapter believe that many women who are severely disturbed have this capacity and can achieve change through psychotherapy. Many such women do benefit from long-term relationship therapy, and the therapist with a feminist perspective will make therapy even more effective.

There was an intense interest in the 1950s and the 1960s in doing individual therapy with people diagnosed as schizophrenic. The feminist movement was reborn in the optimism and idealism of those years, and Chesler's (1972) book is an expression of that zeitgeist. It was the era of Harry Stack Sullivan and Freida Fromm-Reichmann, of the radical therapy of R. D. Laing, who saw truth in the "madness" of the "schizophrenic" and considered the so-called delusions of schizophrenic people to be true perceptions of the reality that existed in the family and in society. This was an optimistic and expansive era, when our theories and therapeutic approaches attempted to encompass all groups in society, even "schizophrenic" people.

Currently, along with the trend in public health to cut services, the field of psychotherapy has moved away from working with more disturbed clients in long-term relationships. In today's competitive world, private-practice therapists are influenced by economic and status considerations. Today's therapists are less likely to take on clients who are difficult to work with and/or unable to pay a full fee.

There are also more personal reasons therapists are reluctant to work with a very disturbed population. First, there is the very intense relationship that is required in this work. The clients have generally been unable to find a trusting relationship in any of the usual ways, so the therapist eventually becomes the one person with whom they have a close, intimate relationship. The bulk of treatment becomes the establishment and maintenance of that relationship. Considerations of trust and safety are primary with such clients, who have frequently been wounded and rejected.

Another consideration is the difficulty of maintaining clear boundaries. The client may relate to the therapist with great intensity, which is intended for others who have abandoned, rejected, or abused her. The client may have very real needs that require concrete help: extra time, reduced fees, or telephone sessions. Defining the boundaries without wounding or abandoning the client may be difficult and a source of stress for the therapist. Women therapists are more likely than men therapists to be supportive and to tolerate fluctuating boundaries between them and their clients (Kaplan, 1979; Lerner, 1988). Maintaining relationships by providing the necessary support is something that women are socialized to do.

This dilemma has many parallels in the roles that women have traditionally played in society, including the strains that go with the role of caretaker to an ill or elderly relative or the role of the single mother. A pattern of ambivalence is often characteristic of the caretaker, who feels guilty and resentful even though she feels caring and loving most of the time. This ambivalence may also be operating in the therapist while treating her disturbed client.

A SURVEY OF PSYCHOTHERAPISTS

A questionnaire was developed by the authors to elicit information from therapists in private practice that might provide some answers to questions raised by the issues outlined above. The authors were interested in collecting data about therapists' experiences with severely disturbed clients and producing a body of information that would be of use to others working with this particular population, in private practice or elsewhere.

The questionnaire was sent to 125 therapists working in New York City; 48 responded. Only 12 had not worked with severely disturbed clients; of the other 36, the majority were women who designated themselves as feminist therapists. Most of them had worked with only one or two very disturbed clients. The data they reported revealed interesting common features about their clients. The fees collected were, on the average, 20% lower than those other clients paid. Half of the disturbed clients were unemployed. Half lived alone. Most had been in treatment before. Several therapists reported good or significant progress. More than half reported at least some progress. The diagnoses given included major depression, bipolar disorder, schizophrenia, paranoia, and atypical psychosis. None had a dual diagnosis.

The problems and symptoms most commonly reported were social isolation, paranoia and suspicion, irrational thinking, and difficulty in dealing with their families. Some features were surprising: most did not hallucinate or have problems with self-grooming, payments, or punctuality; nor was any substance abuse reported. There were no differences reported between these clients and other less disturbed clients in the following areas: hostility and aggression, communication with the therapist, trust in the therapist, or insight.

The therapists' feelings about working with severely disturbed clients were clearly positive in many ways. More information was obtained than can be presented here, but some issues stand out. A large percentage of the therapists reported no difficulty in understanding the clients' thoughts. Very few reported ever feeling uncomfortable or frightened with these clients. Few felt the client was too disturbed to be helped by therapy. Few would refer the client elsewhere "if I had it to do over again." Few had difficulty setting limits, few continued to see their clients solely because of the client's dependency on the therapist, and very few feared leaving the client alone in order to have a vacation. Many therapists reported feeling very close to their clients and found the work to be rewarding. Significantly, 91.6% denied it was embarrassing to discuss these clients with colleagues.

To summarize, it is clear that the results of the survey indicate mostly positive feelings among the therapists about working with severely disturbed clients. The therapists had a strong voluntary commitment to long-term therapeutic relationships and reported that, in most cases, therapy can be very helpful, with slow but steady progress. Most therapists (90%) felt that treatment was successful in the end, however slowly it happened. Each of the therapists reported contact with only one or two severely disturbed clients in private practice, but it is clear that the women therapists questioned did not back off from the challenge and reported that they would take it up again.

It is possible that not many therapists have the patience and understanding to work with severely disturbed people. It also seems likely that those therapists who see only a few such clients don't feel they have sufficient information to present or publish papers about their experiences. It is certainly clear that such clients need long years of treatment and that change occurs at a slow pace. It takes a long time for some degree of trust to develop and for some extension of that client–therapist trust to occur in other relationships.

FEMINIST IMPLICATIONS

The extent of the disorder reported in these clients' lives represents more than inadequate parenting and negative gender-role socialization. They sometimes seem to be hurt past the point of possible recovery. Most of the therapists who responded to the survey, however, were able to report some small progress or maintenance of stability, some greater capacity to find vocational satisfactions and even friendships and relationships. At least, it appears that long-term ongoing therapy is more productive than mere custodial care.

The therapists who reported the best results and progress, described techniques that focused heavily on examination of early life experience. Looking closely at earliest memories of severely disturbed clients may be crucial in treatment. Feminist therapists recognize that "the internal world is inextricably intertwined with the external" (Lerner, 1988, p. 176). Examining the internal world of memory inevitably reveals the traumas and pressures of the sexist society to which these women have been exposed. Feminist therapy offers an analysis of the social, interpersonal, and economic history of the female client and attempts to clarify "pathology" in terms of gender socialization and sexist discrimination.

A feminist theory of personality, in the words of Hannah Lerman (1986) "encompasses the diversity and complexity of women and their lives." In her view, feminist therapy must address "the broad array of female subgroups and types of issues that comprise the female experience" (p. 174). Clearly, women (and men) who are severely disturbed, are an important constituency for feminist therapists. Feminist therapists take an egalitarian position vis-à-vis their clients. Knowledge, experience, and understanding of the female experience are offered to clients in ways that are useful, without hiding behind the cloak of authority. While many severely disturbed people may seem to be childlike and seeking an authority figure to guide them, it is a mistake for the therapist to fall into that role. Who most meets their needs is a down-to-earth person who is able to empathize and self-disclose and who openly discusses and negotiates the contract of therapy and the terms of the therapeutic relationship.

Feminist therapists "promote and reinforce the positive aspects of what it is to be female" (Lerner, 1988, p. 173). It is essential for the therapist to see positive strengths in the client, to include her in the family of women, and to identify with the gender socialization that contributed to her inability to function in the mainstream. Feminists are sensitive to the issues of victimization and powerlessness, and they help clients to understand the sexist forces that are impinging upon them; whenever possible, they help their clients to become more empowered. Assertiveness training, plus the social analysis that we bring to therapy are helpful strategies for those who are disempowered by the economic and social systems. These are ways in which the private practice of feminist therapy is particularly valuable for disturbed clients, in contrast to public clinics and hospitals, which reinforce compliance and passivity in their "patients."

In conclusion, the authors identified a small number of therapists who demonstrated that positive voluntary involvement with severely disturbed clients can help those clients over a long period of therapy. Further study is required to establish the ways in which a feminist analysis can add to the clarity and resolution of the damaging effects of a sexist society.

REFERENCES

American Psychiatric Association. (1980). *Diagnostic and statistical manual of mental disorders* (3rd ed.). Washington, DC: Author.

Ballou, M., & Gabalac, N. W. (1985). *A feminist position on mental health*. Springfield, IL: Charles C. Thomas.

Carmen, E., Reiker, P. P., & Mills, T. (1984). Victims of violence and psychiatric illness. *American Journal of Psychiatry, 141*, 378–383.

Chesler, P. (1972). *Women and madness*. New York: Doubleday.

Craine, L. S., Hensen, C. E., Colliver, J. A., & McLean, D. G. (1988). Prevalence of a history of sexual abuse among female psychiatric patients in a state hospital system. *Hospital and Community Psychiatry, 39,* 300–304.

Eichler, A., & Parron, D. L. (1986). *Women's mental health: Agenda for research.* Washington, DC: National Institute of Mental Health.

Kaplan, A. G. (1979). Toward an analysis of sex role related issues in the therapeutic relationship. *Psychiatry, 42*(5), 112–130.

Lerman, H. (1986). *A mote in Freud's eye.* New York: Springer Publishing Co.

Lerner, H. G. (1988). *Women in therapy.* New York: Jason Aronson.

Rosewater, L. B. (1985). Schizophrenic, borderline, or battered? In L. B. Rosewater & L. E. Walker (Eds.), *Handbook of feminist therapy* (pp. 215–225). New York: Springer Publishing Co.

Sturdivant, S. (1980). *Therapy with women.* New York: Springer Publishing Co.

Test, M. A., & Berlin, S. B. (1981). Issues of special concern to chronically mentally ill women. *Professional Psychology, 12,* 136–145.

Warner, R. (1985). *Recovery from schizophrenia, psychiatry, and political economy.* London: Routledge & Kegan Paul.

■ 7
Family Therapy for Caregivers of Brain-Injured Patients

Rosalie J. Ackerman and
Martha E. Banks

The primary caregivers for brain-injured patients are most often women —
wives, mothers, daughters, and daughters-in-law (Brody, 1981). Brain injury
leads to several unexpected transitions, including severe limitations on traditionally feminine life-style options. In middle-aged and older women, loss
of "ladylike" roles and feminine role behaviors represent major devastations
that are generally overlooked by rehabilitation professionals. This chapter
addresses the issues faced by women who provide care for brain-injured patients. We examine the process of and problems in family assessment and
psychotherapy, with a focus on women's issues. A feminist approach to family psychotherapy is recommended to overcome specific difficulties we have
encountered in our clinical practices.

Family therapy is an important treatment modality within neuropsychological rehabilitation. It helps family members cope with changes in
personality and family roles, those due both to the brain injury and to the
effects of treatment. The goal is to realize the closest approximation of nor-

Portions of this article were presented at the September 1987 conference "Cognitive Rehabilitation: Community Reintegration through Scientifically Based Practice," the March 1988
conference of the Association for Women in Psychology, and the August 1988 convention of
the American Psychological Association.

mality with minimal residual deficits after treatment. Especially important are the realms of social relationships and vocational capabilities (Chance, 1986). Families are provided with information about the psychological and behavioral effects of brain injury, with specific reference to problems that can be anticipated in the patient and to debunk myths and false expectations. The family of the patient entering the rehabilitation setting is seldom prepared for the work that is needed to facilitate growth and adjustment (Evans & Held, 1984). Ways are addressed in which the family can therapeutically interact with the patient. Family psychotherapy serves as a forum for discussion of behavior problems that are sequelae of brain injury. We recommend a feminist approach to family psychotherapy to address the multiple issues faced by women providing care to brain-injured patients.

Rehabilitation programs can leave patients "unrehabilitated" unless they are restored to productivity and satisfying roles in family and society. Many former patients lead lonely, empty lives with minimal social interaction. Brain-injured patients do much better, progress faster, and attain a higher level of functioning if they have a supportive family system (Oddy, Humphrey, & Uttley, 1978; Thomsen, 1974).

Most young brain-injured patients recover basic physical skills and mobility very rapidly, and rehabilitation progress is quite visible. Hospitals are frequently forced by diagnostic-related groups (DRGs) and other cost-limiting factors to discharge patients before persistent and pervasive changes in cognitive, behavioral, and personality interventions can take effect. Long-term models of therapy for the neurological deficits have resulted in extended care or community-based programs (Banks & Ackerman, 1987; Ben-Yishay, 1985; Compton, 1987; Craine & Gudeman, 1981) to treat enduring consequences of neurocognitive deficits. Learning, memory, sensation and perception of the environment, personality, and social interactions impact on judgment in independent living, vocational rehabilitation (McGonagle, Carp, & Balichi, 1983; Prigatano, 1986) and family systems. Therapy can address specific strategies for these deficits.

PROCESS OF FAMILY PSYCHOTHERAPY

Family therapy has been an integral part of neuropsychological rehabilitation in three hospital-based programs: two private, postacute, general rehabilitation hospitals and a federal extended-care geriatric rehabilitation unit. Family therapy in neuropsychological rehabilitation includes assessment of the psychological and physical adjustments necessary for reintegration of the patient into the family and community, treatment for family members coping with changing roles, and maximizing generalization from specific exercises to self-care, family, and community activities. Family members are encouraged to become active in the treatment and/or to continue their emotional support. Two treatment modalities are involved: (1) the family educational conference and (2) family neuropsychotherapy, as suggested by several authors (Ben-Yishay, 1985; Bray, 1987; Diehl, 1983; Rosenthal, Griffith, Bond, & Miller, 1983). In both settings, the family therapy is provided by the neuropsychologist on the treatment team.

Throughout this article, the term "patient" is used to denote the person who has experienced brain injury; this is contrary to the usual practice of family therapists, who view the entire family as the patient. In dealing with brain-injured patients, however, the medical focus on the "identified patient" is clearly indicated. Although the family therapist, as a member of the treatment team, must maintain awareness of the "identified patient," the actual family therapy should be conducted with appropriate attention to the entire family, with an emphasis on empowering primary caregivers and maximizing rehabilitation of the patient. The family therapist should be flexible and willing to use a variety of treatment modalities. Rigid attitudes about "appropriate" roles of family members and "rules" regarding conjoint sessions will impede the rehabilitative process (Ackerman & Banks, 1988a; Goldner, 1985).

Initiation of Therapy

Families consistently report several types of behaviors that make the management of brain-injured patients very difficult (see Table 7.1). Unfortunately, families seldom seek psychotherapy as part of the rehabilitation program and come to the attention of therapists only when there is a breakdown in the caregiving network. Bereavement, increased isolation, and family conflict over the sharing of responsibilities are frequently problematic. Families do not usually seek psychotherapy in response to accidents, illness, financial crises, burglary, fires, or other unexpected life events, yet brain injury is often the result of accidents or illness and leads to financial burden. It is therefore necessary to incorporate family psychother-

TABLE 7.1   Behavior Problems Manifested by Patients in the Home

Memory disturbance
Catastrophic reactions to a variety of irritating problems
Accusing, suspicious, demanding, and/or critical behavior
Communication disturbance of many types
Refusal/inability to bathe, poor self-care
Hiding of objects
Daytime wandering
Night waking and/or disturbances in sleep patterns
Difficulty with meals

apy into the normal therapeutic regimen for brain-injured patients during hospitalization.

Often family members are unaware of available support services. Traditionally, individual therapy was assured. Family neuropsychology is a relatively new treatment modality (Banks & Ackerman, 1987). In the past, the family was minimally educated about brain injury, with little attention given to impact beyond physical difficulties faced by the individual. Cognitive deficits, disrupted family relationships, and constant reassessment of external responsibility for management of personal and interpersonal needs must be considered in a comprehensive and meaningful treatment program.

Identification of Caregivers

Historically, many of the patients in neuropsychological rehabilitation have been young men. The families of such patients often include wives or girlfriends, young children, and middle-aged to elderly parents. Parents of children who have sustained brain injuries are most likely to be involved in the rehabilitation process. In the normal family life cycle, parents expect to raise to adulthood a child who will function independently. When a child or adolescent is brain-injured, the chances of maturing to independence are greatly reduced, thereby causing caregiving parents to maintain that role until death or other intervening illness or disability. The independence and freedom of the "empty nest" are denied to the parental caregivers, and the normal developmental family life cycle is disrupted.

In reality, brain injury can be a problem at any age and is often unacknowledged by clinicians who are not trained in neurology and/or neuropsychology. Women who suffer brain injury as the result of accidents, illnesses, and physical assaults, including rape, are particularly at risk because they are seldom seen by neurologists and neuropsychologists. Another overlooked group of patients for neuropsychological rehabilitation are elderly people who, if given the opportunity, often demonstrate considerable recovery after cardiovascular accidents, falls, or automobile accidents resulting in brain injury, as well as various medical problems that cause periods of anoxia. Avorn (1984) documented discrimination in medical care resulting in elderly patients being excluded from treatment; most of the mistreated elderly are women. For such patients, the family often consists of an elderly spouse, elderly siblings, middle-aged children, and younger grandchildren (Brody, 1981; Gwyther & Blazer, 1984). Frequently, the geriatric brain-injured patient has few family members available who both can and are willing to participate in the arduous process of rehabilitation (Hays, 1984; Weeks & Cuellar, 1981).

The vast majority of primary caregivers are women in a variety of relationships to the patients. For younger patients, the primary caregivers are

TABLE 7.2   Those Identified as Primary Caregivers (in Order of Frequency)

Spouse
Daughter or daughter-in-law
Son
Younger female relative
Younger male relative
Other female relative
Other male relative
Female nonrelative
Male nonrelative

sometimes middle-aged and older parents who are dealing with their own aging and for whom the caregiving involves a major life adjustment. Elderly wives who suddenly become caregivers are seldom prepared to make the drastic change from autonomous "ladies of leisure" to full-time nursemaids; elderly husbands tend to institutionalize their brain-injured wives (Fitting, Rabins, Lucas, & Eastham, 1986). Table 7.2 represents the hierarchy of caregivers for brain-injured and older patients as reflected in several surveys (Banks, Ackerman, & Clark, 1987; Brody, Kleban, Johnsen, Hoffman, & Schoonover, 1987; Fitting et al., 1986; Horowitz, 1985; Mitchell & Register, 1984; Rosenthal, 1986; Stone, Cafferata, & Sangl, 1987; Taylor, 1985). It should be emphasized that daughters-in-law are caregivers more often than sons or other male relatives.

It is extremely important to remember that the "traditional" nuclear family is not always available for support of brain-injured patients. The issues raised in this article pertain to lovers and friends of lesbian, bisexual, and gay patients as well as the significant others of patients. Without the participation of such people in the caregiving role and the treatment planning, patients are sometimes deprived of their rights to treatment and suffer serious setbacks in rehabilitation (Brown, 1988). This concern pertains not only to patients who can expect long lives following brain injury but must include those suffering AIDS-related dementia with poor judgment and need for caregivers (Melton, 1988).

Family Assessment

Family assessment is an important part of the rehabilitation program. Family dynamics examined include coalitions, conflictual relationships, role confusion, boundary enmeshment, and taking on the speaking and decision making of others. Feminist family psychotherapists move beyond traditional gender role expectations in their evaluations, and consider a broad range of issues confronting women and a realistic review of resources needed for appropriate provision of care. Potential stressors on the primary caregiver in-

TABLE 7.3   Problems Frequently Experienced by Caregivers

Chronic fatigue
Anger
Depression
Family conflict
Loss of friends, hobbies, time for self
Worry about self becoming ill
Difficulty assuming new roles and responsibilities
Guilt

clude (1) multiple roles (work, child care, management of one or more households, other illness in the family, recent significant losses, etc.), (2) history of the relationship between the primary caregiver and the patient (e.g., mutual interdependence, dependence, hostility, abuse), (3) economic impact (loss of income, change in living situation, huge medical bills), and (4) perceived personal sacrifice. Such stressors can be manifested in patriarchal families in which women do not traditionally manage financial tasks (e.g., writing checks or filing tax forms).

In families that had relationship problems (both overt and covert) prior to the brain injury, the difficulties intensify with the inability of the patient to participate appropriately in family problem solving. Problems include avoiding and distancing behavior, poor communication, blaming, arguing, autonomy conflicts, ambivalence, manipulation, coercive power struggles, hostility, and submissiveness. It is crucial that information regarding family relationships be gathered, not only from spouses but also from children, siblings, parents, and close friends, whenever possible. Families need to be given information about the patient's illness, problems must be identified, responsibilities and role definitions should be discussed, and social and community links can be established (including legalities such as power of attorney or guardianship). A supportive psychotherapeutic relationships is needed to facilitate such discussion.

Families of brain-injured patients are "suffering just as much as the injured person. And they're not getting much help either" (Jacobs, quoted in Chance, 1986; p. 69). Table 7.3 is a list of the problems most commonly experienced by caregivers (Fitting et al., 1986). Most caregivers are women; social stereotyping has led to the perception of clinical staff that wives, mothers, and daughters are automatically prepared to provide complete physical and emotional care for people who are treated by several nurses and therapists in rotating shifts in the rehabilitation setting. As a result of those stereotypes, requests by caregiving women for assistance or training are not taken seriously by clinicians, insurance companies, or legislators. These women are at risk for having to attend to all of the physical needs of demanding, uncooperative, and potentially dangerous patients, without meaningful relief, for up to 50 years.

The level of stress might engender termination of marriages or long-term separations (Ackerman & Banks, 1988b; Prigatano, 1986).

Before family involvement in the actual rehabilitation sessions is initiated, families should be evaluated to determine whether or not they are able to deal with the patient's disability. Some families are overwhelmed by the simplistic level of rehabilitative tasks and are extremely uncomfortable with the adult patient's difficulty in managing tasks that are easily handled by children. Such families might attempt to complete the tasks for the patient by impulsively giving correct answers while denying the patient's difficulty. Others become disruptive, trying to focus attention away from the exercises, often complaining that the specific tasks are too difficult or irrelevant to the patient's actual abilities. In some instances, family members deny outright the limitations of the patient, insisting that a misdiagnosis was made and that the patient is actually being treated for the wrong disorder; especially in geriatric settings. Some disorders (e.g., senile dementia of the Alzheimer's type) are perceived as more socially acceptable than others. As there is decreased capability for adjustment, such families tend to drop out of their supportive roles, including family therapy. Others act out in various ways that remove or distract attention away from the brain-injured patients, often exhibiting dysfunctional premorbid characteristics.

Families that are well adjusted tend to discuss how therapy exercises might be augmented and/or more closely related to the patient's vocation or to activities that will facilitate return to the home. Such families are able to take a therapeutic role, maintaining the strengthening of skills outside the scheduled sessions and enhancing the rehabilitation.

Educational Conferences

The family conference involves interested family members and multidisciplinary staff. It is a brief meeting, held shortly after admission, to summarize the patient's condition and provide a brief education about deficits. Usually, new information about the problems of the patient adds to the knowledge base of the family about brain injury. The complex nature of consequences of brain injury, the sequelae, prognosis, and management strategies can be briefly and meaningfully explained to the family members. Other sessions occur by appointment following the educational conference. Virtually no psychotherapy is done at this meeting. It is important to follow up with the primary caregiver after the educational conference. Many caregiving women are overwhelmed by the amount of medical information and the number of specialists on the multidisciplinary team.

Family Neuropsychotherapy

The neuropsychological family therapy sessions are, by contrast, psychotherapeutic and delve into family dynamics and emotional reactions about the injured family member (Banks & Ackerman, 1987). Explanations and the implications of what deficits mean in terms of everyday living are carefully described. One of the educative functions of family therapy is to provide a bridge between the rehabilitation exercises and the family routine in order to develop a meaningful and appropriate treatment program for the patient. The family gives feedback about how the patient acted before the illness or injury and describes current levels of activity. Problematic patterns of behavior are identified and discussed. Strategies for dealing with difficult behaviors and training in behavior modification are incorporated into the family therapy sessions. Whenever possible, the patient is present at these sessions. A behavioral contract is made to obtain the cooperation and commitment of the patient and family. Results of the training are evaluated in subsequent therapy sessions. The involvement of the family in treatment-goal planning helps the patient through transitional periods, and it is one of the aids suggested by Anderson and Parente (1985), Parente and Anderson (1986), and Rosenthal and colleagues (1983).

Another aspect of the weekly therapy sessions is review of the patient's progress in individual neuropsychological treatment. This discussion of the patient's progress is held only if the patient has given verbal and sometimes written consent to reveal information. The data are considered confidential and subject to the ethical principles of psychologists. In many instances, memory deficits or other impairing neurological sequelae compromise the comprehension and likely the legal competence of the patient. If a designated person has power of attorney or guardianship, that person is contacted to get permission to release confidential information. Judgment of the (partial) competence of the patient needs to be done early and needs revision as the patient progresses in level of cognitive awareness. Frequent discussion with patient, family, and treatment team of specific areas of competence, incompetence, and potential rehabilitation is important. This must not be limited to the global legal definitions of competence, which minimize individual capabilities.

The family members provide descriptions of behaviors that illustrate the deficits and what is being addressed in rehabilitation interventions. Feedback from the family is very important. It often substantiates patient self-report, adds to the behavioral data base, and provides additional history of the incident and premorbid activities. The family's information can be quite dissonant with the patient's self-report and therefore becomes diagnostic for both the patient and the family dynamics. Especially important is background information about socially inappropriate behaviors, which are then targeted for treatment. For example, one patient refused to carry a pocket calendar or attempt to remember appointments; the family revealed that, despite the patient's apparent premorbid vocational responsibility, he had never successfully kept appointments without assistance. His mother and his wife made all of his appointments for him, frequently calling him at work to remind him of job assignments as well as scheduled family activities. As a result, the patient had no motivation to benefit from memory (re) training involving remembering appointments.

Shaping of acceptable behaviors in therapy ultimately involves psychosocial training in role taking, assertiveness, and reading nonverbal behavioral cues to interpret emotional content in social conversations. Family members are educated about the importance and delivery of positive feedback. Effective interventions are primarily positive reinforcements supplemented by negative reinforcements. For brain-injured patients, punishment is definitely contraindicated (Ackerman & Corbett, 1987).

One aspect of family psychotherapy involves role-identity problems of family members, role reversals in some families, sexual dysfunction in marital dyads, and stressors from consequences of brain injury. Differentiation must be made among adjustments for caregiving spouses, children, and aged parents. Role changes involve determinations of responsibility for housekeeping tasks, financial management, and transportation of the patient and other family members. Some caregiving wives experience difficulty in setting safety limits for their husbands. For example, one woman refused to put recommended dead bolts on her doors to prevent her husband from wandering out of the house during the night. She insisted that the extra locks would be an insult to his masculinity, as he had previously made the rules and similar decisions for the whole family. Family therapists must be prepared to help such caregivers work through the gender-role dilemma.

Family psychotherapists must monitor emotional support for the entire family and assist in preventing social isolation and deprivation. The family experiences multiple losses, such as changes in the patient, financial insecurity, job loss, constriction of the social network, decreased emotional support from family and friends, legal difficulties, and illnesses of other family members, as well as the usual family stressors. It is important to continually assess the primary caregiver's functioning and resources during the course of family psychotherapy; it is this "hidden" victim, the stressed primary caregiver, who needs special attention (Banks et al., 1987; Zeigler, 1987). This issue has been addressed by Steuer and Austin (1980) and Goldner (1985) in their criticisms of the lack of feminist perspectives in traditional psychotherapy. An important focus of therapy, however, is on the caregiver's *perceived* burden of providing supervision for the patient.

Legal and business affairs may need special attention. Sometimes the power of attorney or guardianship has been dealt with by family members. More often, the family is waiting for the recovery of the patient and has done little except pay bills and keep finances from being in extreme chaos. Gentle urging by the neuropsychologist and the social worker is often necessary to get the family to take responsibility for legal and business matters. This is particularly the case when finances were handled exclusively by the male patient and a caregiving woman is expected to manage them. The information from the neuropsychological evaluation is utilized to explain to the family the reasons for such action. Taking over a patient's right to manage business affairs is viewed as extreme by most families. It should be noted, however, that some families have members who rush in to take charge of business and legal matters. Usually, this has a secondary gain for the family member(s). Caution and deliberation are needed in such cases before treatment staff pursue legal interventions. In other family systems, there is no person capable of taking on the guardianship role because of dementia, mental retardation, and/or immaturity. In such cases, the treatment team should assist the court in finding a guardian who is appropriately aware of the numerous and fluctuating needs of the brain-injured patient.

In family neuropsychotherapy, graphic illustrations and discussions of the implications of the performance trends, relevance to the initial treatment goals, inclusion of other therapy goals, and interpretation by the neuropsychologist about the overall performance since the family was last in session are provided. Refined treatment goals of the family are often added during these sessions. This avenue of mutual cooperation accentuates the commitment and motivational levels of the family. Rewarding consequences have been generated from such sessions. The technique of reviewing performance quality often elicits emotional reactions and descriptions of life situations that are problematic to the patient. Treatment can then be formulated to address the "current" problem.

Emotional Issues

A variety of emotional issues are incorporated into the therapy sessions. Often, family members have been actively involved in the acute-hospitalization activities, rescheduling their lives (or have not accepted the disabilities of the patient), resulting in little time for normal grieving. In many cases, they relate that the family neuropsychology sessions are the first forums for candid discussion of the present and anticipated problems faced by the patient. They had been so relieved that the patient had lived that they did not realize that other serious consequences remained to be faced. Another intense and frequent therapeutic issue is the family's management of the changed personality of the patient; for example, one wife complained that, years ago, her husband had left home to go to work and she had not "seen him since."

Patients with high distractibility and severe memory problems should initially work with the therapist alone; as distractibility is reduced and/or memory improves the family can be brought in to observe the actual exercises. Interventions are focused on getting the family to adjust to the agitation of the patient's verbally abusive remarks and/or temper tantrums. In the case of the anxious and agitated patient, family members have more energy to deal with the patient but are extremely frustrated in knowing how to interact. It is also difficult for families to deal with the patient's lack of motivation, apathetic demeanor, and unwillingness to participate in activities (including family therapy). The nonvitality of a patient with depression, emotional lability, crying, and poor tolerance of stress exacerbates a depressive environment in the family system (Banks & Ellett, 1988). Many family members find that very difficult to deal with and will drop out of the help and support mode to carry on with their own lives; divorce is a frequent reaction when families are unable to adjust to the patient's new personality. Interventions with such families are aimed at management of emotions; family psychotherapy can continue to facilitate decision making about and transition toward the most appropriate family arrangement, including separation.

Families of brain-injured patients tend to manifest two types of depression (Lezak, 1978). In the first type, they experience a permanent emotional burden that can persist even after the patient's death. The second type of depression fluctuates with the patient's condition. Families perceived themselves as "going crazy" when they are depressed. One important facet of family psychotherapy is the information that the emotional reactions are normal. Many woman caregivers are given messages by other family members, friends, and clinicians that they are fulfilling expected duties. They are rewarded for being "strong" and noncomplaining and punished for crying or otherwise manifesting expressions of their stress. Psychotherapists can assist caregivers by acknowledging the emotional drain experienced in providing extraordinary care while simultaneously grieving the loss of a fully functioning adult and the concomitant changes in roles.

A review of normal phases of grieving is useful, especially if it is made clear that there are no time limits on the grieving process. The family psychotherapist should assist the family in attending to the emotional, somatic, thinking, and motivational changes that occur as part of normal grieving. Family adjustment to brain injury generally follows an identifiable pattern similar to Kübler-Ross's (1969) stages of grief resolution:

1. There is initially *denial* of the severity of the illness. Psychotherapy during this phase should involve encouragement of open and honest communication, planning for an uncertain future, whole family involvement in decision making, and constructive information for the entire family.

2. During the *anger* phase, family members must discuss feelings and recognize attributional styles such as misperceived locus of control, resentment, and reactive anger.

3. Psychotherapy should focus on control issues, to facilitate the best adaptation to minimize depression and increase self-esteem and the ability to cope.

4. In the resolution phase, the family develops a safe environment for the patient, the patient gains a sense of mastery, the family accepts the patient's disabilities, and strategies for time management and assignment of responsibilities are enhanced. Psychotherapy facilitates all of those activities and provides a forum for discussion of the family's role in the continued rehabilitation of the patient.

PROBLEMS IN FAMILY THERAPY

Rehabilitation Issues

Denial of problems and misconceptions or myths that everything will return to normal are common. Families believe that healing will take place and the "bad dream" will end. Unrealistic expectations for recovery often pervade the discussion until some acceptance of the disabilities is psychologically incorporated. Unfortunately, there is often cooperative support of the healing myth by treatment staff—sometimes inadvertently, at other times overtly and volitionally, but usually in a manner designed to minimize emotional "scenes," reduce a sense of "failure," and provide "hope" when little is warranted. For example, attractive, young, verbal, and bright patients are more positively viewed and endowed with more progress than is appropriate to the patient's actual neuropsychological status.

Families of geriatric and minority patients often are led to believe that there is no chance for rehabilitation. Treatment staff (including physicians ordering therapies) do little to debunk these ageist and racist stereotypes (Banks, 1988; Rosenthal, 1986; Taylor, 1985).

Anger of family members is projected on professional staff and is coupled with a lack of cooperation, which attenuates the effectiveness of treatment, including family therapy. Misinterpretations of information and subsequent contentions that the family members were not informed leads to much distress among the treatment staff and within the family system.

Rejection by the spouse and/or significant others and erosion of a social support system also lead to problematic depression and/or acting out by the patient, and rehabilitation progress is slowed. Family psychotherapy is useful in reframing the dynamics that led to the rejection and may instill in the family a renewed sense of commitment. If such commitment is not attained, the overall treatment of the patient is effectively sabotaged.

Lack of finances leads to premature termination of rehabilitation services, often as the patient is in a rapid state of recovery in the neuropsychological aspects of treatment. As gross motor disabilities and difficulties with activities of daily living are remediated, the patient is perceived as "well" without much regard to intellectual deficits, personality changes, problem-solving capabilities, and other cognitive functioning. Yet these deficits are very often much more debilitating to reentry into the family or community than are physical problems. Professionals, insurance companies, and families need to pay much more attention to these deficits and their remediation.

There are many negative implications of inability to handle money and other financial items. One patient put disability checks into the waste basket until a family member realized what was happening to the checks.

Posttraumatic stress has an adverse impact on family cohesiveness and other dynamics. The emotional fluctuations are viewed in several ways: (1) stigmatizing and to be avoided, (2) nasty to handle, (3) detrimental to health, (4) unnecessary and inconvenient, and (5) embarrassing. Consequently, families avoid dealing with emotions, thus triggering further posttraumatic stress. By contrast, if only physical handicaps are involved, the family social unit is more positively responsive to changes and remains stabilized.

Social deprivation and isolation can result from the family's having to deal with the patient. Such families become a newly formed class of socially deprived individuals and families, as they often lose much of their former social network. Support groups are recommended (Ben-Yishay, 1985; Diehl, 1983) for families and patients, but often such modalities of therapy are unavailable.

Enmeshment and Distancing

There are several maladaptive ways in which caregivers react to their new roles after a patient has sustained brain injury. Some caregivers become enmeshed with the patient. Role assumption or overidentification can limit the recovery and progress of the patient (Banks, 1988). The behavior resulting from brain injury often serves to isolate the immediate family from friends and relatives. Healthy spouses seldom seek substitute caregivers; as a result, there is little opportunity for intervention in the family system unless the patient is rehospitalized. Enmeshed caregivers spend extraordinarily long periods of time during hospital visits, often providing more attention to the patient than is warranted by the level of disability. One patient's daughter often spent up to 10 hours in the hospital daily, taking up to 2 hours to feed the patient, whose primary food intake was through gastrostomy feedings.

Some caregivers take on their new roles as priorities, seeing themselves as altruistic, having increased self-esteem, and developing an increased sense of competence. Such role entrenchment frequently replaces previous roles that have been lost and thus provides the caregiver with a new meaning in life. Active caregiving provides an opportunity to shed unwanted roles and can serve as a substitute for failed marriage, widowhood, or an erratic job history.

Both physical and psychological distancing are often observed, and the patient's recovery is detrimentally affected. Some family members avoid the caregiving situation completely by refusing to become involved with the patient or the primary caregiver. Caregivers sometimes place the patient in a room away from most of the family activities and provide minimal care. The physical distance tends to create considerable conflict that extends beyond the immediate family. In other cases, psychological distancing leads to guilt and resentment at the emotional cost of continued care; caregivers who use psychological distancing are able to meet the instrumental needs of the patient with minimal emotional commitment. In the hospital environment, such caregivers visit often, stay for several hours, and tend to spend more time with staff and other patients than with their own relatives. Unfortunately, these people are perceived inaccurately as being well adjusted and are highly praised for their ability to maintain adequate care for the patient. In reality, they are avoiding confrontation with their anger, guilt, resentment, and/or other emotions about the situation in which they find themselves.

The "Hidden" Victim

During the course of family psychotherapy, the "hidden" victim (i.e., the stressed primary caregiver) receives attention that is often lacking when the focus is on care of the identified patient (Banks et al., 1987). Primary caregivers frequently burst into tears upon initial acknowledgment of their stress. Other family members are unaware of the level of stress endured by the primary caregiver (Jennet & Teasdale, 1983), often perceiving that person as having limited responsibility while the patient is in a hospital or other care facility. It is crucial to continually assess the primary caregiver's functioning and resources during the course of family psychotherapy; this is usually best done in individual collateral sessions rather than in the presence of the identified patient. Caregivers report a variety of problems that interfere with their ability to manage (see Table 7.3). Primary caregivers often complain of feeling trapped and tied down and are fearful of upsetting the patient; they suppress negative emotional expression. Family psychotherapy must address the pathology of such suppression and debunk the myth that the caregiver has control over the patient's emotions and behavior. It is essential to assist primary caregivers in taking care of themselves; that can be reinforced by reminding them that if they do not care for themselves they will not be able to care for the identified patient. In trying to care for her husband, who had had two strokes, one caregiver died within a year of his return to their home. The patient lived for three more years in a long-term nursing care facility. In that case, the family member most available for consideration as a caregiver had health problems that should have precluded her from that role. Similarly, immature children, mentally retarded adult children, and demented spouses and/or parents cannot function as primary caregivers.

Abuse

Many caregivers are the victims of physical abuse (including sexual abuse) from the patient (Lezak, 1978; Zeigler, 1987). Women are particularly at risk because of their small stature and limited physical strength in comparison to the disinhibited men for whom they are providing care. Abusive behaviors include accusing; striking out; hitting; tripping; unreasonable demanding; raging; controllable incontinence; rape; threatening with knives, unconfiscated guns, and other dangerous weapons; and increased abuse of alcohol and drugs resulting in aggression or violence. This behavior is seldom displayed in front of treatment staff and frequently occurs in the home rather than in the treatment setting; complaints by the caregiver are generally ignored or discredited. It is crucial that family psychotherapy be conducted in a supportive manner that allows for adequate trust and safety for family members to discuss the extent of abuse (Bogden, 1984; Willbach, 1989). For some families, behavioral paradigms can be implemented to extinguish such abusive behaviors; but in other instances, community settings outside of the family home are appropriate placements (Adams, 1988). It is important to assist families in making the very hard decision to place a patient in an alternative setting (e.g., nursing home, group home, psychiatric hospital). Families *and therapists* must recognize their limitations in the management of patients from this difficult population; alternative placement does *not* constitute a failure and should not serve as a source of guilt. Ethically, the ultimate criterion for success of treatment is the welfare of the patient.

Another concern is that caregivers who are unable to make healthy adjustments to the patient's illness can become abusive to the patient. Female patients most often report such abuse, but it is clearly not limited to women. The most abused patients are those who are totally dependent on others for nutrition, medication, personal hygiene, ambulation, and/or bed care. Of the physical abuses, the most common is neglect: being left unattended for long periods, lack of changed clothes following incontinence, lack of bathing, and not being repositioned. Other physical abuses include oversedation with medication, withholding of medications, irregular feeding schedules, lack of compliance with prescribed diet, and imprisonment (tying the patient to a chair or bed, placing the patient in a locked room). Verbal and psychological abuse are manifested by infantilization; derogatory statements; threats to institutionalize, abandon, or kill the patient; and placement of necessary items in sight but just out of reach of the patient (O'Malley, O'Malley, Everitt, & Sarson, 1984; Steuer & Austin, 1980). Caregivers who cannot cope with the stress of their situations tend to use mind-altering substances (e.g., alcohol, illicit drugs, pain medications prescribed for the patient), thereby seriously compromising their ability to provide appropriate care for the patient and increasing the chances of abusive behavior.

Much abuse can be prevented if there is early assessment and appropriate intervention. Information about financial and community services, family education about the mechanics of caring for an ill person, supportive assistance in decision making, encouragement of respite care, and resolution of guilt are all important deterrents to potentially abusive situations.

SUMMARY

It is recommended that family therapy be integrated into a comprehensive neuropsychological rehabilitation program. Feminist family psychotherapy is the treatment of choice for addressing the issues faced by caregiving women. In determining the role of the family in neuropsychological rehabilitation, the first step is to assess availability and commitment of family members, with ongoing assessment during treatment. Educational conferences and weekly psychotherapy sessions are used to develop strategies for dealing with difficult behaviors and role changes. Emotional issues are incorporated into the therapy sessions, and appropriate grieving is encouraged. Family adjustment to brain injury follows a pattern similar to grieving and bereavement.

Several maladaptive ways in which caregivers react to their new roles after a patient has sustained brain injury are the reasons that psychotherapy is necessary. It is important to continually assess the primary caregiver's functioning and resources during the course of family psychotherapy; it is this "hidden" victim—the stressed primary caregiver—who needs special attention. Many caregivers are the victims of physical abuse (including sexual abuse) from the patient. Caregivers who are unable to make healthy adjustments to the patient's illness can become abusive to the patient. Much abuse can be prevented if there is appropriate and early intervention.

REFERENCES

Ackerman, R. J., & Banks, M. E. (1988a, August). *Family psychotherapy for caregivers of brain injured patients.* Paper presented at the convention of the American Psychological Association, Atlanta.

Ackerman, R. J., & Banks, M. E. (1988b, March). *Feminist family psychotherapy applied: Caregivers for brain-injured patients*. Paper presented at the convention of the Association for Women in Psychology, Bethesda, MD.

Ackerman, R. J., & Corbett, C. (1987, July–August). *Behavior modification for brain injured patients and families*. Paper presented at Nittany Valley Rehabilitation Hospital, Bellefonte, PA.

Adams, C. (1988). Treatment models of men who batter: A pro-feminist analysis. In K. Yllo & M. Bograd (Eds.), *Feminist perspectives on wife abuse* (pp. 176–191). Newbury Park, CA: Sage Publications.

Anderson, J. K., & Parente, F. J. (1985). Training family members to work with the head-injured patient. *Cognitive Rehabilitation, 4*(1), 12–15.

Avorn, J. (1984). Benefit and cost analysis in geriatric care: Turning age discrimination into public policy. *The New England Journal of Medicine, 310*(20), 1297.

Banks, M. E. (1988, January). *Geriatric family therapy*. Paper presented at the Brecksville Veterans Administration Medical Center, Brecksville, OH.

Banks, M. E., & Ackerman, R. J. (1987). Integrating the family into neuropsychological rehabilitation. *Cognitive Rehabilitation, 5*(4), 19.

Banks, M. E., Ackerman, R. J., & Clark, E. O. (1987). Elderly women in family therapy. In D. Howard (Ed.), *The dynamics of feminist therapy* (pp. 107–116). New York: Haworth Press.

Banks, M. E., & Ellett, B. G. (1988). *Psychological aspects of neurological disease*. Paper presented at the Brecksville Veterans Administration Medical Center, Brecksville, OH.

Ben-Yishay, Y. (1985). Neuropsychological rehabilitation: Quest for a holistic approach. *Seminars in Neurology, 5*, 252–259.

Bogden, M. (1984). Family systems approaches to wife battering: A feminist critique. *American Journal of Orthopsychiatry, 54*, 558–568.

Bray, G. (1987). Family adaptation to chronic illness. In B. Caplan (Ed.), *Rehabilitation psychology desk reference* (pp. 171–184). Rockville, MD: Aspen.

Brody, E. M. (1981). "Women in the middle" and family help to older people. *Gerontologist, 21*, 471–479.

Brody, E. M., Kleban, M. H., Johnsen, P. T., Hoffman, C., & Schoonover, C. B. (1987). Work status and parent care: A comparison of four groups of women. *Gerontologist, 27*, 201–208.

Brown, L. S. (1988). The Sharon Kowalski case: An issue of concern for feminist psychologists. *The Psychology of Women Newsletter, 15*, 1, 3.

Chance, P. (1986, October). Life after head injury. *Psychology Today*, 62–69.

Compton, M. (1987). Computers and cognitive retraining of frontal lobe functions. *MicroPsych Network, 3*, 51–52.

Craine, J. F., & Gudeman, H. E. (1981). *The rehabilitation of brain functions*. Springfield, IL: Charles C. Thomas.

Diehl, L. (1983). Patient-family education. In M. Rosenthal, E. Griffith, M. Bond, & J. Miller (Eds.), *Rehabilitation of the head injured adult* (pp. 395–406). Philadelphia: F. A. Davis.

Evans, R. L., & Held, S. (1984). Evaluation of family stroke education. *International Journal of Rehabilitation Research, 7*, 47–51.

Fitting, M., Rabins, P., Lucas, M. J., & Eastham, J. (1986). Caregivers for dementia patients: A comparison of husbands and wives. *Gerontologist, 26,* 248–252.

Goldner, V. (1985). Feminism and family therapy. *Family Process, 24,* 31–47.

Gwyther, L. P., & Blazer, D. G. (1984). Family therapy and the dementia patient. *American Family Physician, 29,* 149–156.

Hays, J. A. (1984). Aging and family resources: Availability and proximity of kin. *Gerontologist, 24,* 149–153.

Horowitz, A. (1985). Sons and daughters as caregivers to older parents: Differences in role performance and consequences. *Gerontologist, 25,* 612–617.

Jennet, B., & Teasdale, G. (1983). *Management of head injuries.* Philadelphia: F. A. Davis.

Kubler-Ross, E. (1969). *On death and dying.* New York: Macmillan.

Lezak, M. (1978). Living with the characterologically altered brain-injured patient. *Journal of Clinical Psychiatry, 9,* 592–598.

McGonagle, E., Carp, M., & Balichi, M. (1983). An integrated approach to cognitive rehabilitation of the head injured patient. *Cognitive Rehabilitation, 1*(4), 8–12.

Melton, G. (1988). Ethical and legal issues in AIDS-related practice. *American Psychologist, 43,* 941–947.

Mitchell, J., & Register, J. C. (1984). An exploration of family interaction with the elderly by race, socioeconomic status, and residence. *Gerontologist, 24,* 48–54.

Oddy, M., Humphrey, M., & Uttley, D. (1978). Stresses upon the relatives of head-injured patients. *British Journal of Psychology, 113,* 507–513.

O'Malley, T. A., O'Malley, H. C., Everitt, D. E., & Sarson, D. (1984). Categories of family-mediated abuse and neglect of elderly persons. *Journal of the American Geriatrics Society, 32,* 362–369.

Parente, F. J., & Anderson, J. K. (1986, June). *Outpatient cognitive rehabilitation: Affordable therapy in the home.* Paper presented at the Tenth Annual Postgraduate Course on Rehabilitation of Brain-Injured Adults and Children, Williamsburg, VA.

Prigatano, G. (1986). *Neuropsychological rehabilitation after brain injury.* Baltimore: Johns Hopkins Press.

Rosenthal, C. J. (1986). Family supports in later life: Does ethnicity make a difference? *Gerontologist, 26,* 19–24.

Rosenthal, M., Griffith, E., Bond, M., & Miller, J. (Eds.) (1983). *Rehabilitation of the head injured adult.* Philadelphia: F. A. Davis.

Steuer, J., & Austin, E. (1980). Family abuse of the elderly. *Journal of the American Geriatrics Society, 28,* 372–376.

Stone, R., Cafferata, G. L., & Sangi, J. (1987). Caregivers of the frail elderly: A national profile. *Gerontologist, 27,* 616–626.

Taylor, R. J. (1985). The extended family as a source of support to elderly blacks. *Gerontologist, 25,* 488–495.

Thomsen, I. V. (1974). The patient with severe head injury and his family. *Scandinavian Journal of Rehabilitative Medicine, 6,* 180–183.

Weeks, J. R., & Cuellar, J. B. (1981). The role of family members in the helping networks of older people. *Gerontologist, 21,* 388–394.

Willbach, D. (1989). Ethics and family therapy: The case management of family violence. *Journal of Marital and Family Therapy, 15*, 43–52.

Zeigler, E. A. (1987). Spouses of persons who are brain injured: Overlooked victims. *Journal of Rehabilitation, 1*, 50–53.

Part II
Theory

**INTRODUCTION: NEW DIRECTIONS IN
GENDER THEORY**

There has been an explosion of energy among feminist scholars in
the social sciences and humanities as they strike out in new directions to examine issues of interest to women. Psychology has been no
exception; the work of feminist psychologists has enriched and enliv-
ened our field. Feminist psychologists are working in every area of
the discipline, exploring every conceivable issue, and making substantial contributions to gender theory. It would be impossible to
convey the extent of the work in the few pages available to us here.
The following chapters were chosen to illustrate several of the directions in which progress is being made.

We start with a historical perspective. Leonore Tiefer's chapter
presents a thoughtful look back at the changes in sexology research
and theory in the 10 years since she wrote her award-winning critique of the field. In the best women's studies' tradition, Tiefer
places her remarks in personal and social context as she describes
for us her motivation to write the critique and the reaction that followed it before proceeding with her review of what has happened
since then. She concludes that much re-vision is still needed and
suggests ways that sexologists can work to "demasculinize" their
field.

Lesley Diehl's re-vision of psychology includes placing previously ignored women in the history texts. In her chapter she shows
us how she discovered the work of Iva Lowther Peters, a student of
G. Stanley Hall, who received her PhD in sociology in 1918. Al-

85

though Peters taught sociology and economics and spent many years as a university administrator, her work was psychological in nature, and she focused on empowering her women students long before such ideas came into vogue. We think you will enjoy "meeting" Dr. Peters and learning about her early contributions to gender theory.

As Diehl was wondering where we've been, Mary Ricketts wondered where we are. Her chapter presents the results of her research on women graduate students in the United States and Canada. Ricketts compared feminist and nonfeminist students on a variety of personal, political, methodological, and philosophical dimensions and concluded that the reason feminist graduate students often feel like outsiders is that they are. Her choice of the metaphor "stranger in a strange land" is provocative and will certainly lead readers to rethink their own graduate school experiences.

Carole Baroody Corcoran examines the way that traditional gender theory has shaped campus rape prevention programs by suggesting a "victim control" approach; that is, women who refrain from engaging in such risky behaviors as hitchhiking or leaving doors unlocked will avoid being raped. Using examples from her work with college students, Corcoran brings a feminist perspective to illustrate the importance of the empowerment and social change approaches in campus rape prevention programs.

Geraldine Butts Stahly presents a review of the literature and results of her own research to argue that, although all cancer patients may experience stigma, women are affected in unique ways. Her discussion of how gender-role socialization affects the patient's perception of her illness is insightful and interesting and speaks to the need for a re-vision of health psychology.

Finally, Judith Glassgold examines new directions in psychodynamic theories of lesbianism. As she compares theories of women's sexuality to theories that support colonialism, Glassgold takes her readers on a tour of perspectives from early psychoanalysis to recent social constructionism. She points out the benefits and the limits of each theorist's contribution. Her chapter ends with a series of valuable suggestions about the directions in which future theorists, researchers, and practitioners should proceed.

■ 8
Feminism and Sex Research: Ten Years' Reminiscences and Appraisal

Leonore Tiefer

It is important for feminist scholars to reminisce. It contextualizes our work, it builds a sense of group memory and tradition, and it can give us some sense of how we have coped over time with the difficulties of our marginalized position.

This chapter reminisces by looking at a particular article on feminism and sexology (Tiefer, 1978), reviewing its background, its four themes, and how the original talk on which the article was based was received by sexologic colleagues. Then I dwell at some length on what has happened to sex research in the past decade and conclude with a few words on a feminist vision for sex research in the future.

ORIGINS OF THE CHAPTER

In 1969 I earned my PhD at the University of California at Berkeley with a dissertation on hormones and hamster mating behavior supervised by

This chapter is based on a talk given at the 1988 Association for Women in Psychology annual conference. I was invited to mark the passage of 10 years since being awarded a Distinguished Publication award for "The Context and Consequences of Contemporary Sex Research: A Feminist Perspective" (1978).

Frank A. Beach, the noted comparative psychologist (Tiefer, 1970). Beach was a highly influential and much-liked scientist, and a festschrift was being organized for presentation in April 1976 to celebrate his 65th birthday. The previous November, I had received a form letter announcing the event; it had been sent to all of Beach's students from two of his former postdoctoral fellows. "We propose to hold a one-day scientific meeting in Berkeley. . . . the theme of the meeting will be 'Sex research: Where are we now, where are we going?' "[1] The event was to be by invitation only, but the proposed list of speakers was not included, nor did the long letter solicit volunteers. With some trepidation but under the spell of the women's movement, which at that time encouraged taking every opportunity to "speak out," I wrote back volunteering to give a talk on "Changing conceptions of sex roles: Impact on sex research," which I teasingly suggested could be subtitled "The Women's Movement Has Met Frank Beach and He Is Ours."[2]

Most of the others, I knew, would be talking on topics related to hormones and mating/reproductive behaviors, but although I had continued to do animal sex research for several years post-PhD, I was beginning to drift away. In fact, the year the invitation came I was spending a 1975–76 sabbatical at Bellevue Psychiatric Hospital (New York University School of Medicine) in New York City, learning something about human sexuality, specifically about sexual dysfunctions and transsexualism. I was at Bellevue because I had begun to teach human sexuality at Colorado State University (CSU) with only my comparative and physiological background, a poor preparation. I felt I needed to learn a lot more about human beings.

I had begun teaching human sexuality because of feminism. I got involved in feminist activity beginning in 1972, when Dr. Pamela Pearson arrived at CSU from Chicago, relieving my burden of being the only woman in the psychology department and bringing news of a women's "revolution" beginning to take place in the big cities. Within a few months, I helped to found a Fort Collins NOW chapter, a Faculty Women's Caucus, and the Colorado State University Commission on the Status of Women; and, of course, I joined a consciousness-raising group. Feminism was first and foremost a political activity, and much needed to be done.

I actually began teaching human sexuality in 1973 because, as the resident expert on animal mating behavior, I had been invited to a meeting sponsored by the CSU Social Work Department devoted to planning a new, interdepartmental human sexuality course. With my newly sharpened sexism antennae, however, I was horrified by some of the comments made by the meeting convener, and I determined to preempt the interdepartmental planning and offer a course through the Department of Psychology (together with a clinician friend, Joyce Moore-Spinelli). This turned out to be a wonderful experience and ultimately led to a decision to change my area of specialization in psychology.

While I was in New York, I was too busy learning about clinical matters and too intimidated by New York feminist sophistication to get involved in political feminism, but I read a lot. Two books published in 1975 affected me especially. E. O. Wilson's (1975) *Sociobiology* made a big splash in the *New York Times*, and I knew from my comparative and physiological background that this was going to be the beginning of a tremendous growth spurt in biological determinism. The developing feminist in me was not happy about this, and the Beach festschrift offered an opportunity to say something on the subject.

An edited collection in feminist sociology (Millman & Kanter, 1975) gave me some ideas. This truly radical book challenged so much then (and still) prevalent in orthodox academic disciplines (theories, results, methods) that I was swept away by its boldness. I began reading furiously, beginning with many of the references I found in Millman and Kanter. I decided that I would criticize sex research from a feminist point of view, just as their authors had criticized other social science areas.

A letter came back in January 1976, from Ben Sachs, one of the organizers of the festschrift:

> Sorry to be so long getting back to you. Anyway, you can start worrying now about how to say all you want to say about "Changing conceptions of sex roles . . ." in 30–40 minutes. I'll be interested especially since shortly before you arrived in Berkeley Beach was still saying he'd never have ovaries in his lab. (Or have you had some surgery I'm unaware of?)[3]

I didn't recall having heard that, and since I knew that Beach had had female collaborators in the 1940s, I knew it couldn't be completely true. But I think that letter helped steel my resolve.

My talk covered some issues that didn't make it into this chapter, but the themes are the same.

THEMES IN THE 1978 CHAPTER

I tried to organize the chapter in a logical fashion, in part to manage the vast amount of new information I took in during that year of reading and thinking. Building a logical argument also helped me to deal with my fear that these ideas would not be taken seriously.

1. *Exposing and challenging the assumptions.* I had gotten the idea of analyzing the basic assumptions underlying sexology from Millman and Kanter (1975), and I now recognize it as the fundamental first step in all

radical analyses and critiques. *Whose interests are being served?* What questions are being asked and *why?* What research is conducted, why, and how? How are the results interpreted? These are still the fundamental questions.

2. Can we find a masculine bias in sex research? Using some of the notions of "masculine bias" I found in my reading, I suggested that sex researchers seemed possessed of a "phallic fallacy" (a term I found in a 1973 paper by the sociologist Alice Rossi), as indicated by their focus on defining sex as genital copulation, by their disregard of female sexual agency, and by their equating all forms of "sexual outlet" that end in orgasm. I also described how even animal sex research was affected by gender stereotypes because it disproportionately emphasized studies of female *physiology* and male *behavior*. This, I suggested, led us to think of females as more biologically bound and, not incidentally, gave us more information useful for *female* contraception.

In retrospect, I think I was much influenced by the heady experience of working in a psychiatric hospital and, after having spoken with dozens of transsexuals and couples with sexual dysfunctions, was feeling that all animal sex research was totally useless for understanding human patterns! Calling much of the work distorted by "masculine bias" seemed especially legitimate insofar as animal research (including mine) had focused disproportionately on male patterns of behavior. Although Beach had mentioned female patterns of appetitive (i.e., active, soliciting behavior) in many of his papers, he had not emphasized them, giving the impression that male sexuality was much more active and assertive. In the year of the festschrift, a sign of the times appeared, as Beach finally gave a behavioral label, "proceptive," to females' active, soliciting behaviors (Beach, 1976).

3. Biological determinism—the heart of the paper! I had found plenty in my reading to bolster the feminist (but not only feminist) view that an emphasis on biological underpinnings of human behavior is often politically regressive. One monograph documented a high correlation between 24 scientists' philosophic views about the prospects for social equality among groups and their "scientific" explanations for those group differences (Pastore, 1949).

Although Pastore (1949) couldn't say whether his scientists' political views preceded or followed their research, from this study it seemed that the nature–nurture debate—the debate over the validity and extent of biological influences on human capacity and function—was less than "objective": [T]here is interaction of a circular kind between the political and psychological dogmas. Interaction, however, implies some effect of social assumptions upon scientific findings and, correspondingly, some departure from the ideal of objectivity" (Pastore, p. viii).

From a feminist point of view, it was important to show that research with a heavy biological emphasis often went hand-in-hand with less progressive politics and therefore had to be monitored and challenged. I had been keeping a file of biological trends in psychology (growth of neuropsychology, biochemistry of psychopathology, behavioral genetics, etc.), and I argued that the growing emphasis on biological bases of behavior needed to be seen as a trend with important social consequences, not just as new, politically neutral research developments.

Finally, I presented a lengthy discussion of research on prenatal effects of hormones on human sex differences. The paradigm dominant in animal research at the time held that important behavioral predispositions were laid down by prenatal hormones. Research on sex-role behavior in childhood and adolescence seemed to adopt this model uncritically and, again, with negative political consequences. I was very concerned to emphasize *nonbiological* interpretations of the prenatal hormone data. For example, I suggested that maybe individuals with high prenatal male hormone levels behaved more like boys because their parents treated them differently, not because their brains had been programmed to like certain sports and toys. After all, the subjects in these studies were patients in a pediatric endocrinology clinic because of their abnormalities, indicating that their parents were fully aware of their status. *Disputing biological interpretations of sex-role differences was then, is now, and probably always will be a major feminist project* (Bleier, 1986).

4. Conclusion. I concluded with some suggestions for future sex research. That was the part I had the most difficulty with because I really couldn't imagine how to do research different from the type I had been trained to do. But my reading gave me some brand-new ideas of branching out beyond strict quantitative hypothesis testing into more collaborative, qualitative, subjective, and context-related types of methods. I ended with a suggestion that science ought to be socially responsible and anticipate how research results would be used. Again, I was able to find plenty of relevant citations, beginning with Leona Tyler's 1973 presidential address to the American Psychological Association calling for conducting more humanitarian research.

COLLEAGUES' REACTIONS TO FEMINIST CRITICISM

I hope my memory doesn't deceive me when I say that this paper was received with overt amazement. Imagine the situation. After a year's organization and preparation, Frank Beach, an eminent animal sex researcher with over 30 years' productivity and a member of the National Academy of Sciences (a very rare honor for a psychologist) is sitting in a beautiful red velvet jacket, surrounded by students who love and revere him, celebrating his

65th birthday. And I, the only woman on the program, am arguing that some of the very foundations of his work are biased by masculine presumptions and need to be reexamined! My recollection is that Beach himself was taken aback and angrily mentioned something negative about meddlesome people with political perspectives. Later, during cocktails, a few of those present who had left animal research for other domains came up to me and were complimentary, but I remember being upset by Beach's outburst (it's one thing to take intellectual risks and quite another to be emotionally prepared for the consequences). However, in his typical friendly way, Beach later wrote to me:

> . . . Your talk was stimulating and maybe after I get a chance to read it I won't be as alarmed as I was when you read it. Who knows? You may be right. I know we oldsters like to hold tight to old times and old values — often after they are no longer worth preserving. But that's why we always have a "younger generation," isn't it?[4]

I hope I can be as gracious when I am an "oldster"!

After the event, it took months to write up the talk, not the least because I knew the ideas were unpopular and I didn't know whom to turn to for help. I got several letters from colleagues contributing to the festschrift with helpful suggestions, but they all felt I should tone down the feminism! For example, "One other minor criticism which I hate to bring up (for obvious reasons) but I think it would be dishonest to avoid. I think you have overdone the feminist rhetoric. . . . It is too good a paper to be labeled and dated by ideological phrases."[5] The editor of the festschrift volume wrote:

> I must say, Leonore, that I agree with most of the comments [others have] made. . . . Do you think you can modify your chapter to meet these criticisms? You obviously had something on your mind and you got it said to a large, appropriate, and attentive audience. But I'm not sure that putting all your thoughts and speculations in the "permanent record" is a good idea for you, for the point of view you champion, or for the Beach volume itself.[6]

I include these letters because I know they are not unique, and part of my purpose in these reminiscences, as I mentioned earlier, is to show how feminist academicians have been received and how we have had continuously to make choices about what, where, and how to say and write our new ideas. Most of us have received well-meaning but repressive advice from our colleagues about being too "strident," or too ideological or about the negative professional consequences of being labeled "doctrinaire." Yet someone has to write and speak or we'll never move forward, and so the advice must be evaluated in terms of the large goals, not an easy matter.

I ended up asking my younger brother, a biochemistry undergraduate who didn't know anything about my field, to help me figure out if I was making any sense, so that at least the piece would be logical, albeit "ideological." I was extremely relieved when the chapter was finally published (Tiefer, 1978), and you can imagine how validating it was to receive a feminist organization's award.

SEX RESEARCH IN THE SUBSEQUENT DECADE

Let me examine trends in sex research in light of the sort of feminist criticisms I made in that paper.

1. Unfortunately, the first and most important point to make is that the professional sexology literature shows little sign of being influenced by feminist criticisms (Tiefer, 1988). The animal research continues as before, dominated by evolutionary and sociobiology theory and behavioral endocrinology methods and interventions. Human sex research, a field I knew little about in 1976 but have been immersed in for the past decade, is dominated by a medical model of sexuality, depending primarily on physiological measures, usually studying drug/illness/hormone effects, and still preoccupied with a (phallic) genital definition of sexuality. The whole notion of broadening the methods beyond quantitative hypothesis testing has not caught on, and I am still giving papers about it (Tiefer, 1989a, 1989b).

The field of sex research is having a difficult time because we are still in a politically conservative era in which anything resembling the liberalization of sexuality fails to get government support (e.g., sex education, sex research, sexuality clinics). Ironically, AIDS research has injected some new money, visibility, and reputability into sex research, and this may facilitate new growth in the field.

2. Research on sexuality in anthropology, history, and literature: "Interpretive" disciplines have much to say about sexuality and have incorporated feminist methods and concepts much more easily than the sciences have (DuBois, Kelly, Kennedy, Korsmeyer, & Robinson, 1987). In *anthropology*, for example, many books in the 1980s have moved from the "cultural catalog" approach in sexuality to the "cultural meanings" approach (Caplan, 1987; Ortner & Whitehead, 1981). Let me explain the difference and why I think the "meanings" approach takes a more feminist point of view.

The catalog approach describes differences between cultures by statistically analyzing lists: which behaviors are permitted, which are encouraged, which are missing, and so on. Such an approach might consider how many cultures ban prepubertal homosexual play or extramarital sexual liaisons, for example. The "meanings" approach looks at how sexual patterns fit into larger cultural values and patterns of customs regarding gender, the body, fertility, pleasure, and the like. No assumption is made that any particular behavior has the same meaning across cultures. For example, what do people in different cultures think prepubertal homosexual play means? Is it innocent experimenting, harmful training and exposure, OK for one gender but not for the other, or important learning experiences for later social relationships? How does the meaning of this particular activity fit into larger cultural patterns of meaning? For example, if prepubertal homosexual play is banned, might this be part of a culture's view that all sexual experimenting is dangerous because it might lead people to abandon social responsibilities?

The catalog approach, focusing on listing and counting sexual acts, assumes that sexual activities have the same meaning and are the same experience in all cultures. Thus, it makes sense to look at frequency of a particular activity across cultures. Feminists argue, by contrast, that individual activities can mean very different things in different social contexts and that one cannot really understand an activity without looking at the cultural surroundings. Consider age of marriage, for example. It doesn't make much sense to compare age of marriage in two cultures if one of them has marriages arranged by the family for economic purposes and the other leaves marriage completely up to the discretion of individuals who were raised to believe in personal self-determination. Grouping together comparisons of age of marriage, when marriage itself has such different meanings, obscures more than it illuminates.

This is especially problematic with sexual behaviors because every culture seems to have its own idiosyncratic pattern of rules and social customs surrounding sexuality. The experience of masturbation, for example, will be wildly different in permissive or restrictive cultures or in cultures where sex is seen as for the purpose of procreation versus those in which it is for the purpose of celebrating religious ecstasy. Moving from acts to meanings makes culture more fundamental than biology and is consistent with feminist values stressing diversity and the power of social milieu to shape customs and responses.

In *history* there has been an explosion of information about sexuality. Again, moving beyond a catalog approach (e.g., Bullough, 1976), which assumed that a kiss in ancient Greece could be compared to a kiss in modern Brazil, to an approach that emphasizes historical context (e.g., Freedman & D'Emilio, 1988), the "new" social history is consistent with feminist criticisms.

Let me take as an example a chapter written by Atina Grossmann (1983) in a recent feminist collection. Grossmann sets out to examine what was going on with sexuality practice and politics in Germany during the period of the Weimar Republic (the 1920s). She presents us with what seems, on the face of it, to have been tremendous growth of a prowoman political sex reform movement, including agitation for legal abortion, contraception, sex education, women's right to sexual satisfaction, and so on. She describes the social agencies that developed to respond to women's demands and discusses who ran them and what they accomplished. So far, this reads like traditional history: socialworker A did this, and writer B said that, and then a law was passed, and Dr. C opened this clinic, and so on.

But then, *and this is where women's scholarship really makes a difference*, she looks at the context and meaning of these events, not assuming automatically that "abortion" or "sex education" are necessarily good or bad for women. Grossmann (1983) keeps asking: *what was actually happening to women* in this culture? Was any particular social change in sexuality (contraception availability, sex education) really good for women? Did it advance women's autonomy and quality of life? Grossmann describes the German social context for women during the Weimar period: a declining birth rate, a rise in marital age, women moving into the work force, a high incidence of criminal abortions. And she shows (I condense greatly here, and because her article is based on her dissertation it was already condensed) how what seem at first to be gains for women were actually brief, superficial, and easily swept away because they were not based on real changes in social values about gender, they were not based on mass changes in consciousness, they were not based on increased education for women, and they were not rooted in a new relation of women to the society's economic base.

That is, the changes in sexuality were not *grounded in changes in women's political and social context* and therefore could not endure. The changes actually served not to empower women but to make sexuality and family life more controlled by scientifically informed experts who dictated new norms and values. Women themselves were not consulted about the goals of sex—the goals were set out by the experts. (If this sounds something like our contemporary situation, you're getting a point I want to convey.) The experts' goals in Weimar Germany were well intentioned but fundamentally patronizing and disempowering. They made improved sex serve the ends of marriage and motherhood, not the ends of greater control for women over their lives and choices. Women were actually being redomesticated rather than liberated by this prowoman sex reform, and when the Weimar republic was politically undermined and then destroyed by the Nazis, women lost what they thought they'd gained. (Those interested in further study of this period in women's history can consult Bridenthal, Grossmann, & Kaplan, 1984).

In her dissertation, Grossmann (1984) states explicitly how her *choice of question* and *interpretation of research* would be affected by her feminist politics:

This is a history that resonates very profoundly for us today, in a society that ponders the emergence of yet another "new woman" and "new family." A study which examines the political movements and policies which both represented and sought to contain the "new woman" and the "new family" in the "new" Germany of Weimar seems particularly intriguing at a time when . . . the demise of yet another generation of "brave new women" from the 1960s and 1970s is being trumpeted through the media and when headlines suggest the emergence of "post-feminism" or the continuing dilemma of "careers vs. the lure of motherhood." (p. viii)

By looking at the *context* and *meaning* of changes in sexual values, we see that women's conflicts are recurrent and related to larger social forces and meanings. We can learn from the past. Feminist sex history shows us how *the personal is political* in new ways that echo old ways. There are dozens of other wonderful books in feminist sex history, having to do with prostitution or sex abuse or birth control or adultery or children's innocence, that continue and expand these themes.

RELATIONS BETWEEN FEMINISM AND SEXOLOGY

As I mentioned above, it seems to me that professional sexology has not been much affected by feminist criticism and has been continuing more or less in the same way as it had over the past decades. I have elsewhere argued (Tiefer, 1988) that sexology has developed a profoundly neutral, studiously apolitical, "ultrascientific" stance defensively, to avoid charges of sensationalism or politicization that arise because sexuality is such a politicized battleground in our culture. Adhering to the alleged impartiality offered by objective and quantitative methods offered respectability to an otherwise risqué and controversial discipline. The less obviously relevant the work, the less likely it would be to get a mocking "Golden Fleece" award from a senator eager for publicity.

Human sex research thus evolved within this defensive professional stance and inevitably gravitated toward a medicalized frame of thinking, using concepts derived from the most "objectively scientific" type of human research—physiological research, in particular the physiological sex research of Masters and Johnson. Women's own experiences didn't contribute to contemporary formulations in sexology any more than they had in Weimar Germany! Again, it was the experts, benign and well intentioned, who chose language and goals and formulations that fit in with their professional needs.

The irony here is that most people, including most feminists, believe that women's sexuality has been enhanced and that women have been sexually empowered by modern sex research. After all, didn't laboratory research "prove" that men and women were entitled to equal pleasure (i.e., orgasm) because they had similar biology? And didn't laboratory research "prove" that women have orgasm more easily from clitoral stimulation than from intercourse and therefore that sexual activities ought not to revolve solely around the act of intercourse but ought to include more of the types of stimulation women favor?

Atina Grossmann's (1983, 1984) research on Weimar Germany shows us that when *experts* advocate sexual changes for women, without women themselves having more power in society, the changes rarely persist. We are seeing proof of that at this very moment with regard to abortion, as a change won *for* women but not really *by* women is being repealed because women still don't have the political power to make it stand.

The problem with basing women's right to sexual pleasure or particular sexual techniques on biology (as has been done by the experts) is that such arguments affirm and strengthen the right of biology to dictate social arrangements. Biologically deterministic theories about sexuality made me nervous as a beginning feminist in 1976, and they make me just as nervous as an experienced feminist today. The fact that the media continue to be fascinated (one might even say obsessed) with new biological developments isn't any different now than when I observed it a decade ago; only the topics differ (e.g., the new reproductive technologies, PMS). But media fascination with biological bases of behavior has a subtle but persistent consequence of persuading us that biology is the primary influence on our social arrangements, and this is a conclusion feminists must always resist.

Both sexology, because of its worries about professional status, and the media, for its own complex reasons, continue to push toward biological determinism for sexuality, making it more difficult for women to achieve true sexual empowerment. Thus, despite the immense explosion of feminist analysis in the humanities and social sciences pertaining to sexual arrangements, the sorts of criticisms I made in 1978 seem to be still relevant for sex research.

A FEMINIST VISION FOR SEX RESEARCH

I am much better able now than I was a decade ago to articulate what feminist sex research might be like. This is because women's studies has provided so many new models and ideas, and it is always *so much* easier to take something a little bit further or just into a new area than to think of the whole thing from scratch by yourself!

One thing we've learned is that there can be no one model for feminist research; there are just guiding principles — research *of* women, *by* women, and *for* women. When I suggested in 1976 that we ought to have more collaborative and qualitative methods, it was mostly because I was trying to get away from the context-stripped quantitative model of experimentation that dominated sex research. The intervening decade has shown that such research can truly be *for* women, empowering research participants instead of merely using them as "subjects."

If we include women not just as subjects/participants but as co-designers, as evaluators, and as helpers in planning the application of our research, we will move a long way toward a feminist vision. Involving women in choosing questions for research will help us avoid the pitfall of using only past literature to lead us toward our next study, rather than trying to see what needs to be better understood. Research is *not* just for the professional advancement of the researcher!

We will avoid biological determinism in sex research by remembering to take social context into account. Current thinking in sex research suggests that the main factors contributing to sexual activities and choices are a person's own psychology (thoughts, feelings, personal history) and physiology (health/illness, hormone cycle, chronological age, etc). Psychologists are not historians nor sociologists, but psychologists can *embed* their research in social and historical context. They can emphasize the social background of their participants. They can look less for simple or technical conclusions (e.g., women with a history of masturbation are more likely to have orgasm with their partners) and look for socially contextualized conclusions (e.g., white middle-class women whose parents, raised in the "liberated '60s," did not discourage childhood masturbation are likely to value orgasm and to be responsive to socially encouraged partner wishes for orgasm as a measure of the "success" of a sexual encounter).

Reviewing my 1978 paper has shown me that most of the criticisms and suggestions I made are still relevant and meaningful. Through rereading some of my correspondence of the time I have been reminded how difficult it was to figure out the ideas and how anxiety-provoking and frightening it was to say and write them. Now, however, with 10 more years of women's studies to learn from and to stand on, I can see how connected these criticisms and suggestions are to other feminist work in many different academic and nonacademic areas. This gives me continuing confidence to pursue the feminist point of view in sexology, and it gives me greater patience and compassion for those struggling with new ideas in unfavorable situations everywhere.

NOTES

1. Letter to Tiefer from Sachs and Dewsbury, 11 November 1975.
2. Letter from Tiefer to Sachs, 28 November 1975.

3. Letter from Sachs to Tiefer, 19 January 1976.
4. Letter from Beach to Tiefer, 21 April 1976.
5. Letter from Eaton to Tiefer, 3 June 1976.
6. Letter from McGill to Tiefer, 26 July 1976.

REFERENCES

Beach, F. A. (1965). Retrospect and prospect. In F. A. Beach (Ed.), *Sex and behavior* (pp. 535–569). New York: Wiley and Sons.

Beach, F. A. (1976). Sexual attractivity, proceptivity, and receptivity in female mammals. *Hormones & Behavior*, 7, 105–138.

Bleier, R. (1986). Sex differences research: Science or belief? In R. Bleier (Ed.), *Feminist approaches to science* (pp. 147–164). New York: Pergamon.

Bridenthal, R., Grossmann, A., & Kaplan, M. (Eds.). (1984). *When biology became destiny: Women in Weimar and Nazi Germany.* New York: Monthly Review Press.

Bullough, V. (1976). *Sexual variance in society and history.* New York: Wiley and Sons.

Caplan, P. (Ed). (1987). *The cultural construction of sexuality.* New York: Tavistock Publications.

DuBois, E. C., Kelly, G. P., Kennedy, E. L., Korsmeyer, C. W., & Robinson, L. S. (1987). *Feminist scholarship: Kindling in the groves of academe.* Urbana: University of Illinois Press.

Freedman, E. B., & d'Emilio, J. (1988). *Intimate matters: A history of sex in America.* New York: Harper & Row.

Grossmann, A. (1983). The new woman and the rationalization of sexuality in Weimar Germany. In A. Snitow, C. Stansell, & S. Thompson (Eds.), *Powers of desire: The politics of sexuality* (pp. 153–175). New York: Monthly Review Press.

Grossmann, A. (1984). *The new woman, the new family and the rationalization of sex in the sex reform movement in Germany: 1928–1933.* Unpublished doctoral dissertation, Rutgers University, New Brunswick, NJ.

Millman, M., & Kanter, R. M. (Eds.). (1975). *Another voice: Feminist perspectives on social life and social science.* Garden City, NY: Doubleday.

Ortner, S. B., & Whitehead, H. (Eds.). (1981). *Sexual meanings: The cultural construction of gender and sexuality.* Cambridge: Cambridge University Press.

Pastore, N. (1949). *The nature–nurture controversy.* New York: King's Crown Press (Columbia University).

Rossi, A. S. (1973). Maternalism, sexuality and the new feminism. In J. Zubin & J. Money (Eds.), *Contemporary sexual behavior: Critical issues in the 1970s* (pp. 145–174). Baltimore: Johns Hopkins University Press.

Tiefer, L. (1970). Gonadal hormones and mating behavior in the adult golden hamster. *Hormones & Behavior*, 1, 189–202.

Tiefer, L. (1978). The context and consequences of contemporary sex research: A feminist perspective. In W. McGill, D. Dewsbury, & B. Sachs (Eds.), *Sex and behavior: Status and prospectus* (pp. 363–385). New York: Plenum Press.

Tiefer, L. (1988). A feminist perspective on sexology and sexuality. In M. M. Gergen (Ed.), *Feminist thought and the structure of knowledge* (pp. 16–27). New York: New York University Press.

Tiefer, L. (1989a, June). *Qualitative methods in sexology.* Workshop presented at the International Academy of Sex Research, Princeton, NJ.

Tiefer, L. (1989b, August). *Feminist transformations of sexology.* Paper presented at the American Psychological Association, New Orleans.

Tyler, L. (1973). Design for a hopeful psychology. *American Psychologist, 28,* 1021–1029.

Wilson, E. O. (1975). *Sociobiology: The new synthesis.* Cambridge, MA: Harvard University Press.

■ 9
The Discovering of Iva Lowther Peters: Transcending Male Bias in the History of Psychology

Lesley A. Diehl

The role of feminist scholarship as it has been applied to the history of psychology has been twofold. As an accurate portrayal of psychology, a discipline created by both intellectual and social forces, feminist scholarship has documented the traditional or sexist biases of the profession. Such documentation has meant focusing upon negative aspects of the discipline's history, a kind of critical self-examination to tell us where we have been, what talents we may intentionally or unintentionally have wasted, and what forces may continue to shape our discipline should we choose to become less vigilant about the issues of gender, class, and race. Early general analyses of social myth penetrating psychological research and theory in the functionalist movement of the turn of the century have been accomplished in the pioneering work of Shields (1975). Recently, Diehl (1986) has examined the traditional biases found in G. Stanley Hall's theoretical approaches to women's psychological makeup as well as in his policies for women's higher education.

A second role of feminist scholarship in the history of psychology has been to recover or discover the many ways in which women, despite bias and discrimination within the discipline of psychology and other social sciences, have functioned as professionals and made significant contributions to the field. This aspect of feminist contribution to history in psychology has presented a positive, rather courageous view of the woman professional and has corrected possible misinterpretations of the history of women in psychology as the history of women as victims. Rather, it argues that women were actively engaged in resisting exclusions and were finding ways of making their voices heard within the discipline. The work of Shields (1975) and of Diehl (1986) touch on this aspect of feminist scholarship, which is most completely expressed for all of the sciences in Rossiter's (1982) volume on American women of science. More recently, the publication by Scarborough and Furumoto (1987) of their work documenting the lives and careers of the earliest American women psychologists has served as both a correction to traditional history of psychology and an inspiration to present and future generations of women psychologists who have lived far too long without connections to their foremothers.

This chapter is a continuation of the work I began in exploring G. Stanley Hall's theory of woman's psychological development and the educational policies he espoused and developed. Having documented his traditional approaches to women and their education (Diehl, 1986), I will turn more specifically and in greater depth to the lives and careers of the women who came under the influence of Hall. This chapter focuses on discovering the work of Iva Lowther Peters, who had a master's degree from Columbia University (1916) and a PhD degree from Clark University (1918). Although Peters was one of the ablest women to graduate from Clark University, where she studied under Hall, her career did not develop along traditional lines. As was true for other educated women of her time, Peters found the usual academic and state and federal agency work sex-segregated and closed to women, with the exception of a few positions in women's colleges and coeducational institutions. The two decades of the 1920s and 1930s, when Peters was most active, were the years when American women scientists met with increased discrimination and job segregation in public and private agencies and in the colleges and universities (Rossiter, 1982). Many women's colleges, previously the institutions most willing to hire women professionals, began in the 1920s to worry that their reputations for excellence would be better served if they replaced women with men faculty members. Peters's career development during these two decades of discrimination and segregation can be viewed as a reflection of the difficulty of professional development as experienced by the woman social scientist.

The case of Iva Lowther Peters is particularly instructive to the history of psychology and to our search for the contributions of women to the profession, for it suggests that to continue to look for such women in the usual places, such as colleges and universities, is to continue the traditional bias of the field. Within her historical context, Peters represents psychology at its interdisciplinary best, with connections to anthropology, sociology, and economics. Although some might label her a dilettante, Peters's career changes represent not only a survivalist response to the dearth of opportunities for women but, most important, a legitimate expansion and exploration of her intellectual interest in the status of women in her time and world. Using Peters's three career lines of teacher/professor, dean of women and vocational counselor, and researcher on women's careers, this chapter examines her understanding of women's psychology and development in the postindustrial world.

TEACHER, STUDENT, AND PROFESSOR: EDUCATION AND THE INSTITUTIONALIZED SEX TABOO

Several years before applying to Clark University, Peters was corresponding with Clark's president, G. Stanley Hall, concerning her interest in the psychological makeup of the young women she was teaching in the elite Packer Collegiate Institute in New York. Stimulated by discussions with her students, Peters (1916) constructed a questionnaire to explore restrictions in young women's education; the questions were sent to several hundred educators, physicians, social workers, psychologists, and club women — individuals who worked with girls or young women. The replies to the questionnaires, Peters concluded, confirmed her suspicions that social and educational restrictions placed on young women unduly affected their ability to deal with the world, limited social and intellectual development, and even affected psychological and physical health (Peters, 1916). Peters recommended that education for the girl be structured so as to put her in a position "where she will be in control of the situation as the crises of life confront her" (p. 568). Such an educational plan had never been tried and had its "perils for the existing order," Peters warned (p. 568). The recommendation by Peters that women's education might create more than a little discomfort in individuals' lives and that it had implications for changing existing social structures could hardly have been the stuff of which G. Stanley Hall approved. Yet he chose to ignore the more radical message in her work, focusing on the kinds of information she was able to get out of her students. What amazed him about this early work, Hall (1914) commented was

> . . . the intimate acquaintance of these girls with their own inner states and experiences, which is more, it seems to me, than young men ever have, and I wonder if this is what gives girls their amazing power of penetration into human character and motives. (p. 2)

During these years before her study at Clark, Peters began exploring what she referred to as taboos in women's lives, that is, negative attitudes toward women that arose out of history and that shaped women's attitudes toward themselves as well as society's attitudes toward women (Peters, 1916, 1920) Again, her interest in exploring these attitudes developed through her work with the young women of Packer Collegiate Institute. She said of her students that many of them were of the "society type" and "will soon cease to think. They are literally an unutilized by product [sic] of society" (1915, p. 4). Peters did not view the future of these young women as the inevitable outcome of their inherent natures, nor did she see it as the result of their wealthy status; rather, her experiences with these young women, coupled with her knowledge of the history of women's status and her observations of the "new woman" (the educated and financially independent woman), led her to believe that woman's nature and her potential were culturally determined by taboos institutionalized within religion, law, and the family. Further, Peters believed—as her professional life would attest, regardless of the career direction it took over the next several decades—that education and research (the rational) would correct and replace these social biases (the irrational). It was Peters's understanding of the social and cultural basis for women's psychological makeup, which she came to early in her professional development, that became the underlying thesis for what superficially appeared to be a loose aggregate of disjointed career interests. Further, identifying as she did the location of women's psychology within the cultural/historical matrix, Peters chose sociology, rather than the more biologically oriented psychology of the conservative functionalists such as G. Stanley Hall, as her area of concentration for her doctoral work.

Hall's interest in her work led Peters to apply for entrance to Clark University, and she began work on her doctoral dissertation, an explication of the role of taboo in women's development. The dissertation, titled "Woman and the Institutional Taboo" was published as part of the book *Taboo and Genetics: A Study of the Biological, Sociological and Psychological Foundations of the Family* (Knight, Peters, & Blanchard, 1920). The book was co-authored by Knight, Peters, and Blanchard, who each accepted responsibility for one of the three foundations of the family. Peters was responsible for the sociological understanding of the family, and her work focused on tracing the cultural origins of the institutionalized sex taboo, that is, the historical development through culture and religions of primitive controls over women's lives. She argued that these taboos governing women's behavior and interaction with men and other members of society were leftovers from early pre-Christian and Christian times, when taboos were set up to protect others from the "mana," or magic, of women. Thus, these taboos were postulated by Peters to have survived to modern times, although, following industrialization, the taboos only restricted women's freedom and protected them from change (Peters, 1920). Along with Freud, Peters agreed that in addition to fearing the taboo person (i.e., the woman),

man was also fascinated with her, thus creating the paradoxical image of woman as both seducer and innocent.

> Conflicting with his natural erotic inclinations are the emotions of awe and fear which she inspires in him as the potential source of contagion, for there is always some doubt as to her freedom from bad magic, and it is much safer to regard her as unclear. (p. 153)

In the final chapter of her section of *Taboo and Genetics*, Peters examined the institutional sex taboo as it existed in contemporary society and found that, though rationalism and the accumulation of scientific data had led to a somewhat more sane view of woman, her capabilities, nature, and sphere of influence, modern institutions had been shaped by these taboos. She pointed out, for example, that women were still defined as property, that their labor was sex-segregated, that pregnant women were secluded and avoided by others, and that individuals had translated the ancient belief in women's psychic power into the contemporary idea of women's intuition. Further, Peters identified the marriage ceremony and the customs of the family institution as the most direct continuations of the sex taboo.

Marriage, Peters (1920) asserted, was "an accepted exception to the social injunction which keeps men and women apart under other circumstances" (p. 218). The ancient belief that a woman should be kept pure and virginal before the marriage and an obedient mother afterward still governed the life of women, according to Peters. And, she continued, such an attitude toward women on the part of men had created two classes of women, good and bad. Thus, it was Peters's contention that man's making the wife and mother too pure to satisfy his physical needs resulted in the need for prostitutes. Although Peters identified slavery and poverty as the major forces sending women into prostitution, she returned to her indictment of the restrictiveness of the family for women by suggesting that boredom with "the narrowness of family life and desire for adventure" might be another determinant of women's entering into the life of prostitution (p. 225).

Not content with an exposition of the historical antecedents of the institutionalized sex taboo and the identification of the family structure as a major institution reflecting the most direct influence of the taboo, Peters also explained what was dysfunctional about continuation of the taboo and what changes were necessary to create a more rational and functional basis for the family. Thus, like many feminists of her time, Peters was advocating change in the family structure as one vehicle of change in women's status and position in society. In addition, however, Peters also recommended education and careers for women, even relatively nontraditional careers. She placed no restrictions upon the kind of education that should be provided for women, even recommending that sex education become part of the woman's curriculum. In contradiction to G. Stanley Hall's contention that education adversely affected women's reproductive organs, thereby accounting for the fewer children produced by college-educated women, Peters identified the problem as within the institution of marriage itself. As traditionally constituted through taboos, marriage was too restrictive for the educated woman (Peters, 1920). The reason that the highly educated woman did not reproduce herself, Peters contended, was due entirely to the economic penalties of marriage and motherhood.

Peters's position on women's roles, the traditional ones of wife and mother and the emerging role of woman worker or career woman, is open to interpretation. How far-reaching did she mean these changes in family and education to be? Was she subtly pointing to a future where all social institutions would be affected by intentional or unintentional spillover from changes within the American family as the result of alterations in women's education? Or was she simply suggesting that the American family make room for the educated woman by providing more flexibility in the traditional roles of wife and mother? In most instances in which Peters raised the issue of role change, she appeared only to be asking the question of its significance for the future, as in the following example concerning women workers:

These women wage-earners who live away from the tradition of what a woman ought to be will have a great deal of influence in the changed relations of the sexes. The answer to the question of their relation to the family and to a saner parenthood is of vital importance to society. (1920, p. 244)

By the time Peters saw her work in published form, she had had considerable experience, under the most difficult circumstances (World War I), with the kinds of situations to which women could not only adapt but in which they could excel. After completing her degree at Clark, she engaged in war camp community service. Her work was of a most unusual sort. She brought a group of girls to a camp in Virginia, where the girls' duties included offering comfort and hospitality to wounded men returning from the war. The idea to have girls do this work was unique and apparently was proposed by herself. The camp secretary wrote of her work: "By her keen understanding of our problems and by her wisdom in directing the girls under her charge, their work has been such a marked success that we can hardly understand why we tried so long to do this work without them" (Folsom, 1919).

Following her war effort, Peters returned to teaching, as an associate professor of economics and sociology from 1920 to 1922 and professor of economics and sociology from 1922 to 1926 at Goucher College in Towson,

Maryland. The courses she taught at Goucher remained true to her tradition of interest in women; they included courses on social origins, rural sociology, and social psychology. During the Goucher years, she extended her commitment to educating women by developing a program for their vocational guidance. She left Goucher in 1926 to take the position of dean and director of personnel for women at Syracuse University. Her developing interest in the problems of vocational guidance for women also led her to become associated with the Southern Woman's Educational Alliance and she served as its associate college counselor. She eventually published a report on a social and vocational guidance program based on an experimental program set up at William and Mary during the 1924–1925 school year (Peters, 1926a).

Although Peters never again occupied the formal position of college instructor or teacher, her career as a dean and director of vocational guidance programs was a continuation of her interest in freeing women from institutionalized sex taboos.

VOCATIONAL COUNSELOR AND DEAN OF WOMEN: AN OCCUPATIONAL WORLD FOR WOMEN

In encouraging young women to try out careers other than the traditional one of teaching, Peters advocated the development of vocational guidance programs for women's colleges. Under her direction, Goucher College initiated a program in vocational guidance that incorporated two unique features. First, Peters (1923, 1927a, 1927b) insisted that the vocational guidance program be research-oriented, that is, that it develop factual information about women in various occupations through pamphlets, books, and communication with individuals working in the fields and that it follow the career development of its students after their graduation. Peters also established within the community a preprofessional training program, which consisted of paid work in the profession for which the student was preparing. Because vocational guidance for women was a relatively new area of counseling development, Peters felt that the conservative elements of the college could be more easily won over if the program offered exact information rather than advice based on personal opinion (Peters, 1927a, 1927b). For this reason and because she felt that vocational counseling should be built on a realistic consideration of occupations available to women, Peters encouraged the research component of her program. The preprofessional training aspect of the program was included, as it was Peters's philosophy that the social function of her vocational guidance bureau was to link the college to the community (Peters, 1927a, 1927b).

In the winter term of the academic year 1924–1925, Goucher released Peters to the College of William and Mary to attempt an experimental vocational orientation course for 25 young women registered at the college (Peters, 1926a). The success of her experiment in vocational guidance began almost a decade of vocational counseling work, primarily in the position of a deanship at Syracuse University. The vocational course Peters taught at William and Mary incorporated her interest in the historical development of attitudes toward women; however, she chose to take a more optimistic view of history than she had taken in her earlier publications. In the case of the vocational orientation course, she chose to focus on the origins of women's work, stressing the variety of such work historically and connecting contemporary professions to the ancient labors of women.

From the William and Mary experiment, Peters (1926a) produced a monograph outlining in detail her program for a course in vocational orientation. The course was meant to cover an entire semester of work, and it included an extensive list of readings to be completed by the young women. Peters saw the course not only as useful in helping young women decide upon a profession, career, or job but she also viewed the course as necessary regarding "their individual problems of adjustment and also for better understanding of the general changes affecting women today" (p. 4). The structure and content of the course were based on her years of experience in vocational counseling at Goucher and on material and knowledge from several fields: "it may be said that while the material is in the field of economics and sociology, the point of view is that of the psychologist" (p. 5).

The course included readings in the following areas: the education of women, historical occupations of women, economic background of modern society, the effects of industrialization on women, vocational guidance, the new economic status of women, and the physical and mental health of trained women. In addition to the assigned readings, the instructor of the course and/or guest instructors provided lectures in these areas. One month of the course was dedicated to exploring the curriculum with campus instructors serving as lecturers in their areas of expertise. At the end of the course each student was expected to present a report on some area (e.g., mathematics or social work) in which she had become interested. Peters also stressed the importance of a questionnaire on vocational interests to be completed by each student at the beginning of the course.

Although optimistic in encouraging women to explore all career possibilities, Peters also was pragmatic in her understanding that this exploration needed to be balanced with information on the availability of various occupations for women. Included in her monograph and in other writings on vocational guidance for college women (e.g., Peters, 1930) is a cautionary note concerning the variability of opportunity for women in comparison to that of men and the recommendation that vocational counselors explore the opportunities for various professions within their respective colleges' curricula, within the industry nationally, and within their localities.

Coupled with the issue of availability of work for women was Peters's concern for the issue of pay for such work. Ever the pragmatist, Peters (1926a) suggested that less pay for women would have to be taken for granted for "a long time to come" (p. 35) but that there had been since the war some movement toward equal pay for equal work. In addition, Peters suggested, "there are other ways to measure achievement" (p. 35). Peters did not elaborate on what those other ways were, but they certainly were diligently searched for by the women social scientists who encountered sex segregation, low pay, low status, and no opportunity for advancement during the years to follow.

The educational aim of the course was to so stimulate intellectual interest "that the college woman will be aided in becoming a social force through self-discovery" (Peters, 1926a, p. 7). It is not clear how much of a social force Peters intended her students to be, for she seemed to retreat from the implications of this statement by suggesting elsewhere a more conservative end:

> All consideration of changes in the education of women should be related to the study of the family and household.... As the family is and must, for the sake of the state, continue to be of vital importance to woman, and as her emergence into other institutional activities is of such recent date, there should be conscious appraisal of the situation. (Peters, 1926a, p. 9)

If Peters did not fully appreciate the implications of reforming women's education and career orientation for the family and for other social structures—law, politics, and social mores—and it is difficult to believe that she did not, she surely could not have ignored what the students in her vocational orientation course said about the impact of the course on their attitudes:

> So far I have gotten away from the idea that women are inferior to men in occupations—or anywhere. I have also gotten away from the idea that there is a beautiful ideal love into which you must rush quickly—a wonderful knight coming for you on a white charger. (Student comment in Peters, 1926a, p. 11)

Yet another student concluded: "From my reading, I am beginning to believe that woman is not as frail as is generally thought, and that if she attempted and dared to do more, she would succeed as well as man" (p. 12). And finally: "This month has made me realize more than before that women needn't get married or teach school if they don't want to do either. It has made me feel proud to be a woman" (p. 12).

In the 5 years following publication of her vocational guidance book, years she spent at Syracuse in the position of dean and director of personnel for women, she continued her interest in vocational guidance, combining it with her duties as dean of women. In 1930 she was asked to contribute a chapter, "The Dean As a Vocational Advisor" to a book edited by Sturtevant and Hayes (1930), *Deans at Work*. In the chapter she suggested that, for those colleges that were unable or unwilling to provide the students with a trained vocational counselor, the dean and her office could take over some of the necessary duties associated with vocational guidance. Those duties might include collecting relevant written materials on occupations for women and conducting advisory interviews with women each year, or at least in the freshman year. Realizing the amount of work involved in collecting relevant data on occupations and on interviewing and assessment, Peters recommended using the economics department to study occupations and the psychology department to select and administer vocational tests. Because Peters had some considerable experience in interviewing and as the dean of women's office at Syracuse University had been experimenting with a form interview over several years, Peters offered readers of the chapter a personal interview guide, a comprehensive approach asking for information in the areas of family relationships, activities, reading habits, and vocational experiences. She further suggested that the dean's job was to see to it that the young women exiting from college or university were prepared for marriage, career, or both, and that this work was better done with the aid of both a trained psychiatrist and a competent medical advisor. In conclusion, Peters admitted that deans of women usually found themselves too busy to accomplish all she had suggested in the chapter; she recommended that they try both a vocational guidance course, similar to the one she had introduced at William and Mary, and a group approach, a collaboration of dean, departments, and students, to shoulder all of these burdens.

LEAVING THE UNIVERSITY: A RESEARCHER ONCE MORE

When Peters left Syracuse University, she was 55 years old. Whether she was seeking to curtail her activities in preparation for retirement or whether the funding for her position at Syracuse ran out is not clear. An article in the college paper reported that her departure from her post as dean was motivated by "a desire to continue her pioneering work in the field of vocational guidance, which demands so great a share of her time that she feels her duties as dean to be incompatible with it" (*The Daily Orange*, March 31, 1931). The article also reported that she intended, following her departure, to continue her activities in vocational guidance work. However, Peters soon found herself fully occupied with research for the National Federation of Business and Professional Women's Clubs, Inc. The research she accomplished for the Federation was not unrelated to her work in vocational guidance. Beginning in 1924, Peters (1926b), in order to supply her students with pertinent information on new occupations for women, had begun interviewing women representatives of these new occupations. Her interviews led to publication of an article on women business executives, in which she examined the significant role of the Federation of Business and Professional Women's Clubs in the development of an educational program for businesswomen. In 1923, a Department of Research was added to the educational work of the Federation, and Peters was asked to do research for them as a member of the research committee.

Following her departure from Syracuse University, Peters accomplished several studies for the Federation. The first article (Peters, 1935) reported on a preliminary inquiry into the issue of discrimination against women workers following the Depression. In it, Peters examined the impact of the Depression on the existent wage discrimination and job segregation for women, and she optimistically suggested that the time was ripe for a serious consideration of differences in opportunities and earnings for women. Justification for such discrimination, Peters added, "must be expressed in other terms than habit and prejudice" (p. 9). Included in the article were two appendices, one providing a form for a work history interview. The interview was to be conducted with professional and businesswomen and included questions designed to explore factors such as sex, age, dress, appearance, marital status, and the Depression that were thought to be related to job discrimination for women. Appendix B titled "Questions for Forum and Panel Discussion, Connected with Problems of Employability of Women," included questions revealing of the difficulties encountered by women professionals during the decade of the 1930s. For example, the following question recognizes the discrimination and asks for possible responses to it:

> Inasmuch as political opportunity and economic opportunity in the United States have not spread evenly and at the same rate of progress, and as the implications of the New Deal emphasize an increase in economic opportunity, what should be the attitude of progressive women toward the problems involved?
>
> a. Should they emphasize the task of holding the gains of the past decade?
>
> b. Should they concentrate on further gains in the fields in which opportunity was least?
>
> c. Should they concentrate on holding fields in which there is least competition with men? (p. 15)

Questions like those above point out that, as reported in Rossiter (1982), discrimination in terms of sex segregation of employment, wage differential, and lack of promotion increased during the 1920s and 1930s, much to the dismay of those women who had seen the doors of colleges, universities, and federal and state agencies opening to them during the early years of the 20th century. Of little help in averting this decline in opportunities for women was the Depression, which, as Peters indicated in the article, served as yet another reason for continued and increased job discrimination against women workers. It must have been particularly disheartening for someone like Peters, who had dedicated so much of her life's work to encouraging young women to seek careers outside the home, to find society rolling back opportunities for women's professional development.

Of concern to professional women were the strategies that could be developed to counter the declining number of women in the professions. The Federation, wishing to aid young women's careers, was willing to provide some financial assistance to women interested in medicine, but it wanted to know what was to be more successful: assistance to a young woman to enter medicine, where a recession in numbers of women was reported, or assistance in entering a field more open to women, such as public health or bacteriology? Peters's (1935) inquiry into the issue of sex discrimination against women was set up to answer these kinds of questions for the Federation.

The following year the results of the investigation were published (Peters, 1936). Peters had interviewed 212 business and professional women; the women interviewed included those with college educations and those with elementary educations, including clerks, typists, physicians, saleswomen, executives, and teachers at every grade level. Peters explored a number of factors that were hypothesized to be related to occupational discrimination against women. The results showed that education did not protect women from discrimination and that age acted as a factor especially as it related to dress, grooming, and general attractiveness. Women reported difficulties with employers on issues of marital status and social and religious factors, but most important, women reported being denied promotions, being released from their jobs, or receiving less pay in favor of men. Peters concluded that the remarks of the women taken together pointed to the use of the Depression as a scapegoat for the traditional attitudes against women's occupational advancement:

> It was the expressed opinion of many women that in the confusion created by depression [sic] conditions, these old attitudes have emerged in unexpected strength in the midst of modern conditions under which the work of women is a necessity, even in occupations heretofore considered peculiarly their own. (p. 28)

Peters further suggested that to sort out employment, even in the face of overwhelming unemployment, on the basis of sex or marital status was contrary to "American principles," but that until information suggested that public sentiment accepted women as an economic and social asset, women needed to be on their guard. The data on occupational discrimination against women was disheartening, yet Peters chose to remain optimistic, concluding that the future of democracy would find a better plan.

RETIREMENT: LOOKING BACK ON TWO DECADES OF WORK FOR WOMEN

In the *Alumni Directory* (1951) of Clark University, Peters reported herself as a retired professor, writing and doing research. Any record of her professional life seems to have disappeared following her 1936 work for the Federation of Business and Professional Women's Clubs. Neither Clark University nor the colleges, universities, and associations for which she worked or with which she was affiliated report a death date for Peters. It is difficult to believe that the work of a woman described by G. Stanley Hall (1918) as "a lady of a good deal of personal charm, and of unusual tact, sympathy and insight and power to work with others" (p. 1) should so completely have been lost. It can be argued that Peters did more to move information about the similarity of the sexes out of the laboratory and the classroom into the public realm than did most other professionals. In addition, she encouraged young women to operate on this information by freeing themselves from traditional modes of thinking about women's roles through enlightened marriages and/or career selections. That she chose to do her work through vocational guidance programs and research for the Federation has led the search beyond the classroom of the college and university and beyond mainstream publications within the traditional disciplines. The principle that guided Peters's choices of work throughout her career is best expressed in her concluding thoughts for a symposium published as *Women's Coming of Age* (Schmalhausen & Calverton, 1931): "In the presence of the world's need for creative intelligence the friends of the modern woman must steadfastly see to it that she be given her intellectual opportunity" (Peters, 1931, p. 186).

Though the principle exemplified in the quotation above is adequately descriptive of Peters's works, she certainly would have preferred something less pretentious to describe the work of her life, such as the following, written by her earlier in the century and predictive of the enthusiasm and optimism with which she approached each project: "The fact that there has always been more than enough for me to do has probably made me too much of an opportunist" (Peters, 1919, p. 1).

Whether Peters's careers can be viewed as the works of an opportunist, simply responding to what came along, or as a survival response to an increasingly sex-discriminatory work world, or even as an intentional plan developed in accordance with changing and maturing professional interests, her work provides psychology with great insight into and documentation of the social and historical forces that have shaped and continue to shape women's psychological makeup. There is a strong thread of consistency in her work, not in the name with which we label her career—teacher, professor, counselor—nor in the field with which she can be identified—psychology, sociology, economics—but in the question she chose to ask in all of her work: What is it to be a woman in the 20th century? The same question continues to shape contemporary feminist scholarship, and its answer emerges out of an interdisciplinary perspective not dissimilar to that used by Peters. Feminist scholarship as it seeks to find contributions made by women like Peters needs to discard prevailing biases that dictate searches by profession or field of study. Rather, such scholarship needs to adopt a question-oriented approach to inquiry, one that will not limit field of study but will cross disciplines as well as move beyond traditional career lines in psychology (e.g., professor and researcher). Such a search strategy is particularly necessary if we wish to discover women professionals like Iva Lowther Peters, who worked in the lean years of the 1920s and 1930s.

REFERENCES

Alumni directory. (1951) Worcester, MA: Clark University Library.
The Daily Orange (1931, March 31). Syracuse, NY: Syracuse University, The George Arents Research Library.
Diehl, L. A. (1986). The paradox of G. Stanley Hall: Foe of coeducation and educator of women. *American Psychologist, 41,* 686–878.
Folsom, G. I. (1919, July 10). [Letter to whom it may concern], *G. Stanley Hall Papers,* Clark University Archives, Goddard Library, Clark University, Worcester, MA.
Hall, G. S. (1914, July 2). [Letter to Peters], *G. Stanley Hall Papers,* Clark University Archives, Goddard Library, Clark University, Worcester, MA.
Hall, G. S. (1918, June 25). [Letter to Women's Educational and Industrial Union], *G. Stanley Hall Papers,* Clark University Archives, Goddard Library, Clark University, Worcester, MA.
Knight, M. M., Peters, I. L., & Blanchard, P. (1920). *Taboo and genetics: A study of the biological, sociological, and psychological foundations of the family.* New York: Moffat, Yard, and Company.
Peters, I. L. (1915, July 9) [Letter to Hall], *G. Stanley Hall Papers,* Clark University Archives, Goddard Library, Clark University, Worcester, MA.
Peters, I. L. (1916). A questionnaire study of some of the effects of social restrictions on the American girl. *Pedagogical Seminary, 23,* 550–569.
Peters, I. L. (1919, August 5). [Letter to Hall], *G. Stanley Hall Papers,* Clark University Archives, Goddard Library, Clark University, Worcester, MA.

Peters, I. L. (1920). The institutionalized sex taboo. In M. M. Knight, I. L. Peters, & P. Blanchard (Eds.), *Taboo and genetics: A study of the biological, sociological, and psychological foundations of the family* (pp. 131–244). New York: Moffat, Yard, and Company.

Peters, I. L. (1923). A two-year experiment with vocational guidance in a woman's college. *Pedagogical Seminary, 30,* 225–240.

Peters, I. L. (1926a). *Social and vocational orientation for college women.* Richmond, VA: The Southern Woman's Educational Alliance; Baltimore: Goucher College.

Peters, I. L. (1926b). The woman business executive. *Industrial Psychology, 1,* 288–292.

Peters, I. L. (1927a). The function of vocational guidance in a woman's college. In F. Allen (Ed.), *Principles and problems in vocational guidance* (pp. 267–272). New York: McGraw-Hill.

Peters, I. L. (1927b). The practice of vocational guidance at Goucher College. In F. Allen (Ed.), *Principles and problems in vocational guidance* (pp. 272–279). New York: McGraw-Hill.

Peters, I. L. (1930). The dean as a vocational advisor. In S. M. Sturtevant & H. Hayes (Eds.), *Deans at work* (pp. 189–210). New York: Harper and Brothers.

Peters, I. L. (1931). The psychology of sex differences. In S. D. Schmalhausen & V. F. Calverton (Eds.), *Women's coming of age: A symposium* (pp. 163–186). New York: Horace Liveright.

Peters, I. L. (1935). *Occupational discriminations against women: An inquiry into the economic security of American business and professional women.* New York: National Federation of Business and Professional Women's Clubs.

Peters, I. L. (1936). *A study of employability of women in selected sections of the United States: Interview study of 212 business and professional women.* New York: National Federation of Business and Professional Women's Clubs.

Rossiter, M. W. (1982). *Women scientists in America: Struggles and strategies to 1940.* Baltimore: The Johns Hopkins Press.

Scarborough, E., & Furumoto, L. (1987). *Untold lives: The first generation of American women psychologists.* New York: Columbia University Press.

Schmalhausen, S. D., & Calverton, V. F. (Eds.). (1931). *Woman's coming of age: A symposium.* New York: Horace Liveright.

Shields, S. (1975). Functionalism, Darwinism, and the psychology of women. *American Psychologist, 30,* 739–754.

Sturtevant, S. M., & Hayes, H. (1930). *Deans at work.* New York: Harper and Brothers.

■ 10
The Feminist Graduate Student in Psychology: Stranger in a Strange Land?

Mary Ricketts

Recently, interest has been shown in the development of psychometric measures of psychologists' epistemological values, to profile the value systems of distinct interest groups within the profession (Coan, 1979; Kimble, 1984; Krasner & Houts, 1984; Unger, Draper, & Pendergrass, 1986). The reconceptualization of psychology as a value-laden, rather than value-free, science (Kuhn, 1970) has provided the impetus for documenting the notion that adherents of conflicting paradigms within the field hold incompatible epistemological values (Buss, 1979b), which underlie the seemingly irresolvable theoretical and methodological controversies among various groups within psychology (Koch, 1981).

This chapter is based partly on survey data from the author's doctoral dissertation, conducted under the supervision of Henry L. Minton at the University of Windsor. The contributions of Rhoda Unger and Jeri Wine, as external co-chair and examiner, respectively, are gratefully acknowledged. Thanks are also due to Doris Howard of AWP and Meryl Cook of CPA SWAP for their assistance in distributing the questionnaires and to the attendees at both conferences, who returned them. Janice Ristock at OISE and Olga Malott and Doris Swan at the University of Windsor assisted in data collection at those institutions. Wilfrid Laurier University supplied a $300 initial research grant in support of this project, and Diane Wright and Sandra Brown surveyed WLU graduate students and alumni in connection with their Honours BA thesis projects under the author's supervision. Diane and Sandra also carried out the data entry and statistical analyses for this research, and I am grateful for their dedication and competence.

Coan (1979) developed the Theoretical Orientation Survey (TOS) to measure the contrasting epistemological positions of objectivism and subjectivism, which reflect the scientist/humanist value dichotomy considered endemic in psychology (Kimble, 1984). The scale consists of 32 5-point Likert-type items. Objectivism encompasses endorsement of impersonal causality, behavioral content emphasis, elementarism, physicalism, and quantitative methods in psychology. Subjectivism involves a preference for free will, experiential content, holism, rejection of physicalism, and qualitative methods in psychology. In a survey of 866 American Psychological Association (APA) members, Coan (1979) found that clinical and personality psychologists were more likely to hold subjectivistic views, whereas psychologists in areas of specialization such as behavior analysis, developmental, learning, and physiological psychology tended to be objectivists. Academic psychologists generally tended to be somewhat more objectivistic than were practitioners. Male psychologists scored higher on all five of the components of objectivism than did females, and objectivism was found to be negatively correlated with both age and religiosity in the sample. King (1980) administered Coan's (1979) TOS to students ($N = 514$) and professors ($N = 27$) in 27 different undergraduate psychology courses, ranging from first to fourth year. There were no significant differences in average TOS scores associated with level of course, nor did the students' scores on the components of objectivism differ from the professors', except on the issue of impersonal causality, where the students more strongly endorsed the notion of free will. King (1980) concluded that students come to the study of psychology with preexisting, rather firmly set epistemological values.

Kimble (1984) has also documented the existence of incompatible epistemological values among various interest groups in psychology. Kimble's Epistemic Differential (ED) scale contains 12 items and reflects the basic concept of a scientist/humanist dichotomy of values in its organization. The ED was distributed to a random sample of 400 APA members, each of whom belonged to only one of the following divisions: Division 3 (Experimental), Division 9 (SPSSI), Division 29 (Psychotherapy), and Division 32 (Humanistic). The percentage of respondents with scores in the scientific direction for members of Divisions 3, 9, 29, and 32 were 95%, 47%, 23%, and 28% respectively. In a sample of introductory psychology students ($N = 100$), the distribution of scores on the ED was continuous; there was no clear evidence of two distinct values cultures existing prior to exposure to psychology courses. However, data for graduate students in psychology in a program organized into separate social science and natural science divisions ($N = 59$) showed the same polarization of values as that between members of Division 3 and the other APA divisions tested.

Krasner and Houts (1984) administered Coan's (1979) TOS to a group of senior psychologists who were founders of the behavior modification movement during the 1950s and to a comparison group of their nonbehaviorist contemporaries. The behavior modification group scored significantly higher on all components of objectivism, though the two groups did not differ on any of the eight measures of personal values, which were also assessed by means of a Values Survey (VS) designed by the researchers. The comparison group's scores quite closely resembled those of Coan's (1979) normative male sample. Ricketts (1986) surveyed feminist psychologists, utilizing the same measures of theoretical and personal values employed by Krasner and Houts (1984). TOS scores of feminist psychologists were markedly more subjectivistic than those of the female APA members contained in Coan's (1979) normative TOS data. No significant differences in epistemological values were found between feminist graduate students and PhDs in the sample. Although Krasner and Houts (1984) found personal values to be poor predictors of TOS scores among their sample, for the feminists, the scales that assessed general attitudes about the role of science in society were found to be useful predictors of epistemological values. Specifically, endorsement of a value-laden concept of science was found to be associated with a preference for subjectivist epistemology. Within the feminist sample, academics tended to be somewhat less subjectivistic than were practitioners, and heterosexuals were also somewhat less subjectivistic than were lesbians.

Unger's (1984–1985) Attitudes About Reality (AAR) scale contains 28 Likert-type items and was constructed to reflect Buss's (1979a) description of objectivist versus subjectivist epistemologies as a continuum ranging from belief that reality constructs the person to belief that the person constructs reality. High scores on the AAR reflect a belief that reality is stable, irreversible, and deterministic. Low scores reflect a belief that reality is changeable and that alternative views of reality may be equally valid. Unger (1984–1985) found that a sample of feminist leaders in psychology scored significantly lower on the AAR than a comparison group of psychology professors and a sample of college students enrolled in psychology of women courses. The biggest differences in opinion between the feminist psychologists and comparison groups involved beliefs about biological determinism and scientific objectivity; feminists tended to be more rejecting of both notions. In related research, Unger et al. (1986) have suggested that one's epistemological values may be influenced by the social groups with which an individual identifies. People who have experienced a relatively problem-free relationship with society tend to give more credence to notions of "objective" reality, and those who have experienced social oppression are more inclined to the view that reality is a matter of cultural definition and individual perspective. "Thus feminists, who identify with women as a deprived group, appear to have a particularly strong disposition to endorse the view that reality is socially constructed" (p. 76).

Unger et al. (1986) conclude that what the AAR is measuring "parallels," or is conceptually similar to, the epistemological positions of objectivism and subjectivism assessed by Coan's (1979) TOS. Brown (1986) tested the concurrent validity of Unger's (1984–1985) AAR, Coan's (1979) TOS, and Krasner and Houts's (1984) VS on a sample of 100 senior undergraduate psychology majors and graduate students in psychology and found the AAR scale to be significantly correlated with two components of TOS objectivism, Impersonal Causality ($n = .22$, $p < .05$) and Physicalism ($r = .40$, $p < .001$), as well as the composite Objectivism score ($r = .27$, $p < .01$). The AAR score was also positively correlated with TOS Biological Determinism ($r = .29$, $p < .01$). These results substantially support Unger's (1984–1985) assertion that the AAR is conceptually similar to the TOS, though the AAR also includes some sociopolitical content that the TOS does not assess. Brown (1986) also found significant positive correlations between the AAR and several VS scale scores: Science and Ethics ($r = .31$, $p < .001$), Science and Theism ($r = .40$, $p < .001$), Social Philosophy ($r = .48$, $p < .001$), and Health Care ($r = .24$, $p < .01$). Wright (1986) found that MA students enrolled in a general experimental psychology program scored significantly higher on the AAR than did MA students in a social/community psychology program offered by the same department.

The main focus of the present investigation is the epistemological values of graduate students who identify as feminists. A subset of Ricketts's (1986) survey of feminist psychologists was composed of current graduate students, mainly from human service–related areas of specialization within psychology. The present study attempts to provide a fair and realistic comparison group for this sample, composed of graduate students from programs in which the prototypical student could reasonably be expected to hold fairly liberal, humanistic, social change–oriented views. The objective is to explore the extent and nature of differences in epistemological values between feminists and their hypothetical "peer group" in graduate school. Such differences may contribute to the "outsider" phenomenon commonly experienced by women who go through graduate training in psychology as identified feminists, which Lott (1985) has described as the feeling that "we both belong and do not belong to the primarily male establishment and are thus both insiders and outsiders" (p. 156). Generally, it is predicted that the feminist graduate students will tend to be more subjectivistic in their theoretical views and less conservative in their sociopolitical views than the comparison group.

METHOD

Sampling Procedures

Feminist graduate students

A questionnaire was included in the registration kit presented to all participants at the 10th National Conference of the Association for Women in Psychology (AWP) in New York City in March 1985 and at the Canadian Psychological Association Section on Women and Psychology (CPA SWAP) annual meeting held in Halifax, Nova Scotia, in June 1985. Additional questionnaires were distributed early in 1987 to students in the doctoral program in community psychology at the Ontario Institute for Studies in Education (OISE) in Toronto, a graduate program that professes a feminist orientation, to include more Canadian students in the composition of the feminist sample ($N = 52$).

Comparison group

A questionnaire was distributed early in 1987 to current MA students and recent graduates of the Psychology Department at Wilfred Laurier University, Waterloo, Ontario. The department offers a terminal MA degree with a specialization in general experimental or social community psychology. Questionnaires were also distributed around the same time to current students in the PhD program of the Psychology Department at the University of Windsor, Windsor, Ontario, in order to include doctoral-level graduate students in the comparison group. The department has a strong applied focus and offers PhD degrees with a specialization in clinical, developmental, or social/community psychology. Responses from the graduate students surveyed at Wilfred Laurier University and the University of Windsor were combined to form the comparison group ($N = 62$).

Measures

Theoretical Orientation Survey (TOS)

This 32-item, 5-point Likert-type scale developed by Coan (1979) assesses respondents' epistemological assumptions about psychology. The TOS has been shown to have adequate reliability and validity and factors into eight subscales, five of which define the contrasting viewpoints Objectivism and Subjectivism. Krasner and Houts's (1984) factor analysis replicated the eight factors reported by Coan (1979).

Values Survey (VS)

This 43-item, 5-point Likert-type scale was developed for Krasner and Houts (1984) by a panel of eight experts in the area of science and ethics, to assess the personal and sociopolitical values of psychologists in eight broad domains: science/ethics, scientists' social responsibility, science/theism, social philosophy, political philosophy, health care delivery, environmentalism, and research/ethics. Krasner and Houts describe the reliabilities of the

VS subscales as "adequate" but do not specify further. Houts (personal communication, 1986) has expressed only guarded confidence in the psychometric properties of the VS scales. Ricketts's (1986) factor analysis of the VS found that the Social Philosophy and Political Philosophy scales have adequate validity, but the rest are questionable.

RESULTS

Table 10.1 summarizes the sex and age composition of the feminist and comparison graduate student samples and indicates the range of areas of specialization represented in each group. The feminist sample is 96% female, whereas the comparison group is nearly 50% male. These figures are in line with the typical proportions of men and women found in feminist organizations and graduate programs in psychology, respectively. The average age for the feminist sample is approximately 3 years higher than that of the comparison group, which may reflect the fact that many feminists tend to be "mature" graduate students who are several years older than their classmates and following a nontraditional path to the PhD. Over 80% of the feminists and 70% of the comparison group indicated clinical, community, counseling, or applied social psychology as their principal degree subfield,

TABLE 10.1 Summary Table of Demographic Variables for Feminist and Comparison Graduate Students in Psychology

Variable	Feminist (*N* = 52)		Comparison (*N* = 62)	
	n	%	*n*	%
Sex				
Male	2	3.8	29	46.8
Female	50	96.2	33	53.2
Age[a]				
20s	21	40.4	31	50.0
30s	24	46.1	27	43.5
40s	7	13.5	4	6.5
Specialization				
Clinical	23	44.2	9	14.5
Community	8	15.4	24	38.7
Counseling	10	19.2	0	0.0
Applied social	1	1.9	11	17.8
Other	10	19.3	18	29.0

[a]Feminist mean age = 32.9 years; comparison mean age = 30.2 years.

TABLE 10.2 Results of Analysis of Variance of TOS and VS Scale Scores for Feminist and Comparison Graduate Students in Psychology

Scale	Feminist (N = 52)		Comparison (N = 62)		F
	M	SD	M	SD	
Factual Orientation[a]	7.79	2.27	8.26	1.72	1.58
Impersonal Causality	8.33	2.61	8.92	2.77	1.36
Behavioral Content	7.69	1.92	9.63	2.84	17.48***
Elementarism	8.15	2.60	9.65	3.05	7.73**
Biological Determinism	9.58	2.96	10.21	3.58	1.03
Environmental Determinism	11.15	3.28	11.31	2.13	.09
Physicalism	7.87	2.18	9.55	2.67	13.28***
Quantitative Orientation	8.54	2.98	10.74	3.21	14.23***
Objectivism[b]	40.58	8.95	48.48	10.97	17.33***
Endogenism[c]	48.42	4.68	48.90	4.44	.31

[a]Range for each scale is 4–20. Higher score indicates endorsement of the labeled dimension role.
[b]Range is 20–100.
[c]50—(Biological–Environmental) Determinism scale scores.
**p < .01.
***p < .001.

so students in both samples are drawn primarily from the liberal, humanistic, service-oriented specialties within psychology.

The prediction that feminist graduate students would tend to be more subjectivistic than the comparison group in their theoretical views was supported. Table 10.2 contains mean TOS scale scores for the feminist and comparison groups. Multivariate analysis of between-group differences for the eight TOS subscales yielded a significant multivariate effect, Hotelling-Lawley Trace $F(8, 105) = 2.89$, $p < .01$. Scores for the feminists were significantly lower than for the comparison group on four of the five components of Objectivism, Behavioral Content Emphasis, $F(1, 112) = 17.48$, $p < .001$; Elementarism, $F(1, 112) = 7.73$, $p < .01$; Physicalism, $F(1, 112) = 13.28$, $p < .001$; and Quantitative Orientation, $F(1, 112) = 14.23$, $p < .001$, as well as the composite Objectivism score, $F(1, 112) = 17.33$, $p < .001$. The feminist and comparison graduate students did not differ significantly in their endorsement of a theoretical rather than factual orientation in psychology, in a preference for free will over impersonal causality, or in their views on biological and environmental determinism. Both groups are markedly exogenist in their views on the sources of individual differences; that is, they place more emphasis on environmental than on biological determinants, as indicated by their low Endogenism scores.

Table 10.3 contains mean VS scale scores for the feminist and compari-

TABLE 10.3   Results of Analysis of Variance of VS Scale Scores for Feminist and Comparison graduate Students in Psychology

Scale	Range	Feminists (N = 52)		Comparison (N = 62)		F
		M	SD	M	SD	
Science and Ethics	4–20	9.37	2.93	9.84	2.57	.84
Scientists' Responsibility	5–25	18.25	1.98	17.97	2.86	.36
Science and Theism	5–25	16.13	3.19	16.92	3.30	1.65
Social Philosophy	7–35	15.40	3.43	17.88	3.26	15.48***
Political Philosophy	6–30	16.52	4.09	19.69	3.66	19.09***
Health Care	4–20	7.40	2.69	7.92	2.59	1.08
Environmentalism	5–25	11.19	2.33	12.56	2.40	9.51**
Research Ethics	7–35	29.27	3.20	29.28	3.16	.01

**p < .01.
***p < .001.

son groups that support the prediction that feminists would differ in their sociopolitical values from hypothetical graduate school peers. Multivariate analysis of between-group differences on the eight VS scales yielded a significant multivariate effect, Hotelling-Lawley Trace $F(8, 105) = 12.22$, $p < .001$. Feminists tended to be significantly more liberal than the comparison group in their social and political values, as indicated by their lower scores on the scales for Social Philosophy, $F(1, 112) = 15.48$, $p < .001$; Political Philosophy, $F(1, 112) = 19.09$, $p < .001$; and Environmentalism $F(1, 112) = 9.51$, $p < .01$. The feminist and comparison graduate students did not differ significantly on any of the scales that assess general attitudes about the role of science in society and the social responsibilities of the researcher.

Individual item analyses were performed for those TOS and VS subscales where significant differences in average scores were found between the feminist and comparison groups. Table 10.4 contains results of the item analysis for four TOS scales and indicates 10 items on which feminists were more likely than the comparison group to take a position of *strong* agreement or disagreement. Feminists were more likely to *strongly agree* with the following statements:

Item 4. Psychologists should be as concerned with explaining private conscious experience as they are with explaining overt behavior.
Item 12. The individual subject's personal account of his/her private conscious experience is one of the most valuable sources of psychological data.
Item 20. Psychologists can gain many valuable insights through medi-

TABLE 10.4 Item Analysis of Four TOS Scales for Feminist and Comparison Graduate Students in Psychology

Scale	Feminists (N = 52)		Comparison (N = 62)		
	M	SD	M	SD	F
Behavioral Content					
Item 4	1.67	.62	2.03	.90	5.89*
Item 12	1.71	.64	2.53	1.14	21.31***
Item 20	2.17	.86	2.66	1.20	6.02*
Item 28	2.13	.82	2.40	.91	2.69
Elementarism					
Item 5	2.35	.97	2.98	1.21	9.65**
Item 13	1.64	.69	2.35	1.01	16.32***
Item 21	2.12	.89	2.10	1.11	2.84
Item 29	2.04	.71	2.22	.94	1.16
Physicalism					
Item 7	1.98	.87	2.34	1.05	3.79
Item 15	1.63	.71	2.11	.91	9.50**
Item 23	2.07	.86	2.32	1.02	1.88
Item 31	2.17	.98	2.77	.97	10.77***
Quantitative Orientation					
Item 8	2.21	1.14	2.89	1.18	9.45**
Item 16	2.13	.91	2.34	.99	1.29
Item 24	1.90	1.09	2.69	1.25	12.67***
Item 32	2.29	.96	2.82	1.17	6.97**

$*p < .05.$
$**p < .01.$
$***p < .001.$

tation and other procedures designed to expand or illuminate private experience.

Item 5. For many research purposes, it is best to permit many relevant variables to interact in a natural fashion and then analyze the results, rather than try to effect strict control.

Item 13. Highly controlled experiments often give a misleading picture of the complex interactions that actually occur under natural circumstances.

Item 8. The use of mathematical models and equations in theory often serves to create a false impression of scientific respectability instead of furthering our understanding.

Item 24. A strong insistence on precise measurement and quantification is likely to cause psychologists to neglect important areas of research.

TABLE 10.5 Item Analysis of Three VS Scales for Feminist and Comparison Graduate Students in Psychology

Scale	Feminists (N = 52)		Comparison (N = 62)		
	M	SD	M	SD	F
Social Philosophy					
Item 4	1.85	.94	4.02	1.31	105.48***
Item 11	2.35	1.08	2.81	1.21	4.49*
Item 13	1.56	.64	1.63	.71	.31
Item 16	2.08	1.01	2.29	1.04	1.22
Item 25	2.23	.93	3.77	1.17	61.81***
Item 34	2.12	.92	2.21	.70	.38
Item 39	2.00	.89	2.39	.91	5.23*
Political Philosophy					
Item 5	2.29	1.21	2.87	1.29	6.12*
Item 10	3.62	1.01	4.06	.72	7.60**
Item 20	2.60	1.14	3.27	1.07	10.64***
Item 32	3.37	.99	3.92	.91	9.66**
Item 33	2.27	.66	2.68	1.02	6.15*
Item 40	2.38	.99	2.89	1.04	6.86*
Environmentalism					
Item 7	4.06	.96	4.32	.76	2.70
Item 21	1.75	.95	2.58	1.11	18.08***
Item 23	1.83	.88	1.85	.83	.03
Item 27	1.62	.63	1.82	.80	2.29
Item 31	1.94	.92	1.98	.93	.05

*$p < .05$.
**$p < .01$.
***$p < .001$.

Feminists were more likely to *strongly disagree* with the following statements:

Item 15. It is best to define perception just in terms of stimulus–response relationships, rather than in terms of internal events that cannot be publicly observed.

Item 31. As far as possible, the stimulus and response variables used in psychological theory should be defined in strictly physical terms.

Item 32. A good indicator of the maturity of a science is the extent to which its explanatory principles are stated in precise quantitative form.

Table 10.5 contains results of the item analysis for three VS scales and indicates 11 items on which feminists were more likely than the comparison group to take a *strong* position. Feminists were more likely to *strongly disagree* with the following statements:

> Item 4. All things considered, competition is the best relationship between people in a society.
> Item 11. Material and class equality are idle dreams.
> Item 39. In science as in life, the best results follow when one is engaged in a competitive struggle for knowledge and resources.
> Item 5. Private property and private ownership of production are necessary to have optimal personal freedom.
> Item 33. Individual liberty should take precedence over social goals and collective restraints on liberty.

Feminists were more likely to *strongly agree* with the following statements:

> Item 25. The affluent of the world have a moral obligation to respond to the needs of the less well-off.
> Item 21. The solution to the environment crises requires new values, new social systems, and new political structures.

Feminists were much less likely than the comparison group to respond in the politically conservative direction (in favor of a free enterprise economic philosophy) on the following items:

> Item 10. Goods and services are best provided by centralized government agencies as opposed to local agencies and private corporations.
> Item 20. Goods and services are best provided by private corporations as opposed to government agencies.
> Item 32. Capitalism should be eliminated.
> Item 40. Socialism is a desirable goal.

DISCUSSION

As defined by Kuhn (1970), a "paradigm" represents the necessary consensus of a group of scholars about the nature and purpose of research in their field. A paradigm has two components, a "disciplinary matrix" and "shared exemplars." The disciplinary matrix is a set of fundamental assumptions that are simply accepted as givens, which categorically determine the direction of theory construction and hypothesis testing. Shared exemplars are approved models of good research that provide methods and precedents for investigating problems. The field of psychology has long been dominated by a paradigm that can basically be characterized as imitative of the outlook and methods of 19th-century natural scientists. The central assumptions that form psychology's disciplinary matrix were heavily influenced by positivism: "a philosophical tendency oriented around natural science and striving for a unified view of the world of phenomena, both physical and human, through the application of the methods ... whereby the natural sciences have attained their unrivaled position in the modern world" (Leichtman, 1979, p. 50). Early in the 20th century, the controlled laboratory experiment became established as the dominant shared exemplar in North American psychology. Gergen (1979) has argued that when psychologists became committed to experimentalism, an underlying "mechanistic" concept of human psychological functioning was simultaneously absorbed that has significantly limited it "in the range of its concerns, in the types of behaviour singled out for study, in the selection of explanatory constructs, and in its vision of human potential" (p. 194).

Feminist psychology is particularly inspired by a keen sense of betrayal at the biased way women's behavior and experience have traditionally been treated as subject matter by men in the field. "The response is one of outrage that these procedures could have been used in a field we thought was what it said it was: scientific, an honest search for truth using a particular kind of method" (Parlee, 1985, p. 195). Feminist psychology has been described as having progressed rapidly through an "imitation" and a "protest" phase with respect to traditional positivist assumptions and methods (Wine, 1985). These developments parallel concurrent progress within mainstream social psychology, which for a long time identified itself as an empirical science, then experienced a "crisis of confidence" (Elms, 1975) about the objectivity and value neutrality of the knowledge produced by such methods. Several recent reviews of the progress of feminist psychology suggest that the field is now moving into a third phase, which focuses on the uniqueness of much of female experience, "with the growing awareness that the categories, hierarchies, structure, and research methods developed to describe male experience are simply not adequate to the task of describing ours" (Wine, 1985, p. 187). Parlee (1985) has called research on topics that deal with aspects of female specificity "phenomena in search of a paradigm" (p. 197). Henley (1985) concluded that "feminist psychology attempts to move from a compensatory and revisionist approach toward one that is transformative" (p. 119). These descriptions suggest that feminist psychologists are a group whose paradigm, or necessary consensus about the nature and purpose of research in their field, is presently in transition (Rosnow, 1981).

What appear on the surface to be "methodological" controversies probably have their roots in conflicting epistemological values or beliefs about the nature of reality and what constitutes valid knowledge about reality. Un-

128 :: Theory

ger et al. (1986) found that feminists, because they identify with women as an oppressed group, tend to reject objectivist notions of reality as stable, irreversible, and deterministic. Gergen (1985) has commented that feminists have been frontrunners in the social constructionist movement in modern psychology, a perspective critical of traditional empiricism. What appear on the surface to be "sociopolitical" differences probably have their roots in conflicting philosophies of human nature. Wine (1982) has commented that the nature of the ideal human being that is evident in psychology is directly tied to its empiricist methods. The guiding image is the "abstracted, separated, self-interested, context-free individual" (p. 69). Androcentric individualism values separation, domination, rationality, and egocentrism and is a view of human nature that is antithetical to the gynocentric principle of relationality that informs feminist views of human development and social interaction. "Relationality refers to consciousness of the necessary interdependence of human beings, to a sense of connectedness to others, to awareness of one's embeddedness in human, social and historical contexts, to the maximization of well-being for all persons, and to commitment to nonviolence" (p. 68).

The results of this study suggest that feminists' views on both methodological and philosophical issues in psychology place them at odds with mainstream thinking, even within their own chosen areas of specialization in the field. Feminist students tend to be more critical of traditional empiricism and its underlying assumptions and more skeptical of the power of "number crunching" research methods to produce valid knowledge about reality. Feminist students tend to be more attuned to flaws in the traditional theory canon that result from unexamined acceptance of individualism. The findings provide insight into the sense of being an "outsider" that many feminists experience as graduate students.

REFERENCES

Brown, S. M. (1986). *Personal epistemology and values of "potential" psychologists.* Unpublished Honours BA thesis, Wilfred Laurier University, Waterloo, Ontario, Canada.
Buss, A. R. (1979a). *A dialectical psychology.* New York: Irvington.
Buss, A. R. (Ed.). (1979b). *Psychology in social context.* New York: Irvington.
Coan, R. W. (1979). *Psychologists: Personal and theoretical pathways.* New York: Irvington.
Elms, A. C. (1975). The crisis of confidence in social psychology. *American Psychologist, 30,* 967–976.
Gergen, K. J. (1979). The positivist image in social psychological theory. In A. R. Buss (Ed.), *Psychology in social context* (pp. 193–212). New York: Irvington.

Gergen, K. J. (1985). The social constructionist movement in modern psychology. *American Psychologist, 40*, 266–275.

Henley, N. M. (1985). Psychology and gender. *Signs, 11*, 101–119.

Kimble, G. A. (1984). Psychology's two cultures. *American Psychologist, 39*, 833–839.

King, D. J. (1980). Values of undergraduate students and faculty members on theoretical orientations in psychology. *Teaching of Psychology, 1*, 236–237.

Koch, S. (1981). The nature and limits of psychological knowledge. *American Psychologist, 36*, 257–269.

Krasner, L., & Houts, A. C. (1984). A study of the "value" systems of behavioral scientists. *American Psychologist, 39*, 840–850.

Kuhn, T. S. (1970). *The structure of scientific revolutions*. Chicago: University of Chicago Press.

Leichtman, M. (1979). Gestalt theory and the revolt against positivism. In A. R. Buss (Ed.), *Psychology in social context* (pp. 47–75). New York: Irvington.

Lott, B. (1985). The potential enrichment of social/personality psychology through feminist research and vice versa. *American Psychologist, 40*, 155–164.

Parlee, M. B. (1985). Psychology of women in the 80s: Promising problems. *International Journal of Women's Studies, 8*, 193–204.

Ricketts, M. (1986). *Theoretical orientations and values of feminist psychologists*. Unpublished doctoral dissertation, University of Windsor, Windsor, Ontario, Canada.

Rosnow, R. L. (1981). *Paradigms in transition*. New York: Oxford University Press.

Unger, R. K. (1984–1985). Explorations in feminist ideology: Surprising consistencies and unexamined conflicts. *Imagination, Cognition, and Personality, 4*, 297–405.

Unger, R. K., Draper, R. D., & Pendergrass, M. L. (1986). Personal epistemology and personal experience. *Journal of Social Issues, 42*, 67–77.

Wine, J. D. (1982). Gynocentric values and feminist psychology. In A. R. Miles & G. Finn (Eds.), *Feminism in Canada: From pressure to politics* (pp. 67–88). Montreal: Black Rose Books.

Wine J. D. (1985). Models of human functioning: A feminist perspective. *International Journal of Women's Studies, 8*, 183–192.

Wright, D. (1986). *Theoretical orientation and area of specialization in WLU psychology students and alumni*. Unpublished Honours BA thesis, Wilfrid Laurier University, Waterloo, Ontario, Canada.

■ 11
From Victim Control to Social Change: A Feminist Perspective on Campus Rape Prevention Programs

Carole Baroody Corcoran

The speaker started off by telling us a little about what acquaintance rape actually was. She had indicated that acquaintance rape accounted for at least 70% of rape cases. I guess this surprised me a little because I always thought of rape as when you get attacked in a parking lot at night by a stranger. [Comment from a female student following a presentation on acquaintance rape]

The group as a whole seemed educated about the myths of rape and misconceptions. However, through slips of the tongue and the way they phrased certain statements, it became clear to the facilitators that other things were operating. It seemed that people were not convinced that rape is *never* the fault of the victim. Some believed that they would never act the same way a victim of the scenarios did—shocked, confused, and helpless. . . . It became frustrating to try to lead the discussion when people were so closed-minded. [Comment by a female resident advisor after co-facilitating a dormitory workshop on acquaintance rape]

While we were watching the film that depicted a situation leading up to a date rape, some men in the group started yelling, "when are we going to get to the good part?" [Female student's comment about a film and discussion on acquaintance rape]

Myths surrounding the causes and prevalence of acquaintance rape are alive and well on today's college campuses. Educational attempts to counter these beliefs can be frustrating at best, and often they are met with resistance and open hostility. After a brief review of the evidence pertaining to students' beliefs about rape myths and the prevalence of date and acquaintance rape on college campuses, several issues will be addressed concerning rape prevention and education efforts by examining three approaches to the problem: victim control, self-empowerment, and social change (Morgan, cited in Bateman, 1987). In addition, this chapter will stress the importance of maintaining a feminist perspective in sexual assault programming because it provides a cogent analysis of the causes of sexual violence and it suggests specific strategies for the prevention and, ultimately, the elimination of rape.

Recent research indicates that a substantial minority of college students subscribe to rape myths and that gender differences exist, with women being less accepting of rape myths than are men (Giacopassi & Dull, 1986; Gilmartin-Zena, 1988). Further, certain factors, such as the type of dating activity and who initiates and who pays for the date, influence male students' judgments concerning the justifiability of date rape (Muehlenhard, Friedman, & Thomas, 1985). Gilmartin-Zena's (1988) findings suggest that college students experience confusion (i.e., they tend to agree or are undecided) with respect to the following rape myths:

> Rape is an act of sex rather than violence.
> Being out alone at night may be a cause of rape.
> The suggestive dress of women may be a causal factor.
> Women can protect themselves from ever being raped.
> Women often falsely accuse men of rape.
> The attractiveness of the woman may be a cause of rape.
> Prostitutes comprise a problematic category.
> Many men would not rape, even if they thought they could get away with it.
> After their assaults, women should be visibly upset.
> Society does not play a role in causing rape.
> Women must fight off their assailants.
> Men rape due to uncontrollable passions.
> If women say "no" to sexual advances, they may not really mean it. (p. 284)[1]

Acceptance of rape myths is similar to what Hall, Howard, and Boezio (1986) call rape tolerance, and it may contribute to the tendency to blame the victim and/or minimize the seriousness of rape. Their study of adolescents and university students supports the view that rape tolerance (or acceptance of rape myths) is correlated with sexist attitudes toward heterosexual relationships (beliefs that men should dominate women and that sex involves conquest and the perception of the other sex as sex objects). In addition, their male university subjects were more rape-tolerant and sexist in their attitudes toward heterosexual relationships than female university subjects were. Although the Hall et al. study does not address the issue of whether sexist attitudes and rape tolerance in men are directly associated with the tendency to engage in sexually coercive behavior, their results and similar findings (e. g., Burt, 1980) lend credence to the notion that fostering egalitarian, nonsexist attitudes and challenging rape-tolerant beliefs should be central components of campus rape education programs.

The results of studies examining the prevalence and scope of sexual abuse and assault on college and university campuses are alarming. For example, Mary Koss and her colleagues' survey of a representative national sample of 6,159 students at 32 institutions of higher education reveals that 53.7% of the 3,187 female respondents have experienced some form of sexual victimization (Koss, Gidycz, & Wisniewski, 1987). Although 12.1% of the women report experiences that meet the legal definition of attempted rape and 15.4% describe experiences that legally are rape, only 27% of the women who report having intercourse against their will through the use of verbal and physical coercion label their experiences as rape. Further, 84% of the women know the men who raped them, only 5% report their rapes to the police, only 5% seek rape crisis assistance, and 42% tell no one about their experience.

Data from the 2,972 males in the study indicate that 25.1% of the men admit to engaging in some form of sexual aggression and 7.7% report perpetrating an act that meets the legal definition of rape or attempted rape. Again, only 1% of the men acknowledge that the incident is, in fact, rape. The Koss et al. (1987) findings are important for several reasons. First, beyond demonstrating the pervasiveness of sexual assault, they illustrate that both college men and women do not perceive and label these occurrences as rape. This study also supports Johnson's (1980) contention that it is unlikely that a "small lunatic fringe of psychopathic men" (p. 146) are responsible for these widespread acts of sexual coercion. Indeed, many feminists view rape as an exaggeration of the unequal power in "normal" heterosexual relationships, where the male assumes a dominant role and the female is passive. Finally, although one would not expect the frequencies reported by female and male students to match, the discrepancies between victimization experiences reported by women and sexually aggressive acts reported by men imply that there is a gender gap in perceptions of what constitutes "real rape."

A number of colleges and universities have begun to offer programs designed to increase rape awareness, with a particular emphasis on date and acquaintance rape. In fact, the increasing quantity and quality of resource materials for these efforts is encouraging (see, e.g., Parrot, 1986; Warshaw, 1988). However, many sexual assault education and prevention programs place responsibility for rape avoidance on women and therefore indirectly (and perhaps unintentionally) support a victim-precipitation model. Amir (1967) describes the concept of victim-precipitated rape as follows:

> If the victim is not solely responsible for what becomes the unfortunate event, at least she is often the complementary partner. . . . Theoretically, victim precipitation of forcible rape means that in a particular situation the behavior of the victim is interpreted by the offender as a direct invitation for sexual relations or as a sign that she will be available for sexual contact if he will persist in demanding it. (p. 493)

Given males' greater sense of entitlement and their responsibility for initiating sexual activity, college women may find themselves in the "gatekeeper" role of setting sexual limits and taking responsibility for men's ("uncontrollable") sexual arousal. This feeling of responsibility for men's sexual arousal is illustrated in the following female student's comments from a dormitory workshop on acquaintance rape:

> From our personal discussion, something was brought into focus which I sometimes have ignored. One male pointed out that sometimes a woman will do something just out of affection for a man, and a man will take it the wrong way and get sexually turned on by it. If more women realized this, perhaps fewer date rapes would occur.

Further, if a man believes that when a woman says no, she means maybe or yes, he may ignore her protests and force sexual intercourse. Perceptions such as this are common among college males, as is evident from the comment below:

> The two short movies on acquaintance rape clarified the thought I had that men and women interpret messages differently. Through the discussion after, I found that the girls most often felt that the fault was the man's, whereas in my view the fault could not have been fully either party's. I feel that a girl often does not make her intentions clear. Although she says "NO," the way she says it is interpreted as "maybe" by the male.

Unfortunately, some women also share this view, and thus when an acquaintance or dating situation goes awry, both partners may construe it as the woman's fault.[2]

By examining three general approaches (victim control, self-empowerment, and social change) and applying them to acquaintance rape, it is possible to explore the implications for developing effective campus education and prevention programs. These three perspectives are also useful for describing the level of awareness that characterizes students' thinking about acquaintance and date rape. Consequently, students may respond differently and take away different messages from education programs as a function of their underlying assumptions about the nature of rape.

VICTIM CONTROL

Historically, this has been the traditional approach to rape education and prevention. The idea is that if a woman refrains from engaging in certain "risky" behaviors (e.g., going out alone at night, hitchhiking, leaving a door unlocked), she will be able to avoid rape. This follows from the victim-precipitation view, and because, until recently, rape has meant stranger rape, education programs have primarily included prevention tactics that are consistent with a victim-control model. These rape prevention strategies (such as a woman who lives alone listing only her first initial in the phone book) do not apply to acquaintance rape situations. However, the victim-control perspective is also evident in education about date and acquaintance rape. For example, to avoid acquaintance rape, a woman should not drink, dance provocatively, or wear miniskirts. Thus, the cause of rape is simply attributed to a different set of "risky" behaviors.

The following excerpt from a student evaluation of a dormitory acquaintance rape workshop illustrates a perception of rape that reflects the assumptions of the victim-control stance:

> I felt that sometimes women could invite rape by behavior and that rape is motivated by a need to overpower. Men need to feel superior and women sometimes ask for rape by acting provocative or "teasing" men. A lot of the girls felt that it shouldn't matter what girls wear because men have no right to violate any woman's body—prostitute or not. . . . The discussions were very intense, and I found that I tended to side with the opinions of most of the guys.

This student feels that women can prevent rape by controlling and restricting their behavior, that is, by not acting and dressing in a "provocative" manner. For many students, the victim-control point of view (along with other rape myths) can serve a self-protective function. It may preserve one's belief in a just world (Lerner, 1970) and reinforce the idea that "rape won't happen to me."

Obviously, there are a number of problems associated with the victim-control model. This view places responsibility for rape prevention on the intended victim and does not challenge the existing social conditions that cause and allow rapes to occur. It suggests that, to prevent rape, women should restrict their freedom and limit their actions. Associated with victim control is victim blame. Thus, if a woman is raped, she (and others) may feel that she is to blame because she failed to engage in the necessary victim-control strategies (e.g., "this wouldn't have happened if I hadn't been drinking, invited him in, kissed him," etc.). In addition, this viewpoint allows the rapist to justify his behavior ("she asked for it") and divert the responsibility for sexual assault from the rapist to the victim. Finally, unless all women lock themselves away or perhaps wear rape-proof armor, this approach does not affect the incidence of rape. The restriction and control of women is a heavy price to pay, particularly because victim-control strategies will not significantly reduce or eliminate the occurrence of rape.

SELF-EMPOWERMENT

Empowerment strategies do not seek to limit a woman's freedom; rather, they try to provide women with more options and to strengthen their ability to resist and avoid rape (e.g., instead of staying home, park in a well-lit parking lot and pay attention to surroundings when walking at night). Other practices consistent with the self-empowerment approach would include providing accurate information about the definition of rape and its prevalence, assertiveness training, and self-defense skills.

The following student comment pertaining to an invited speaker on acquaintance rape embodies the self-empowerment model applied to dating situations:

> In conclusion, what I got out of the whole program was that date rape happens a lot because there is a communication gap between two people and a preventative measure may be to bridge this gap. . . . I was reminded that although rape is the attacker's fault, I can help protect myself by being more aggressive, giving firm answers, clear signals, and by communicating with the male.

Instead of restricting her behavior to prevent rape, this student feels that a woman should be more forceful or assertive in her communication with male acquaintances. Most date rape programs promote this message, and indeed, self-empowerment (both physically and verbally) may help women avoid rape (Bart & O'Brien, 1985). It is interesting that, although research evidence supports the efficacy of *physical* resistance, most acquaintance rape programs stress misinterpretation as the cause of date rape and therefore suggest that the remedy lies in assertive *verbal* communication on the part of the female. In some education programs, there is also the undertone that women are sending out subtle nonverbal "signals" of which they may not be aware.

Self-empowerment is certainly a preferable alternative to fear or restriction, but the burden for rape prevention is still placed on the woman. Whenever the responsibility for rape avoidance remains with women, the potential for victim blaming is not far away. If a woman does not employ empowerment strategies (or if they are not effective), there is the danger that she will blame herself ("I must have miscommunicated or not communicated assertively enough") or be blamed by others for her rape ("Why didn't you fight or resist?"). It is troubling to think that the major focus of most college acquaintance rape education programs can easily be twisted into yet another version of blaming the victim. Further, it may be misleading to overemphasize assertive communication as a rape avoidance strategy when there is no evidence that a man whose goal is to have sexual intercourse (with or without consent) will be dissuaded by such a tactic. For example, consider what the following female student learned from an acquaintance rape discussion in her dorm:

> The group discussed teasing a man, and leading him on when you are not meaning to. It was interesting because there were four girls and two men. I learned a lot about communication, to say no and explain yourself, and if you do communicate then you will not be forced to do anything you don't agree with, or feel comfortable with.

Yet many women who forcefully protest, scream, and physically fight are still the victims of acquaintance rape. Assertive communication is important; however, additional strategies may be necessary yet not sufficient to avoid rape (see, e.g., the Levine-MacCombie & Koss, 1986, findings on effective avoidance strategies for acquaintance rape). Finally, although empowerment strategies may prevent a particular individual woman from being raped, this approach does not directly affect the overall incidence of rape. If a rapist is deterred, he will probably seek another "more vulnerable" target. As Swift (1985) points out, "The net effect of successful rape avoidance, then, may be to displace victimization from informed women, prepared women, and women proficient in self-defense to the very young, the physically or mentally disabled, or the elderly" (p. 418).

SOCIAL CHANGE

This approach does not view rape as a woman's problem or an individual interpersonal act. Rather, rape is a societal and structural problem, the product of a patriarchal culture that promotes and allows rape through gender socialization, the acceptance of interpersonal violence, and institutionalized misogyny. Although this perspective, unlike the others, does not place the responsibility for rape prevention on women, it also does not provide specific rape avoidance or self-protection strategies (Bateman, 1987). Admittedly, it is a bit overwhelming to consider changing family, educational, legal, political, and economic systems as rape prevention strategies. Current research findings indicate that we cannot clearly discriminate between men who will or will not rape (this is consistent with the feminist position that our culture accepts and maintains rape-supportive beliefs and values). However, we do know the attitudes and behaviors that are linked to rape as well as what we would have to change in order to dismantle our rape-supportive culture. These factors (eliminating rape myths, fostering male–female relationships that are egalitarian and nonexploitative, and reducing aggression and violence) are amenable to educational programs.

The vast majority of rape education efforts are aimed at women, and in fact, very little is said about men. If you were unfamiliar with our culture and you happened to attend a typical college date rape program, you might have a hard time figuring out that men have any responsibility for rape or rape prevention. It is impolite to say that men rape and outrageous to point out that the only way to change the incidence of rape and eliminate rape is for men to stop raping. The following female student's comment on an invited speaker on acquaintance rape exemplifies the social change perspective:

> She was a good speaker, but I feel that too much time was spent on concentrating on women and how they might "lead someone on" and not enough time was spent telling people that regardless of what a woman wears she is *never* to be blamed for being raped. I wanted more time spent on how men can prevent rape.

This remark also illustrates how the same speaker (mentioned previously in a comment as emphasizing assertive communication) or program can have a very different message and impact as a function of the student's level of understanding about rape. This particular student would like to see a shift from placing responsibility on women to examining rape-supportive attitudes and men's responsibility for rape prevention. This type of reaction to acquaintance rape education programs is least common, and it is expressed only by a minority of students who have developed a certain degree of feminist awareness. Students whose understanding of acquaintance rape is consistent with the victim-control or self-empowerment approaches may become very defensive or uncomfortable at the mention of men and rape.

Because acquaintance rape is typically viewed as a woman's problem, when sexual assault education programs are presented on college campuses, they are automatically considered to be programs for women. The topic of rape certainly can be quite threatening to men. Part of the threat is that it will hit too close to home, and men will have to identify themselves as part of the problem. This is one reason for the "conspiracy of silence" among men on the subject of rape. Instead of getting upset about not being distinguishable from men who do rape and breaking the silence, men tend to distance themselves from the topic. The following comments from a male student concerning rape awareness activities illustrate this:

> I found this movie very interesting, and felt sorry for these women because they seem to have had to make changes in their lives due to the fear of rape. Being a male, I had a hard time identifying with the women, and I was kind of ashamed to be part of a race which was causing this fear in their lives. . . . The other activity I attended was the rape awareness workshop. . . . I have only one complaint. I kept hearing the phrase "every man is a potential rapist." I will agree that every man has the apparatus with which to rape, but I do not agree that every man is a potential rapist. I know that I could never rape anyone.

Many rape educators have to exercise considerable ingenuity to get any students (and particularly men) to attend programs. One activity that attracted a great number of men on our campus was a program entitled "What Does *Animal House* Have to Do with Rape Awareness Week?" As advertised, the movie *Animal House* was shown, but students were unaware that it would be immediately followed by a powerful documentary describing a program in which incarcerated rapists are confronted by women who have been raped. The following two male students' comments show that if you can find "a hook," men can and will learn more about rape:

> First we watched a movie called *Animal House* which had many incidences of males taking advantage of females, which, in fact, was made to be a comedy. I have seen this movie many times before, but it was different to look at it from the perspective of rape. There was a scene in the movie where a girl who was naked passed out in a guy's bed, and he had to ask himself whether or not he would have sex with her. This would have clearly been an example of rape because consent was not given.

> I was very pleased with all the forums, panels, films and lectures that took place during Rape Awareness Week. I really learned more than I expected to. I think more people should become aware of the problems surrounding rape and do something to help. I am very glad and pleased with myself that I went.

Finally, more acquaintance rape programs are beginning to emphasize social change and, in particular, how the differential socialization of girls and boys contributes to the likelihood of sexual coercion and assault. Men have also begun to organize and present workshops to educate and enhance their own understanding of rape and to work toward its elimination. See, for example, the curriculum guide developed for men by Ohio State University (Stevens & Gebhardt, 1984).[3]

How can we best reach students at these various levels of rape awareness, facilitate their understanding, and help them to analyze the problem from a more sophisticated feminist standpoint? The popular conception of acquaintance rape (as personal and individually caused) must change, and students need to recognize the political nature and social causation of sexual violence. As a first step, it is imperative that we examine the actual versus intended effects of our rape education programs, with an eye toward individual differences in our students. Clearly, there is a great need for research that assesses the scope and effectiveness of our intervention programs. It is important that feminist theories redirect and inform rape education efforts as we continue to study and understand the complex nature of gender socialization and rape-tolerant attitudes. Our greatest hope for altering the incidence of rape is through awareness and education. The task of changing a "rape culture" is at the same time formidable and mandatory.

NOTES

1. Gilmartin-Zena (1988) discusses the lack of agreement concerning two of these myths: Rape as violence rather than sex and the likelihood of men raping.

2. Recent research (see, e.g., Muehlenhard, 1988) suggests that a minority of college women report saying no to sexual intercourse when they really mean yes because of the sexual double standard ("nice women don't say yes"). Although these women are being dishonest, saying no indicates a lack of consent (even though they may be insincere); and if a man ignores such a refusal, it is rape.

3. Schedules of various rape awareness activities and a workshop designed for Residence Life Staff are available from the author.

REFERENCES

Amir, M. (1967). Victim precipitated forcible rape. *Journal of Criminal Law, Criminology, and Police Science, 58,* 493–502.

Bart, P. B., & O'Brien, P. H. (1985). *Stopping rape: Successful survival strategies.* New York: Pergamon.

Bateman, P. (1987, September). *Sexual assault prevention: A comprehensive approach.* Paper presented at the meeting of Virginians Aligned Against Sexual Assault (VAASA), Charlottesville, VA.

Burt, M. R. (1980). Cultural myths and supports for rape. *Journal of Personality and Social Psychology, 38,* 217–230.

Giacopassi, D., & Dull, R. T. (1986). Gender and racial differences in the acceptance of rape myths within a college population. *Sex Roles, 15,* 63–75.

Gilmartin-Zena, P. (1988). Gender differences in students' attitudes toward rape. *Sociological Focus, 21,* 279–292.

Hall, E. R., Howard, J. A., & Boezio, S. L. (1986). Tolerance of rape: A sexist or antisocial attitude? *Psychology of Women Quarterly, 10,* 101–118.

Johnson, A. G. (1980). On the prevalence of rape in the U. S. *Signs, 6,* 140–153.

Koss, M. P., Gidycz, C. A., & Wisniewski, N. (1987). The scope of rape: Incidence and prevalence of sexual aggression and victimization in a national sample of higher education students. *Journal of Consulting and Clinical Psychology, 55,* 162–170.

Lerner, M. J. (1970). The desire for justice and reactions to victims. In J. Macauley & L. Berkowitz (Eds.), *Altruism and helping behavior: Social psychological studies of some antecedents and consequences* (pp. 205–229). New York: Academic Press.

Levine-MacCombie, J., & Koss, M. P. (1986). Acquaintance rape: Effective avoidance strategies. *Psychology of Women Quarterly, 10,* 311–320.

Morgan, M. K. (1986). Conflict and confusion: What rape prevention experts are telling women. *Sexual Coercion and Assault, 1,* 160–168.

Muehlenhard, C. L. (1988). "Nice women" don't say yes and "real men" don't say no: How miscommunication and the double standard can cause sexual problems. *Women & Therapy, 7,* 95–108.

Muehlenhard, C. L., Friedman, D. E., & Thomas, C. M. (1985). Is date rape justifiable? The effects of dating activity, who initiated, who paid, and men's attitudes toward women. *Psychology of Women Quarterly, 9,* 297–310.

Parrot, A. (1986). *Acquaintance rape and sexual assault prevention training manual.* Ithaca, NY: Cornell University.

Stevens, M., & Gebhardt, R. (1984). *Rape education for men: Curriculum guide.* Columbus: Ohio State University.

Swift, C. F. (1985). The prevention of rape. In A. W. Burgess (Ed.), *Sexual assault: A research handbook* (pp. 413–426). New York: Garland.

Warshaw, R. (1988). *I never called it rape.* New York: Harper & Row.

■ 12
Cancer and Stigma: Problems of Seriously Ill Women

Geraldine Butts Stahly

Women victims of violence often find that the initial traumatic event is followed by secondary victimization, stigma and blame by others that may increase emotional trauma and block recovery. The consequences of such blame may be devastating. For example, in studies of battered women (Stahly, 1978; Walker, 1978), the victim often feels embarrassed, ashamed, and guilty. The social support network shrinks. The victimized woman suffers loss of self-esteem, followed by a sense of helplessness and hopelessness. Depression and despair immobilize the woman, making it difficult to seek help or to find alternatives to the cycle of violence in which she is caught. Even when alternatives are offered, a sense of worthlessness, hopelessness, and despair may make it difficult for her to take action.

Although the woman with cancer is not a "victim" in the sense of a battered woman, it is clear that the effects of stigmatization, a sense of lowered self-esteem, lost status and social support, and consequent helplessness and despair make the cancer patient a disadvantaged person who suffers many

The author's research, cited in this article, was supported by a California Divisions Cancer Society Postdoctoral Research Fellowship No. P-15-83. The author gratefully acknowledges the help and support of Dr. Robin DiMatteo of the University of California, Riverside, sponsor of the ACS postdoctoral research project cited above; Dr. Sonia Blackman of California State Polytechnic University, Pomona, for contributing some germinal ideas on the relative stigma of cancer and heart disease; and Charlene Neighbors for her invaluable assistance in the preparation of this manuscript.

of the psychosocial consequences experienced by victims of violence (Stahly, 1988). However, the social-psychological perspective of "victimization" is just beginning to be considered in evaluating the psychosocial environment of the cancer patient (Dunkel-Schetter & Wortman, 1982; Taylor, Wood, & Lichtman, 1983; Wortman, 1983).

STIGMA AND VICTIM DEROGATION

Social psychologists have found that most people believe in what has been called the just world hypothesis (Lerner & Simmons, 1966). This is the belief that people generally get what they deserve, that in the long run good things happen to good people and bad things to bad people. Such an attitude results in blaming the victim's behavior or character when something bad happens. Such victim blaming does not result from cruelty or lack of concern for the victim's plight; rather, it is based on the profound need of observers to believe that they have some control over their own lives and will be able somehow to prevent tragic things from happening to themselves. By finding fault with the victim's behavior or character, individuals reassure themselves that they can escape the victim's fate.

The derogation of the victim, even a victim who is perceived to be "innocent," is well established in psychological literature (Lerner, 1971; Lerner & Mathews, 1967; Lerner & Simmons, 1966; Mills & Egger, 1972; Shaver, 1970). In a classic study that established the paradigm for much of the research of victim derogation, Lerner (1971) suggests a just world explanation of the phenomenon that is motivational and based on elements of equity theory (Walster, Berscheid, & Walster, 1973), the theory of cognitive dissonance (Festinger, 1954), and balance theory (Heider, 1958).

The belief in a just world is not limited to observers. Victims may also believe that their behavior determines their outcomes. When tragedy strikes, it may bring with it a dramatic reappraisal of individuals' beliefs about themselves and the world (Janoff-Bulman & Frieze, 1983). The victims' first response may be to review their behavior looking for a clue to "where I went wrong." Such a causal review is found in cancer patients, who may become preoccupied with understanding "why me?" as they blame everything from old bruises to distant ancestors for their illness. The search for a behavioral link is often seen as morbid self-pity or neurotic self-blame by others. However, there is some evidence that victims may be trying to regain a sense of control of their fate (Janoff-Bulman, 1979; Janoff-Bulman & Frieze, 1983). When victims cannot find a behavioral reason for a negative occurrence, their sense of powerlessness may be profound. Such individuals may feel helpless, worthless, vulnerable to future risks (Perloff, 1983), and even somehow deserving of bad things, but they are unable to identify how to change. The finding that victim derogation is greater where the victim's behavior cannot be faulted, is a related phenomenon (Lerner & Simmons, 1966). To adjust emotionally to a crisis, whether it is victimization or disease, it is necessary for the individual to feel hope and some power to control future outcomes. Stigma, and the rejection and isolation it brings, may be directly related to the observers' perception of a victim as helpless and out of control. Such a perception may be frightening to the observers and lead them to take increased social distance from the unfortunate victim.

Cancer arouses fear. In spite of AIDS, cancer remains the most feared disease that the general public believe could attack "people similar to themselves" (Leishman, 1987). Because the cause of the disease is generally unknown, the patient appears innocent and helpless, unable to prevent the onset or improve the outcome of disease (Maguire, 1985). The "victim derogation" findings in social psychology suggest that it is just such innocence and helplessness that maximizes stigma and derogation. Although heart disease is a greater killer, it is believed by the public to be largely preventable through life-style changes: heart patients do not suffer the stigma, social isolation, or rejection of cancer patients (Katz, 1981; Stahly & Blackman, 1985). The just world hypothesis would suggest that heart patients' "complicity" in their disease through smoking, overweight, lack of exercise, and so on, makes them seem more in control of their fate; they are therefore less threatening to an observer and are consequently less stigmatized.

STIGMA AND SOCIAL STRESS

To the extent that the cancer patient is seen as helpless and the disease as powerful and out of control, others may respond to the patient with discomfort and social distance. The withdrawal of support from the patient can lead to serious problems with interpersonal relationships. Such problems have been described at length in the literature (Cobb & Erbe, 1978). Marital and family problems have also been discussed (Greenleigh & Associates, 1979; Meyerowitz, 1980). Dunkel-Schetter and Wortman (1982) note that patients have difficulties in relationships with friends and may perceive that their social life is damaged by their "cancer patient" status. Such responses may be seen as an important aspect of stigma.

In a study of adaptation and coping conducted by the author (Stahly, 1988), 30 female and 20 male patients participated in semistructured clinical interviews and completed a questionnaire that included a measure of stigma. The patients interviewed had diagnoses of either breast, gynecological, lung, or colorectal cancer. The partner or another close family member of each patient also completed the interview and questionnaire. Patients scoring highest on the Stigma Inventory (Stahly & Blackman, 1985) reported higher levels of social stress (Stahly, 1988). Findings of the study indicate that gender and age of the patient are significantly correlated with scores on the Stigma Inventory.

Patients under 50 years of age scored highest on the stigma measure of the inventory, indicating difficulties in social presentation and interpersonal interactions. In interviews, younger patients were more likely to spontaneously mention embarrassment and shame regarding their illness. These patients appear to suffer greater social stress than do older patients, a contrast that is especially poignant in the descriptions patients gave of the effect of cancer on their social lives and friendships.

Female patients reported significantly more experiences of stigma than did male patients. Women were more likely to report rejection from closest family members, especially their partners and, to a lesser extent, their children. Female patients were also more likely to be divorced or widowed at the time of diagnosis. Those in marital or dating relationships were more likely than male patients to have the relationship end after the diagnosis.

One aspect of the stigma that can be particularly disconcerting for the cancer patient is the persistent myth of contagion. Many patients have reported that friends are unwilling to visit or, when visiting, unwilling to take food in the patients' homes. Some patients have even had the experience of being the only one served on paper plates at a formal dinner, of being asked not to use the restroom or swimming pool ("Cancer," 1977). Those patients who scored highest on the Stigma Inventory were more likely to report fear of contagion as a problem for their friends or family (Stahly, 1988).

The diagnosis of cancer brings great anxiety for a patient. In times of anxiety the needs for social support and social comparison may be intensified (Schachter, 1959). Yet the anxiety of the patient is often matched by the anxiety the diagnosis brings to family members and even the physician who must deliver the dreaded news. Doctors and nurses are not immune to the stigma of cancer. Interaction with the cancer patient can be stressful and can lead to derogation of the patient. In a study of stress, nurses on a cancer unit were found to have levels of stress only slightly less than that of new widows measured on the Goldberg Health Questionnaire (Brooks, 1979). Another study found that residents and interns hold significantly more negative attitudes toward cancer than toward heart disease (Kaye, Appel, & Joseph, 1980).

Social stress appears to be further heightened for patients who have received a terminal prognosis (Stahly, 1988). Terminal patients were among those scoring highest on the Stigma Inventory (Stahly & Blackman, 1985), perhaps supporting the theoretical notion that part of the stigma that patients experience results from the difficulty friends and family may have with the possibility of death. The patient may respond to such difficulties with either withdrawal or anger that increases social distance and isolation.

How do the stress and negative attitudes of others affect the patient? When patients reach out for support, clarification, and comfort, they may discover that others are uncomfortable with the reality of the patient's condition and unsure of how to communicate with and support the patient. Among the greatest fears patients may experience at the earliest stage of cancer is that they will be rejected and abandoned by loved ones (Sutherland & Orbach, 1953). For the woman patient, especially, this fear often becomes a reality (Stahly, 1988). Likewise, communication that could reassure the patient of support from significant others, clarify the patient's medical condition, and help the patient mobilize the psychological and physical strength to deal with the disease are often lacking. In the author's study, a 37-year-old with metastatic cancer reported that the most difficult aspect of her illness was her father's reaction: "He was in a daze for months and couldn't stand to hear me talk about my fear of dying" (Stahly, 1988). The loss of the ability to discuss her fears with her father was particularly distressing for the patient because her father is a physician and she depends on him for informational as well as emotional support. In a review of their experiences conducting support groups, Dunkel-Schetter and Wortman (1982) report that patients, especially women, are often disturbed by spouses' unwillingness to discuss their disease and its ramifications. Likewise, patients often report that friends seem to avoid them and are awkward and tense in their presence.

STIGMA AND NONVERBAL COMMUNICATION

A patient may well interpret overt social rejection and others' fear of contagion as stigma, but the sense of stigma may also derive from covert and subtle cues in interpersonal interactions. In fact, the attitude of others toward the cancer patient may be one of ambivalence, expressing both sympathy and discomfort; this may present the patient with confusing messages (Katz, 1981). To delineate the aspects of stigma, it is necessary to go beyond the direct questioning of attitudes to the subtle cues that may be found in nonverbal communication. Cancer patients may identify some nonverbal cues, as in their sense that people take increased personal distance (Hall, 1966); more often, the patients sense a discomfort with others that they cannot quite identify.

Women are, in general, socialized to greater interpersonal sensitivity to emotional communication and generally score higher, as a group, on measures of nonverbal sensitivity. Women cancer patients may report greater perception of stigma because of their sensitivity to subtle nonverbal communication from those around them (Friedman, Prince, Riggio, & DiMatteo, 1980; Rosenthal, 1979).

When individuals are under conditions of anxiety, they become especially attuned to interpersonal cues and seek social comparison; cancer patients' fear of their disease may make them especially sensitive to the physicians' unintentional messages of discomfort and ambivalence. Just as individual physicians may differ in skill as encoders, so patients may differ in their decoding ability (Friedman et al., 1980; Rosenthal, 1979). Some patients may be better at identifying the "leakage" and sensing conflicting cues; such patients may become more anxious and vigilant and perhaps even distrustful and hostile toward others. The role of nonverbal communication in the perception of stigma is an important area of empirical investigation. Nonverbal skills can be taught in order to enhance the social-emotional aspects of patient care and to enhance patients' satisfaction and compliance with their medical regimens (DiMatteo & DiNicole, 1982). Intervention strategies aimed at the family and other support systems may also be enhanced by nonverbal-skills training.

STIGMA AND FAMILY ROLES

Patients' experiences differ widely in the willingness of family and friends to be supportive, open in communication, and tolerant of negative emotions (Stahly, 1988). Straus (1973) has described a family system's response to crises as consisting of antecedent variables, precipitating variables, and consequent variables. The antecedent variables include demographics, ethnic and subcultural family styles, personality and experiential differences in family members, differences in communication styles, and attitudes toward disease in general and cancer in particular. These variables may predict that a family will be flexible and supportive in crises or at risk of maladaptive response.

Precipitating variables are defined as aspects of the crises causing tension and distress in the family system. A diagnosis of cancer is invariably a family crisis, but the degree of crisis may be related to the recommended treatment and prognosis for the disease as well as the age, sex, and role expectations of the patient. In a family where the patient is the principal breadwinner and the disease and the treatment regimen mean loss of income, the crisis will be intensified. Because women were more likely to be alone at the time of diagnosis, they were frequently without an adequate means of support when they were unable to work. Although the male patients appeared to suffer more loss of role identity when they were unable to work, their wives often provided a financial backup that the single women patients lacked.

Likewise, if the patient is a mother who is primarily responsible for providing warmth, nurturance, and emotional support for family members, the family may be deprived of this role function. Further, if there is no family member who is able or willing to assume her supportive function, the woman patient may find herself without nurturance or support when she needs it most. The nurturing, caretaking role becomes especially critical during the period of treatment and the long period of chronic illness that may follow a cancer diagnosis. In families in which gender roles are rigidly adhered to, the woman's partner and even her children may be unprepared to assume the nurturing role. The more rigid the system, the more likely the disintegration of that system, which leaves the woman alone in her time of greatest need. Interventions with cancer patients and their families that strengthen family cohesion and reduce the distress of necessary role changes may reduce patients' perception of the stigma of their illness.

Consequent variables consist of the family's coping mechanisms. If these reinforce the negative responses to the crisis, they may cause further stress. Thus, if the family system cannot cope with the disease, it may begin to disintegrate and lose the ability to cope in other areas as well. The parent of a child patient may withdraw from the spouse or find it difficult to hold a job or care for the other children. The spouse of a patient may withdraw emotionally and physically from the patient and may even seek a relationship outside the marriage, thus accelerating the system's deterioration.

If, on the other hand, the family system copes effectively with the crisis, it can be a time of growth despite the fear and pain. Family members may learn new roles and exhibit courage and love beyond their former experiences together; they may sense a greater closeness and come to cherish each other and life itself. The differences in positive and negative coping by the family may make a significant difference for the patient in terms of emotional adjustment and compliance with treatment and prognosis.

To determine the impact the system has on the patient, one aspect of study assesses the coping strategies from a "family system" perspective. Role displacement appears to contribute to the interpersonal difficulties reported by the patients (Stahly, 1988). A 34-year-old female patient, married, with small children, described the biggest change cancer had made in her life as the loss of her caretaking role: "Other family members have to do for me, when I used to be the one doing for others" (Stahly, 1988). In general, younger patients were much more likely to report changes in their roles in the family. Loss of role function appeared to contribute significantly to the higher scores on the Stigma Inventory of younger patients as well as of the women patients in our study (Stahly & Blackman, 1985).

When the family system remains cohesive, it may ameliorate the experience of social isolation and loss of support that characterizes the experience of patients who feel stigmatized. Married patients, overall, scored lower on the Stigma Inventory than single or divorced patients; this trend was also significant for patients over age 50 (Stahly, 1988). As one 79-year-old woman stated, "When you've been married 56 years, you've dealt with worse problems than cancer."

Women patients in our study were much more likely to be alone at the time of diagnosis, widowed or divorced, and thus unable to benefit from the positive support of a long-term marital relationship. Women in relationships at the time of diagnosis were more likely than male patients to be left by their partners. Generally, those women blamed the cancer and their partners' inability to cope with it for the end of the relationship.

SOCIAL SUPPORT

The importance of social support for patients is well documented in the health care literature; such support is credited with promoting recovery and improving coping with serious injury or illness (DiMatteo & Hays, 1981). Even in studies of the terminally ill, social support is crucial (Carey, 1974); Weisman and Worden (1975, p. 61) found that the "patients who lived significantly longer were those who had maintained cooperative and mutually responsive relationships with others" (Weisman & Worden, 1975; see also Carey, 1974).

An important aspect of social support may be the opportunity it provides for social comparison. Under stress, individuals express an increased need for self-evaluation, and the cancer patient may look to others to judge whether their response to the crisis of their diagnosis is appropriate. In a study of breast cancer patients, Wood, Taylor, and Lichtman (1985) found that patients actively sought social comparisons and preferred to compare themselves with others who were coping less adequately. By finding examples of people who were worse off than themselves, the patients appeared to build their self-esteem and reduce their sense of victimization. Taylor, Wood, and Lichtman (1983) have incorporated these findings into a theory of response to victimization called Selective Evaluation.

Because the role of the victim is aversive, individuals seek to end their perception of themselves as victims by finding examples of how "things could be worse"; they may even distort reality in order to make a downward comparison. Such a comparison may also be a way of reducing stigma. Patients who lack a downward comparison may feel more stigmatized than those who can find a more unfortunate individual with whom they can compare their plight. The finding that patients over 50 years score lower on the Stigma Inventory (Stahly, 1988) may be due, in part, to the greater ease an older patient may have in finding downward comparisons. That is, advancing age may bring death and serious disability to others within the patient's network of friends and acquaintances, and cancer patients who compare their illness with Alzheimer's disease may decide that they are fortunate.

STIGMA AND PATIENT COMPLIANCE WITH MEDICAL REGIME

Patient compliance is an issue of concern to a wide range of health providers. There is extensive research that indicates that the socioemotional aspects of the physician–patient interaction may be central to both patient satisfaction and patient compliance with the medical regimen (DiMatteo & DiNicole, 1982). For the cancer patient, compliance may be a life-and-death issue. In a study of malignant melanoma patients, Temoshok (1983) and her colleagues (Temoshok et al., 1985) found that one of the predictors of negative outcome (defined as recurrence of cancer at an 18-month follow-up) was patient failure to keep follow-up appointments.

Temoshok (1983) suggests that delaying and noncompliant behaviors are indicative of a personality style characterized by denial, passivity, and a high need for social approval. This personality constellation has been labeled Type C. These patients may be too "too nice"; in their anxiety to please they may ignore their own health needs, not wanting to "bother the busy doctor" or "inconvenience" family or friends. Not surprisingly, these overadaptive, self-sacrificing responses were most typical of women patients in Temoshok's study.

It is somewhat difficult to believe that need for social approval is the primary explanation for so profoundly dangerous a behavior as missed appointments following treatment for cancer. An alternative explanation could include consideration of the women patients' sense of stigma. Given these women's high need for approval, their denial and destructive noncompliant behavior may be increased by their perception of the changes their "cancer patient" status has brought to their role in their family and social support system. Because the woman generally fills the role of family caregiver, both she and those around her may be resisting the role changes that the status of cancer patient may bring by denying the seriousness of the illness. Likewise, the loss of a woman's accustomed position in the family system may result in feelings of depression and covert rage, expressed indirectly through self-destructive noncompliance. A careful analysis of the family system and social support network is necessary to deepen understanding of both the phenomenon of stigma and the role of the patients' support systems in facilitating or discouraging compliance with the medical regimen.

The literature of victimization associates helplessness and despair with immobilization. Stigma may well be a victimizing and immobilizing force. Angry, demanding patients may be reacting against their sense of powerlessness and helplessness; to the extent that they feel empowered, they may be willing to be active, compliant participants in even a very difficult medical regimen. Type C patients may appear to be highly cooperative, the epitome of the "good patient" that a physician prefers (DiMatteo & DiNicole, 1982; Pratt, 1978). However, if such patients are denying the reality of their illness and feeling stigmatized and helpless, they may, in fact, be the least cooperative in the long run. They appear to be cooperative in attitude but fail to follow through with behaviors that are medically necessary.

EMOTIONAL FACTORS AND POSITIVE OUTCOMES

There is some empirical evidence that mood state may predict medical outcome for the cancer patient. Temoshok et al. (1985) found better outcome at 18 months in melanoma patients who initially scored high in anger, anxiety, hostility, and depression. Likewise, Derogatis, Abeloff, and Melisaratos (1979) found the best prognosis in patients described as "angry" and "obnoxious." Because anger is generally more consistent with male gender role–stereotyped behavior, it is more likely to be men who manifest these apparently beneficial emotions. Although it may not be possible or desirable to create an intervention that makes "nice" women patients into obnoxious ones in order to improve their prognosis, it is possible to improve women's sense of personal efficacy.

Bloom (1979) demonstrated that giving mastectomy patients information about their disease and encouraging their participation in decisions about their treatment significantly changed their scores on the Fate subscale of the Health Locus of Control Scale (Wallston, Wallston, Kaplan, & Maides, 1976). The patients' sense of personal efficacy appeared to be improved by the intervention strategy. These findings suggest that information, choices, and participation may be the key to successful intervention and will be especially beneficial to women patients in terms of both improved compliance and prognosis.

Although anger may increase the patients' sense of power and the will to fight their illness, hostility may have some disadvantages as well. In a study conducted by the author (Stahly, 1988), the patients expressing the highest levels of anger also reported the greatest loss of social support and scored highest on the Stigma Inventory. Angry patients may alienate their support system. The relationship between patients' anger, perception of stigma, and loss of social support is certainly not clear. Patients who respond to the crisis of their illness with anger may alienate their support system and experience the subsequent withdrawal of others as stigma. In addition, the experience of being rejected and stigmatized may lead to anger and hostility in the patient. In either case, the process is interactive, and interventions are needed both to lower the patients' hostility and to reduce the stigmatization of the patient by others. Dealing effectively with a patient's anger may be the first step in opening positive communication between the patient and salient others and ensuring that the patient receives needed emotional support.

Longitudinal studies of psychosocial adaptation to cancer are needed. Findings of the author's study of psychosocial adaptation to cancer indicate that the effects of gender role–stereotyped behavior and role expectations may be another area of adaptation to cancer that needs to be explored (Stahly, 1988). The gender differences are important both in understanding the special problems women patients face and in designing gender-appropriate supportive interventions. The results of long-term studies can contribute significant information on the social and psychological aspects of cancer that may be as disabling as the disease itself. Better understanding brings the hope of more effective interventions to reduce social morbidity in cancer patients and their families.

REFERENCES

Bloom, J. (1979). Psychosocial measurement and specific hypothesis: A research note. *Journal of Consulting and Clinical Psychology, 47*, 637–639.

Brooks, A. (1979). Public and professional attitudes toward cancer: A view from Great Britain. *Cancer Nursing, 2*, 453–460.

Cancer: More than a disease, for many a silent stigma. (May 5, 1977). *New York Times*, p. A16.

Carey, R. G. (1974). Emotional adjustment in terminal patients: A quantitative approach. *Journal of Counseling Psychology, 21*, 433–439.

Cobb, S., & Erbe, C. (1978). Social support for the cancer patient. *Forum on Medicine, 1*, 24–29.

Derogatis, L. N., Abeloff, M. D., & Melisaratos, N. (1979). Psychological coping mechanisms and survival time in metastatic breast cancer. *Journal of the American Medical Association, 242*, 1504–1508.

DiMatteo, M. R., & DiNicole, D. D. (1982). *Achieving patient compliance: The psychology of the medical practitioner's role.* New York: Pergamon Press.

DiMatteo, M. R., & Hays, R. (1981). Social support and serious illness. In B. Gottlieb (Ed.), *Social networks and social support* (pp. 117–148). Beverly Hills, CA: Sage.

Dunkel-Schetter, C., & Wortman, C. (1982). The interpersonal dynamics of cancer: Problems in social relationships and their impact on the patient. In H. S. Friedman & M. R. DiMatteo (Eds.), *Interpersonal issues in health.* New York: Academic Press.

Festinger, L. (1954). A theory of social comparison processes. *Human Relations, 7,* 117–140.

Friedman, H. S., Prince, L. M., Riggio, R. E., & DiMatteo, M. R. (1980). Understanding and assessing nonverbal expressiveness: The effective communication test. *Journal of Personality and Social Psychology, 39,* 333–351.

Greenleigh & Associates. (1979, May). *Report on the social, economic, and psychological needs of cancer patients in California.* San Francisco: American Cancer Society, California Division.

Hall, E. T. (1966). *The hidden dimension.* Garden City, NY: Doubleday.

Heider, F. (1958). *The psychology of interpersonal relations.* New York: John Wiley & Sons.

Janoff-Bulman, R. (1979). Characterological versus behavioral self blame: Inquiries in depression and rape. *Journal of Personality and Social Psychology, 37,* 1798–1809.

Janoff-Bulman, R., & Frieze, I. H. (1983). A theoretical perspective for understanding reactions to victimization. *Journal of Social Issues, 39,* 1–17.

Katz, I. (1981). *Stigma: A social psychological analysis.* Hillsdale, NJ: Lawrence Erlbaum Associates.

Kaye, J., Appel, M., & Joseph, R. (1980). Attitudes of medical students and residents toward cancer. *Proceeding of the 14th Annual Meeting of the American Association of Cancer Education, 1,* 367.

Leishman, K. (1987). Heterosexuals and AIDS: The second stage of the epidemic. *Atlantic, 259,* 39–69.

Lerner, M. J. (1971). Observers' evaluation of the victim, justice, guilt and veridical perceptions. *Journal of Personality and Social Psychology, 20,* 127–135.

Lerner, M. J., & Mathews, G. (1967). Reaction to suffering of others under conditions of indirect responsibility. *Journal of Personality and Social Psychology, 5,* 319–325.

Lerner, M. J., & Simmons, C. H. (1966). Observer's reaction to the "innocent victim": Compassion or rejection? *Journal of Personality and Social Psychology, 4,* 202–310.

Maguire, P. (1985). The psychological impact of cancer. *British Journal of Hospital Medicine, 2,* 100–103.

Meyerowitz, B. E. (1980). Psychological correlates of breast cancer and its treatment. *Psychological Bulletin, 87,* 108–131.

Mills, J., & Egger, R. (1972). Effects of derogation of a victim on choosing to reduce his distress. *Journal of Personality and Social Psychology, 23,* 405–408.

Perloff, L. S. (1983). Perceptions of vulnerability to victimization. *Journal of Social Issues, 39,* 41–61.

Pratt, L. V. (1978). Reshaping the consumer's posture in health care. In E. G. Gallagher (Ed.), *The doctor-patient relationship in the changing health scene* (pp. 197–214). Washington, DC: U. S. Government Printing Office.

Rosenthal, R. (Ed.). (1979). *Skill in nonverbal communication: Individual differences.* Cambridge, MA: Oelgeschlager, Gunn & Hain.

Schachter, S. (1959). *The psychology of affiliation.* Stanford, CA: Stanford University Press.

Shaver, K. G. (1970). Defensive attribution: Effects of severity and relevance on the responsibility assigned for an accident. *Journal of Personality and Social Psychology, 14*, 101–113.

Stahly, G. B. (1978). A review of select literature of spousal violence. *Victimology, 2*, 591–607.

Stahly, G. B. (1988). Psychosocial aspects of the stigma of cancer: An overview. *Journal of Psychosocial Oncology, 6*, 3–27.

Stahly, G. B., & Blackman, S. (1985, April). *A comparison of the stigma of cancer and heart disease: Test of the Stigma Inventory.* Paper presented at the Western Psychological Association Convention, San Jose, CA.

Straus, M. (1973). A general systems approach to a theory of violence between family members. *Social Science Information, 12*, 105–125.

Sutherland, A. M., & Orbach, G. E. (1953). Psychological impact of cancer and cancer surgery: 2. Depressive reactions associated with surgery for cancer. *Cancer, 6*, 958–966.

Taylor, S. E., Wood, J. V., & Lichtman, R. R. (1983). It could be worse: Selective evaluation as a response to victimization. *Journal of Social Issues, 39*, 19–40.

Temoshok, L. (1983). *Psychosocial aspects of malignant melanoma.* Riverside: University of California. Health Psychology Colloquium.

Temoshok, L., Heller, B., Sagebiel, R., Blois, M., Sweet, D., DiClemente, R., & Gold, M. (1985). The relationship of psychosocial factors to prognostic indicators in cutaneous malignant melanoma. *Journal of Psychosomatic Research, 29*, 139–153.

Walker, L. (1978). Battered women and learned helplessness. *Victimology, 2*, 525–534.

Wallston, B. S., Wallston, K. A., Kaplan, C. D., & Maides, S. A. (1976). Development and validation of the health locus of control scale. *Journal of Consulting and Clinical Psychology, 44*, 580–585.

Walster, E., Berscheid, E., & Walster, G. (1973). New directions in equity research. *Journal of Personality and Social Psychology, 25*, 151–176.

Weisman, A. D., & Worden, J. W. (1975). Psychosocial analysis of cancer deaths. *Omega, 6*, 61–75.

Wood, J. V., Taylor, S. E., & Lichtman, R. R. (1985). Social comparison in adjustment to breast cancer. *Journal of Personality and Social Psychology, 49*, 1169–1183.

Wortman, C. B. (1983). Coping with victimization: Conclusions and implications for future research. *Journal of Social Issues, 39*, 195–221.

■ 13
New Directions in Dynamic Theories of Lesbianism: From Psychoanalysis to Social Constructionism

Judith M. Glassgold

Fifty years ago the psychology of women was described as "the dark continent," yet to be fully discovered and understood (Freud, 1933/1964). Freud's choice of the metaphor "dark continent" was apt, as women's psyche was unexplored and hidden. However, in this metaphor was another more insidious meaning: "dark continent" was used by Europeans to describe Africa during its period of colonialism. Freud's use of this metaphor reminds us that the psychology of women was once the territory of foreign (male) experts.

Recently, feminist scholarship has begun a revolt against this foreign authority. By challenging traditional male views, feminist scholars have taken back much of the territory of women's sexuality and identity. These advances, however, have not completely displaced previous views. Fifty years later, the psychoanalytic views of women are still shackled by the colonial legacy of the dark continent. Inherited definitions of gender, sexuality, and normalcy remain so embedded in many psychoanalytic theories that feminist scholars continue to incorporate them unquestioningly into modern revisions of psychoanalysis.

Understanding the weaknesses in modern psychoanalytic theories becomes particularly important when trying to apply these theories to clinical practice. Despite many therapists' greater interest in the techniques of psychoanalytic practice, theories of development and psychopathology are intrinsic to their practice. Clinical decisions in treatment are often based on the clinician's conceptualization of the client's problems. Thus, understanding how a theory explains sexual orientation and its relationship to developmental psychopathology is essential for those therapists working with lesbians.

This chapter will provide the reader with an overview and criticism of the common problems in psychoanalytic theories of lesbianism. It focuses on some of the limitations common to most psychoanalytic theories, using examples from well-known theories. It then provides an alternative focus for dynamic theories that incorporates new trends in feminism and psychology.

Psychoanalytic theories of lesbianism epitomize the difficulty of liberating feminist theory from the past. Traditionally, psychoanalytic theorists viewed lesbianism (or female homosexuality) as deviant and developed a theory of etiology based on traditional views of gender roles and sexuality. Many feminists trying to use psychoanalytic theories reject the view that lesbianism is always pathological. As a result, two distinct types of psychoanalytic views of lesbianism currently exist: those that remain close to the traditional or classical formulations, such as Eisenbud (1982), McDougall (1970, 1980), and Siegel (1988), and those that use Chodorow's (1978) feminist revision of object relations theory, such as Burch (1982, 1985), Elise (1986), and Lindenbaum (1985). The more classical theorists focus on etiology and deficits in development. Those who are influenced by feminist object relations theory try to illuminate difficulties that lesbians face in intimate relationships (Burch, 1982, 1985; Elise, 1986; Lindenbaum, 1985).

Although these two perspectives are very different, they have some very similar problems stemming from the psychoanalytic assumptions used. The problematic assumptions can be summarized as follows: (a) psychosexual development results in a heterosexual adult without exception; (b) an individual is an isolated entity only influenced by family dynamics and the unfolding of biological development; (c) the view of adult development and consciousness excludes an understanding of subjectivity and provides an incomplete version of psychological change; and (d) the view of a woman's development confuses social traditions with psychological normalcy and provides overgeneral templates for normalcy that exclude human diversity.

Classical psychoanalysis is unique in its view of the relationship of sexuality and development. The two are integrated and represent increasing stages of maturity. This is seen in Freud's zones of development (oral, anal, phallic, genital) and the psychosexual impact of the Oedipal phase, which is crucial for the development of sexual and ego structure. Departure from the heterosexual outcome is indicative of a personality deviation, and the only way to achieve health is through a change of sexual orientation to heterosexuality.

The early stages of child development of both classical analysis and object relations theory presume inevitable heterosexuality in a teleological manner. Thus, a deviation of adult sexuality is usually linked to a childhood disturbance. Closely linked to this view of development is the assumption that one can discover the key historical events in psychological development. For instance, through analysis a historical reconstruction of a person's development can occur, creating causal links between early events and later issues. This allows analysts to postulate the genetic (early) root of a disorder in childhood to establish the disorder's etiology and sites for intervention.

A focus on the etiology of a disturbance relies on a transparent interpretation of the psyche that seems to simplify and minimize the psychoanalytic belief in the unconscious vicissitudes of development. These theorists assume that a clear linear relationship exists between the insults of childhood and adult personality, ignoring the process of the unconscious and the variety of mediating variables and individual responses. This interpretation may be due in part to an attempt to determine causal relationships in order to change the personality. However, such causal interpretations are overly historical and teleological, and they do not incorporate the complicated and as yet undetermined relationships between the outside world and the developing psyche.

Further, early events are assumed to determine adult sexual orientation, which then is assumed to be permanently fixed. Kinsey's original research (Kinsey, Pomeroy, & Martin, 1948) indicated that sexual orientation is not so exclusively heterosexual and is not necessarily dichotomous (either heterosexual or homosexual). Many more-recent studies illustrate that women's sexuality is more fluid (Golden, 1987; Lowenstein, 1984/85) and can change throughout life. It is not uncommon for a woman to recognize or change her sexual orientation late in life as a result of social and psychological issues, particularly cultural repression. These works indicate that early events and relationships may be only one part of a much more complex picture of sexuality.

The more modern psychoanalytic perspectives focus their understanding of lesbianism on the preoedipal phase of development, which stresses the relationship of the developing child with its mother. In such theories early deviation or disturbances in development are seen as indications of greater pathology in the development of the self, relationships, and reality testing, such as in borderline or narcissistic disorders. Although this point of view has gained much popularity in understanding personality disorders, it was expanded universally to homosexuals by McDougall (1970), Siegel (1988), Socarides (1988), and others. Most often, lesbianism, defined as an erotic attachment to a woman (who is viewed as mother surrogate), is seen as incomplete separation or a lack of individuation from the mother (Siegel, 1988; Socarides, 1988).

McDougall's (1970, 1980) work illustrates very clearly the consequences of this view of lesbians as suffering from serious early deficits. McDougall sees the adoption of homosexuality as a way of stabilizing an unstable personality. The assumed identification with the father protects the girl against a "psychotic restructuring" (1980, p. 209): "The homosexual pays dearly for a fragile identity that is not her own. Yet she is compelled to play this role, for the alternative is the death of the ego" (1980, p. 210). McDougall assumes that this "fragile identity" is a result of having been a damaged child suffering from severely problematic relationships, which often result in sadistic and masochistic elements in later relationships.

Ruth-Jean Eisenbud (1982, 1985) takes a more middle ground, trying to maintain a developmental and etiological focus with a more affirmative view of lesbianism. Her work is a good example of the difficulty of successfully achieving this goal. Although Eisenbud accepts that lesbianism can be a healthy choice for a particular woman, she still focuses on etiology of sexual object choice from the context of a linear developmental theory in which the outcome is heterosexuality. Her model proposes that deficits and abnormalities in the early mother–daughter relationships cause lesbian object choice: lesbianism would not occur if development were optimal — if all goes well, the child is heterosexual. However, she does not assume that lesbians are as seriously disturbed as do McDougall (1970, 1980), Siegel (1988), or Socarides (1988). For instance, Eisenbud (1982) states that lesbianism occurs when the preoedipal period is prematurely eroticized. The mother is either seductive, excluding, or incorporating. Eisenbud sees the lesbian choice as a progressive move to cope with a deficit.

Eisenbud and other theorists confuse sexual object choice with separation–individuation of the self. They assume that, to separate, the girl needs to develop an erotic attachment to the father and renounce phallic desire for the mother. Thus, the girl must give up the original love object (the mother) in order to individuate. They do not consider that women can remain erotic objects for the girl although the individuation has occurred. However, for men, the erotic object can remain the mother although individuation occurs. What is especially problematic is that the above basic description of the female oedipal period is the codification of a teleological explanation of why adults are heterosexual rather than an exploration of childhood development.

Psychoanalytic theory has so incorporated heterosexuality into its view of normalcy that heterosexuality has become part of the definition of gender. If a person loves a woman, s/he is assumed to be a man or manlike. Similarly, if a person is attracted to a man, s/he is assumed to be female or feminine. Thus lesbians are like men and gay men are like women.

In psychoanalytic theory, socially endorsed gender roles and definitions of female sexuality are often completely intertwined. Psychological health is equated with the characteristics that make the traditional mother, and sexual normalcy is defined as behaviors that result in reproduction. The past focus on female frigidity—a discomfort with or rejection of intercourse—and the debate over the vaginal versus clitoral orgasm defined normal female sexuality in the context of reproduction. The psychoanalytic model of sexuality is thus functionalist, assuming that reproduction and motherhood are, respectively, the appropriate sexual and psychological endpoints. This again differs from norms for men. Although heterosexual genitality was seen as normal, the focus on parenting is not as all-encompassing. Psychoanalysis thus endorses the current accepted role for women and performs a conservative social function by making normalcy synonymous with social roles.

Another common problem is that psychoanalysts generalize from their patient populations to the general population. By confusing their clinical population with a normative population, they are led to assume that their homosexual clients are representative of all homosexuals. However, in generalizing from individual clients, there is the possibility of generalizing unique or extreme elements of pathology. For instance, although McDougall (1970) does accept that many homosexuals have no psychiatric symptoms and little impairment in social relations and creativity, most of the cases of homosexuality she discusses are examples of severe ego deficits and extreme personality dysfunction. These clients then become models for her general view of the dynamics of homosexuality. McDougall thus confuses the etiology of personality disorders with the etiology of lesbianism. Siegel (1988), Socarides (1988), and Eisenbud (1982, 1985) make some of these very same assumptions. Even those feminist writers who focus solely on lesbian couples and who are lesbian-affirmative make this same error.

The body of work applying feminist object relations theory to lesbianism originates in the growing field of couples therapy, rather than from individual psychoanalysis. For instance, see the literature on fusion and merger in lesbian couples (Burch, 1982, 1985; Elise, 1986; Lindenbaum, 1985), incest and lesbians (Starzecpyzel, 1987), and the dynamics of lesbian communities (Pearlman, 1987).

These writers base their work on Chodorow's (1978) revision of object relations theory because of its feminist approach and emphasis on the preoedipal phase of development. However, because of problems with Chodorow's work, many of the problems already mentioned above reoccur.

Chodorow (1978) bases her work on traditional psychoanalytic sources and makes similar assumptions about sexual development as classical sources (Glassgold, 1990). Chodorow's analysis of a woman's preoedipal phase focuses only on heterosexual development and does not include a discussion of lesbians. Chodorow's work is based, in fact, on the universal response of a mother to her child determined by the mother's heterosexual orientation. Most of these applications of Chodorow's work seem to assume that heterosexual women and lesbians have similar early experiences and similar personality traits, although the basis for this assumption is unclear (except that they may accept that sexuality remains undetermined until the Oedipal phase).

Further, these feminist theorists (Burch, Elise, and Lindenbaum) do not examine or challenge any aspects of the overall psychoanalytic developmental theory that they incorporate. By focusing on the early determinants of lesbian object choice within the framework of object relations theory, they have difficulty avoiding the implication that the choice is the result of a more disturbed relationship. For instance, they propose the concept of fusion that assumes a lack of differentiation between self and other. By basing this concept on object relations theory, in which a lack of differentiation implies more serious pathology, they replicate the assumptions of traditional psychoanalysts. Further, the theory of separation–individuation is founded on the view that change of object (from mother to father) occurs during childhood, an assumption based on a belief in normative heterosexuality.

Certain feminist theorists go further and use non-lesbian-affirmative sources in their work. For instance, Lindenbaum (1985) accepts McDougall's assertion that a faulty early mother–daughter tie is the cause of later problems in lesbian relationships. McDougall is actually pointing to a serious ego deficit in lesbians. By not criticizing these comments and by generalizing these clinical cases to all lesbian couples, Lindenbaum furthers the error and reproduces McDougall's overgeneralizations.

Even if one adopts a perspective that values the importance of early childhood relations, one could omit the devaluation of homosexuality and the functionalist emphasis on heterosexuality. Based on logic similar to traditional object relations theory, a completely opposite case could be made. Positive, not negative, relations with the mother could leave a child desiring the same-sex love object. Disappointments with the mother or a poor relationship could cause the child to change sexual and love objects (as Freud [1933-1964] actually suggested had to happen) and move to heterosexuality.

In addition to not distinguishing between a normative and a clinical population, both the nonaffirmative traditional and the feminist object relations approaches group together women (and men) with varying degrees of same-sex attraction, desire, attachment, fantasies, and overt sexual behavior. Thus, psychoanalytic theories often suffer from the problem of overgeneralization and lack of specificity and attention to particular individual characteristics. These generalizations falsely dichotomize sexuality and ignore other aspects of diversity that affect identity and sexuality, such as age, generation, culture, geography, religion, ethnicity, and race.

The above psychoanalytic assumptions cannot clarify the differences between degrees and kinds of same-sex desire and love and the process of affirming (or denying) those feelings. Thus, the lack of specificity in psychoanalysis greatly limits the usefulness of psychoanalytic theory in understanding the phenomena of "coming out" and lesbian identity formation. A more genuinely affirmative theory would transform many of the problematic elements of past theories by shifting focus from the areas outlined above. Clearly, the basic psychoanalytic concepts must more closely match the diversity of actual lives. Rather than create a theory of lesbian development from frameworks that ignore lesbians or view them as pathological, it is more useful to incorporate the concept of difference. This allows for a psychodynamic theory of early development and interpersonal relations that includes lesbianism as one of many positive and healthy possibilities. The capacity to develop stable internal representations of self and other and a capacity for mature attachments can be the focus of such a lesbian-affirmative theory that views diversity as intrinsic to sexuality and love.

Psychoanalysis has pointed to the importance of incorporating relationships of the developing child into personality structure. However, most psychoanalysts take a narrow view of the interaction of the internal and external world. The external world is usually defined as only the parents, leaving out the larger family and sociocultural context. Further, the direction of influence travels in only one way: from the outside in, from more powerful forces onto the individual.

An improved psychodynamic theory must acknowledge the psychological repercussions of a larger number of relationships. Family and society experienced through cultural images, political relationships, language, and nonverbal representations, transmit important values and perceptions of self and others. Sexual identity in the modern world is not a neutral position and is not independent from society at large. Rather, sexual identity is socially constructed; that is, it develops within a network of linguistic, cultural, historical, racial, and ethnic patterns. Sexuality and identity are shaped by culture and are not independent or universal, as they are often presented in psychoanalytic theory. Those who are defined as different contend with the negative messages or invisibility that shape the developing child and then must cope with a stigmatized identity as an adult.

The incorporation of the influence of the larger world is just the first step. A new model must specify the particulars of such a relationship more clearly. For instance, in theories based on Marxism the individual is often presented as having little free will and as unable to resist the messages of the larger society. This is clearly inaccurate, as resistance and rebellion do exist; yet at the same time, resistance is shaped by the types of social structure present.

One of Freud's most useful discoveries—the importance of individual insight—can be reframed to help us move away from psychologically or socially deterministic views of development while recognizing that the individual is not an isolated being. He recognized that an awareness that life is determined by forces outside of oneself can lead to personal change. Freud may have been the first to acknowledge that insight into the factors influencing one's life can lead to psychological growth.

Freire (1970), a social critic, put this realization slightly differently: "Only beings who can reflect upon the fact that they are determined are capable of freeing themselves" (cited in Rich, 1979, p. 67). An awareness of the psychological impact of personal history and social location can alter the perception of oneself and of one's previous life. A shift in consciousness, identity, and personal history can emerge from individual efforts, as in psychotherapy, or through group and political efforts such as occurs for individuals involved in social movements (e.g., civil rights, feminist, black, Latino, gay/lesbian).

This view recognizes the power of the larger world but goes beyond that potentially disempowering realization. In actuality, social context is not simply restricting but is part of a fabric of life that has many potential outcomes; it is actually the substance of meaning and possibility (Lauretis, 1986). Individuals are shaped by the world and shape the world; change is inevitable and endemic. Identity is not fixed by the end of childhood as in a traditional psychoanalytic approach; rather, the awareness of self that emerges in adolescence is a starting point for a process that has no clear endpoint.

Subjectivity emerges from one's embeddedness in society and by the attributes (gender, race, class) that are labeled or recognized by society as important—and how these attributes are labeled (valued, devalued, mixed). But because of the emphasis on a person's active engagement with the environment, the person's psyche is not overdetermined by social forces. Self-representation changes with the available meanings and conditions: "Consciousness of self, like class consciousness or race consciousness . . . is a particular configuration of subjectivity, or subjective limits, produced at the intersection of meaning with experience" (Lauretis, 1986, p. 8). Because individual subjectivity develops through an active engagement with these conditions, it is always in flux: "Consciousness, therefore, is never fixed, never attained for once and for all, because discursive boundaries change with historical condition" (Lauretis, 1986, p. 8).

Sexual preference is an individual process of making meaning within a total context, but the individual may not be aware of the context or its influence. The personal meaning and experience of lesbianism varies and is shaped by (sub)culture, race, religion, and historical context. Thus, for human beings, difference is not only "sexual or racial, economic or (sub)cultural, but all of these together, and often at odds with each other" (Lauretis, 1986, p. 14).

This type of approach allows for sexuality, gender, or any other aspect of internal life to change meaning through alterations in context and personal experience. Women (and men) use the available and constantly changing definitions (as well as their own experiences even if in contradiction to these meanings) to make sense of their lives. Thus, when a woman states that she is a lesbian, it is a personal interpretation of such feelings and concepts as desire, love, sexuality, and relationships and perhaps many more similar issues). The meanings of these feelings and labels originate from the world around her but eventually take on an individual flavor due to the uniqueness of her experiences and way of making meaning.

A focus on the individual's capacity to create meaning allows theorists to conceive of human beings as being able to understand and interpret society as well as to maintain some independence from these external forces and discourses. This helps explain the resistance to socialization that is evident in particular individuals and in the social protest movements that center around issues of personal identity (e.g., gay/lesbian pride, feminism, black consciousness).

In such a dynamic therapy, a therapist would focus on the meaning and function of a person's view of his or her own sexuality and gender. A therapist would attempt to understand how others understand and live their lives "by searching out and analyzing the symbolic forms—words, images, institutions, behaviors—in terms of which, in each place people actually represented themselves to themselves and to one another" (Geertz, 1983, p. 58). However, these structures are not assumed to be universal or fixed but are webs of meaning that evolve and change. Both therapist and client must come to terms with existing meanings and forces that impinge on the past and present. Once those structures are transformed, the client can look more openly to the future and see new possibilities.

This focus on meaning addresses the lack of attention paid in psychoanalytic theory to the subjective experience of women (and men), although awareness or the lack of awareness become issues during the course of therapy. This model diverges from a causal interpretation of psychological development and events to a focus on the human being as a meaning-making entity, interpretive and creative. When the client is seen as having a role in interpreting and constructing the world, agency is restored to the person, even in a world defined and limited by discourse and political and economic forces.

This view of dynamic change also allows for a new focus for psychotherapy, gaining the awareness that results in change. The focus on meaning and individual interpretation alerts therapists to examine the absence of meaning making or consciousness of social influences in an individual client. In some ways this focus on awareness and its absence recalls the concept of repression, but in a new light. The focus in Freud's work was on the repression of traumatic past events. In this view, the focus is on the repression of awareness (of the socially constructed nature of the self). The transformation would be found not only in intellectual understanding but by focusing on what prevents awareness. This means one must address the fear, emotional pain, and sense of inadequacy (to name just a few negative feelings) left from growing up in the world. Through the processing of these feelings about past and present events, a client's view of his/her position in the world shifts, and choice of future actions changes.

Psychological theories are embedded in a nexus of social forces and can be as repressive as any socializing force. The exclusion of the issues mentioned in this chapter from psychoanalytic theories and the predominance of other factors reflect the prejudices of our times and the limits of our field. Until unrecognized aspects of lesbian lives and psychological experience are explored and integrated into future theories, even affirmative theories of homosexuality will be burdened by inherited methodologies and categories from a prejudiced science. These permit the psychology of women to reflect the attitudes of its colonizers and thus remain a dark continent.

Theorists and therapists concerned about the psychology of lesbian experience must direct their attention to their own assumptions, focusing on the intellectual and social repercussions of the particular theories they adopt. The task is to redefine the approach of psychological theory so that it empowers, not colonizes, women.

REFERENCES

Burch, B. (1982). Psychological merger in lesbian couples: A joint ego psychological and systems approach. *Family Therapy, 9*(3), 201–277.

Burch, B. (1985). Another perspective on merger in lesbian relationships. In L. B. Rosewater & L. Walker (Eds.), *A handbook of feminist therapy: Women's issues in psychotherapy* (pp. 100–109). New York: Springer Publishing Co.

Chodorow, N. (1978). *The reproduction of mothering: Psychoanalysis and the sociology of gender.* Berkeley: University of California Press.

Eisenbud, R. J. (1982). Early and later determinants of lesbian choice. *The Psychoanalytic Review, 69*(1), 85–109.

Eisenbud, R. J. (1985). Women feminist patients and a feminist woman analyst. In T. Bernay & D. Cantor (Eds.), *Psychology of today's woman* (pp. 273–290). Hillsdale, NJ: Analytic Press.

Elise, D. (1986). Lesbian couples: The implication of sex differences in separation–individuation. *Psychotherapy, 23*(2), 305–310.

Freire, P. (1970). *Cultural action for freedom.* (Monograph Series No. 1). Cambridge, MA: Harvard Educational Review and Center for the Study of Development and Change.

Freud, S. (1964). Femininity. In J. Strachey (Ed. and Trans), *New introductory lectures on psychoanalysis* (pp. 112–135). New York: Norton. (Original work published 1933).

Geertz, C. (1983). "From the native's point of view": On the nature of anthropological understanding. In C. Geertz (Ed.), *Local knowledge* (pp. 55–93). New York: Basic Books.

Glassgold, J. M. (1990). *The construction of feminist psychoanalysis: Nancy Chodorow's* The reproduction of mothering (Doctoral dissertation, Rutgers–The State University of New Jersey, G.S.A.P.P., 1989). *Dissertation Abstracts International, 51*(2), 984B.

Golden, C. (1987). Diversity and variability in women's sexual identities. In Boston Lesbian Psychologies Collective (Eds.), *Lesbian psychologies: Explorations and challenges* (pp. 18–34). Urbana: University of Illinois Press.

Kinsey, A. C., Pomeroy, W. B., & Martin, C. E. (1948). *Sexual behavior in the human male.* Philadelphia: W. B. Saunders.

Lauretis, T. de (Ed.). (1986). *Feminist studies, critical studies.* Bloomington: Indiana University Press.

Lindenbaum, J. P. (1985). The shattering of illusion: The problem of competition in lesbian relationships. *Feminist Studies, 11*(1), 85–103.

Loewenstein, S. F. (1984/85). On the diversity of love object orientations among women. *Journal of Social Work and Human Sexuality, 3*(2/3), 7–24.

McDougall, J. (1970). Homosexuality in women. In J. Chasseguet-Smirgel (Ed.), *Female sexuality: New psychoanalytic perspectives* (pp. 171–212). Ann Arbor: University of Michigan Press.

McDougall, J. (1980). *Plea for a measure of abnormality.* New York: International Universities Press.

Pearlman, S. F. (1987). The saga of continuing clash in the lesbian community, or will an army of ex-lovers fail? In Boston Lesbian Psychologies Collective (Eds.), *Lesbian psychologies: Explorations and challenges* (pp. 313–326). Urbana: University of Illinois Press.

Rich, A. (1979). *On lies, secrets, and silence.* New York: Norton.

Siegel, E. E. (1988). *Female homosexuality: Choice without volition.* Hillsdale, NJ: Analytic Press.

Socarides, C. (1988). *The preoedipal origin and psychoanalytic therapy of sexual perversions.* Madison, WI: International Universities Press.

Starzecpyzel, E. (1987). The Persephone complex. In Boston Lesbian Psychologies Collective (Eds.), *Lesbian psychologies: Explorations and challenges* (pp. 261–282). Urbana: University of Illinois Press.

Part III
Research

INTRODUCTION: NEW DIRECTIONS IN
FEMINIST RESEARCH

In addition to their many contributions to theory and practice, feminist psychologists have made innumerable contributions to psychological research. From critiques of the scientific method, to the development of qualitative methodologies, to the pioneering of new topics, feminist researchers have suggested new directions in every area of the discipline. Perhaps the most progress has been made in social psychology, the area in which most of our authors work.

The first two chapters focus on the effects of institutionalized sexism. Mykol Hamilton and her colleagues examined the possible bias against women defendants when jury instructions are worded in the masculine generic. What happens, they wondered, when the jury is instructed to consider whether "he [the female defendant] has a right to stand his ground." This is only one of a series of Hamilton's studies on the psychological effects of language use: her research is adding up to an important body of work as she argues powerfully for the use of inclusive language.

Eugenia Proctor Gerdes and her students examined bias in hiring decisions, using a standard social psychology paradigm. Subjects were asked to imagine that they were personnel officers and to rate the qualifications of applicants after reading their résumés. The results of this study strongly support the continued need for affirmative action plans.

The next two chapters consider reactions to the victimization of women. Debra and John Hull and their students, motivated by the

165

high frequency of date rape on college campuses, examined college students' perceptions of how they could avoid this experience. The subjects read and completed a story about a hypothetical date in which the man began to abuse the woman. The authors found a number of interesting differences in the ways their female and male subjects perceived and reacted to the situation. They end with some practical suggestions on how to avoid date rape.

One of the biggest controversies in the feminist community in recent years has been the question of how to fight pornography. Everyone agrees that pornography contributes to the degradation and victimization of women, but not everyone agrees that legislative action to control it is appropriate. Gloria Cowan and Geraldine Stahly examine several classes of variables that might predict attitudes toward pornography control. They studied personal values, experiences with victimization, attitudes toward pornography, and attitudes toward censorship. The results were analyzed in light of Gilligan's theory of divergent models of moral reasoning.

The last three chapters in this section are concerned with gender-role socialization and stereotyping. Karen Keljo Tracy examined the similarities and differences in middle-aged, highly educated men's and women's reactions to a stimulus ad in the personals columns of the newspapers. The wording of the ad was the same except that one version described a female and the other a male heterosexual "attractive professional." The results are examined in light of social psychological theories of courtship initiation.

Beverly Ayers-Nachamkin examined the effects of gender-role orientation on causal attributions for success and failure. Apparently, gender-role socialization remains strong; Ayers-Nachamkin found that in making attributions about their behavior women, unlike men, must decide which self to serve—the feminine or the competent.

Gender-role stereotyping also remains strong. Michele Larrow and Morton Weiner found that their subjects discriminated easily among the roles of men and women. Societal changes were, however, reflected in the fact that there was more variation among the roles for women and that extreme masculine traits are no longer seen as desirable in most roles. The authors discuss the need for behavioral measures to track further changes in gender roles.

Our goal in presenting these papers was to encourage readers to wonder about other lines of research in feminist psychology and to investigate further. If we've been successful, you should put down this volume and begin to plan a scholarly inquiry of your own. Although we've come a long way in our understanding of the psychology of women and gender, much remains to be done. All of our talents and energy are needed.

■ 14
Jury Instructions Worded in the Masculine Generic: Can a Woman Claim Self-Defense When "He" Is Threatened?

Mykol C. Hamilton,
Barbara Hunter, and
Shannon Stuart-Smith

Masculine generic terms, or the use of such words as "man" and "he" to refer to both sexes, have come under fire for their inherent male bias. Psychologists, linguists, and sociologists have gathered empirical evidence indicting masculine generics; lawyers, editors, and others have put forward cogent arguments against the use of masculine generics in their respective fields. The predominant theme has been that masculine generics exclude women, promoting an androcentric point of view and ignoring women individually and collectively.

The empirical evidence for cognitive exclusion of women is strong. Masculine generics lead to male-biased mental imagery in both the communicator (Hamilton, 1988b) and the audience (Hamilton & Henley, 1982; Martyna, 1978, Experiments 1 & 2). People who are asked to create or select drawings to illustrate titles or stories written in the masculine generic (e.g., "Urban Man") tend to produce exclusively male drawings (Harrison &

Passero, 1975; Schneider & Hacker, 1973). Several studies have found that subjects are likely to believe a woman does not "fit" in a sentence worded in the masculine generic (Martyna, 1978, Experiments 3 & 4; MacKay & Fulkerson, 1979; Silveira, 1980).

The complaints go even deeper than cognitive exclusion, and research has also demonstrated behavioral implications. For example, job advertisements worded in the masculine generic have a negative effect on women's job interest (Bem & Bem, 1973; Stericker, 1981), and a study by Henley, Gruber, and Lerner (1984) indicates that alternatives to the masculine generic may positively affect the self-esteem of young girls. Hamilton (1988a) found that use of another male-biased term ("homosexual") in media reports leads some people to believe that lesbian sexual behaviors are as likely to put one at risk for contracting AIDS as are heterosexual or gay male sexual behaviors. Another study (Hamilton, 1989) showed that a proposed (and now adopted) nonsexist version of Maine's constitution affected young women's beliefs, attitudes, and self-assessments positively, when compared with the original male-biased version.

A chief complaint of legal scholars from the United States, Great Britain, Australia, and Canada has been that statutes worded in the masculine generic are subject to extremely inconsistent interpretation. ("Conveyancer's notebook," 1985; Cox & Ray, 1986). For example, despite the fact that sections (rules) guiding interpretation state that words such as *man* and *he* should always be seen as including women as well as men, statutes written in the masculine generic have been used to exclude women from male-dominated professions. For example, in an 1875 case, Lavinia Goodell was denied admission to the bar because the statute regulating bar admission referred to attorneys as "he." Her petition to the court asserted that the statute should be interpreted in accordance with the earlier section stating that "every word importing the masculine gender only may extend and be applied to females as well as to males" (cited in Cox & Ray, 1986, p. 23). The court denied her petition, asserting that "the language of the statute, of itself, confessedly applied to males only" (p. 23). Several writers (Baron, 1986; "Conveyancer's notebook," 1985; Kanowitz, 1973; Ritchie, 1975; Scott, 1985) have noted that the selective application of rules governing linguistic interpretation is still quite common. As Scott (1985) states:

> Where a statute imposed duties or penalties on persons, where the masculine form was used it was asserted that women were included. . . . Yet where a statute imposed privileges or benefits upon persons, the opposite was the case: courts held that women were not intended to be included within the terms of the legislation. . . . To deprive women of rights, privileges, or benefits, the judiciary manipulated the law. (p. 164)

Selective interpretation has had, then, concrete negative effects on women's lives.

Recently, the possible impact of masculine generics in another legal context has been spotlighted. Attorney Elizabeth Schneider successfully argued to the Supreme Court of the state of Washington (*Washington, State of, v. Yvonne Wanrow*, 1977) that the jury in a 1973 murder case may have been unable to consider adequately the female defendant's plea of self-defense, due in part to the masculine generic wording of the judge's instructions concerning the self-defense decision. The jury was instructed, for example, to consider whether "he [the person who is claiming self-defense] has a right to stand his ground," and Schneider claimed that such wording may have prevented the jury from putting themselves in defendant Yvonne Wanrow's shoes, assessing risk of death or bodily harm from *her* personal point of view.

Schneider's claim, while intuitively plausible, could be only speculative. The present study is a direct laboratory test of the hypothesis that a decision about the reasonableness of a woman's self-defense claim is affected by the pronouns used in jury instructions. We tested the hypothesis by giving college students the facts of the Wanrow case in writing, then asking them to read the original (masculine pronouns) or modified (non-male-biased pronouns) jury instructions concerning the issue of self-defense, and finally soliciting their opinions about whether Ms. Wanrow had acted in self-defense, what crime she had committed, and what her punishment should be.[1]

METHOD

Subjects

Seventy-two introductory psychology students from the University of Kentucky participated in the experiment for course credit; 37 were males, 33 were females, and 2 subjects did not indicate their sex. Ages ranged from 17 to 27 years of age, with a mean age of 19.35. Subjects were approximately evenly distributed by sex across the three conditions.

Procedure

Subjects were told they were participating in a study on jury decision making and that they were to imagine that they were members of an actual jury while completing the experimental tasks. They were given a brief written description of the facts of the Wanrow case, which they read silently as the female experimenter read it aloud to them; then they spent 4 minutes studying the description individually. The case involved a confrontation between Ms. Wanrow and Mr. Wesler, a man she suspected had tried to molest her young son. Under a rather ambiguous set of circumstances,[2] she ultimately shot Mr. Wesler at close range, killing him. The defense claimed Wanrow shot Wesler in self-defense. There is considerable question as to whether this claim was warranted, and the written description given to subjects reflected the ambiguity of the facts. For example, subjects were told that there were other people nearby when the shooting took place, implying that Ms. Wanrow should perhaps have solicited aid rather than shooting Wesler. On the other hand, subjects learned that Ms. Wanrow was rather small, had a broken leg, and was using a crutch, all of which could have increased her fear of bodily harm from a threatening individual.

After the 4 minutes, the descriptions were collected and subjects were given a written transcript of the actual jury instructions defining self-defense. They were told to read the instructions carefully to themselves twice. One-third of the subjects received jury instructions worded in the original masculine generic, one-third read instructions using "he or she" constructions in place of the "he" constructions, and one-third read instructions containing "she" constructions throughout. Below is a transcript of the jury instructions in their original form (boldface ours; not presented in boldface to subjects:

> When there is no reasonable ground for the person attacked to believe that **his** person is in imminent danger of death or great bodily harm, and it appears to **him** that only an ordinary battery is intended and is all that **he** has reasonable grounds to fear from **his** assailant, **he** has a right to stand **his** ground and repel such an assault. But **he** has *no right* to repel a threatened assault by the use of bare hands or a deadly weapon, unless **he** believes, and has reasonable grounds to believe, that **he** is in imminent danger of death or great bodily harm.

Subjects were next asked to respond to opinion questions concerning the case. The first question was "Do you think the defendant acted in self-defense?" Subjects marked "yes" or "no." We hypothesized that subjects who read the original "he" version would be less likely to believe Wanrow had acted in self-defense than would subjects in the other two groups. The use of two different non-male-biased versions was exploratory.

The second question concerned the severity of the crime: "If the jury decided that the defendant did not act in self-defense, what crime do you think she should be convicted of?" Subjects had four choices, presented in decreasing order of severity: first-degree murder, second-degree murder, manslaughter, and negligent manslaughter. Definitions were given for each of these crimes. Subjects were then asked: "If the defendant is found guilty, what punishment do you think the judge should decide on?" Subjects were to check one of seven recommendations for punishment, ranging from the most severe punishment—the death penalty—to the least severe punishment: less than a year of incarceration. On the last page of the questionnaire, subjects were asked to indicate their age, sex, and any guesses they might have as to the hypotheses of the experiment.

Hypotheses

The central hypothesis was that subjects in the "he" condition, because of their relative inability to take the defendant's point of view, would be less likely to believe Wanrow had acted in self-defense than would subjects in either of the other two conditions. We also hypothesized that those in the "he" condition would attribute a worse crime to Wanrow (when asked to assume her guilt) than would subjects in the other two conditions and would recommend harsher punishment. Our reasoning here was that because subjects in the nonsexist-language conditions would more likely believe Wanrow had acted in self-defense (first hypothesis), they would have difficulty assuming she was guilty and would therefore be more lenient in ascribing a crime and recommending punishment.

We also hypothesized some sex-related differences. Calhoun, Selby, and Warring (1976) found that women tend to identify with rape victims more than men do, and research by Towson and Zanna (1983) demonstrated that women make more lenient legal judgments than do men concerning retaliation of a rape by the victim or her fiancé, as well as viewing a retaliatory act as more justified. Though Wanrow was not a victim of sexual assault nor the fiancée of a victim, she believed her son had narrowly missed being sexually assaulted by Wesler; thus, her point of view may have been analogous to that of an assault victim's fiancé. We hypothesized that female subjects in our study might identify with Wanrow more than would male subjects and thus might be more likely to believe she had acted in self-defense and make more lenient judgments concerning punishment and the crime committed.

RESULTS

None of the subjects' guesses about the hypotheses came near the truth. The few who ventured a guess believed we were studying moral reasoning or attitudes toward crime. Thus, demand characteristics were probably not high.

As predicted, opinion as to whether Yvonne Wanrow had acted in self-defense differed significantly depending on pronoun condition, $\chi^2(2) = 10.24$, $p < .01$. (See Table 14.1 for frequencies of "yes" and "no" responses on the self-defense question.) Further, in a series of pairwise planned comparisons, we found the following. Subjects in the "he" condition were significantly less likely than subjects in the "he or she" condition

TABLE 14.1 Number of "Yes" and "No" Responses to the Self-defense Question, Broken Down by Pronoun Condition

Response	Pronoun Condition		
	He	He or She	She
Yes	5	16	11
No	19	8	13
Total	24	24	24

to believe Wanrow had acted in self-defense (5 out of 24 vs. 16 out of 24, respectively), $\chi^2(1) = 10.24$, $p < .005$. More subjects marked "yes" for self-defense in the "she" condition (11 of 24) than in the "he" condition (5 of 24), though this difference did not reach significance, $\chi^2(1) = 3.38$, $p < .06$. There was no significant difference between the two non-male-biased conditions (16/24 vs. 11/24 "yes" responses).

The second hypothesis concerning self-defense, that more female than male subjects would believe Wanrow had acted in self-defense, was also tested by chi square. Results of this test were not significant. (See Table 14.2.)

Next we analyzed subjects' ratings of the severity of the crime (Crime Severity), using a two-way analysis of variance with pronoun condition and subject sex as independent variables (see Table 14.3). The predicted main effect for pronoun condition was not significant. There was, however, a significant effect for subject sex in the predicted direction, with male subjects viewing the crime as more severe than did female subjects ($MM = 2.82$ vs. $FM = 3.31$, respectively, on the 4-point scale; smaller numbers indicate a more serious crime), $F(1, 68) = 4.26$, $p < .02$. The interaction effect was not significant, as expected.

Next we looked at what punishment subjects felt the defendant should receive (Punishment Severity), assuming the jury found her guilty. A two-way analysis of variance revealed that neither pronoun condition nor sub-

TABLE 14.2 Number of "Yes" and "No" Responses to the Self-defense Question, Broken Down by Subject Sex

Response	Subject Sex	
	Male	Female
Yes	15	16
No	22	17
Total	37	33

TABLE 14.3 Number of Male and Female Subjects Choosing Each Crime Severity Rating

	Pronoun Condition					
	He		He/She		He	
Crime Severity	Males	Females	Males	Females	Males	Females
First-degree murder	2	0	1	0	3	0
Second-degree murder	0	0	0	3	2	0
Manslaughter	8	7	7	4	7	6
Negligent manslaughter	2	5	3	4	2	4

ject sex had a significant effect on punishment. An interaction effect had not been predicted and was not found.

DISCUSSION

Our central hypothesis was confirmed: for our "jurors," masculine generic wording of jury instructions concerning self-defense gave Yvonne Wanrow less chance of winning her claim of self-defense than did the two non-male-biased versions, with significance obtained for one non-male-biased pronoun and a trend toward significance for the other. We had not hypothesized a difference between the effects of the two non-male-biased pronouns, "he or she" and "she." As it turned out, only "he or she" produced a significantly different result from "he" on Self-defense, with the "she" condition producing a nearly significant difference. Nevertheless, because the two non-male-biased pronouns did not behave significantly differently from each other, it seems likely that the two non-male-biased pronouns in fact function in the same way. We believe that our results indicate that such an effect could have been operating in the actual trial, as Elizabeth Schneider argued in the appeal, and could operate in other legal situations where a woman's behavior is measured against a male standard.

The effect of pronoun was not strong enough to cause a difference in subjects' responses about the severity of Wanrow's possible crime or their recommendations for her punishment. We had hypothesized that if the male pronoun led to fewer decisions of self-defense, this would in turn cause subjects in the male pronoun condition to give more severe ratings on Crime Severity and on Punishment Severity. A look at the frequencies of the four possible responses to the crime question reveals that the nonsignificant pronoun effect could be due to the lack of variation in responses. Eighty-four percent of the respondents believed the crime Wanrow committed, assuming she was found guilty, was either manslaughter or negligent manslaughter. Perhaps the details given about the possible crime were sufficiently clear that they overrode any possible pronoun effect. There was considerably more variation on the punishment question, so a similar explanation for the nonsignificant pronoun effect is not suggested.

We had hypothesized a main effect of subject sex on Self-defense, Crime Severity, and Punishment Severity, believing that female subjects would be more lenient toward Wanrow in each decision than would male subjects. The hypothesis was confirmed for Crime Severity but not for Punishment Severity or Self-defense. The finding for Crime Severity corroborates Towson and Zanna's (1983) finding that female subjects are more lenient in their legal judgments than are male subjects about someone who retaliates against her own sexual assault or that of someone close to her; the findings for Punishment Severity and Self-defense do not.

CONCLUSIONS

The results of the present study indicate that the most important decision before the jury in many murder trials, the decision concerning self-defense, might potentially be affected by the pronoun used in jury instructions. In exploring this particular use of the masculine generic, however, we looked at only one very specific instance in which masculine pronouns are used in a legal setting. There are many other areas in which male-biased language is used in the law, and it seems reasonable to speculate that there would be similarly serious effects in such instances. For example, in deciding a standard of conduct in negligence, jurors have traditionally been instructed to apply the "reasonable man" standard—would the reasonable man have behaved as the defendant did under like circumstances? The reasonable man has been defined as someone of reasonable prudence, someone who would exercise reasonable caution; one definition describes him as follows: "He is an ideal, a standard . . . one who never drives his ball until those in front of him have definitely vacated the putting-green which is his own objective; who never from one year's end to another makes an excessive demand upon his wife, his neighbors, his servants" (Herbert, cited in Keeton, Dobbs-Keeton, & Owen, 1984, p. 174-175). In recent years the standard applied is often that of the "reasonable person," but this has not completely replaced the "reasonable man" standard. The results of the present study, in combination with all else we now know about the masculine generic noun and pronoun, tell us that the days of the reasonable-man standard and of other uses of a "generic" masculine should be over. As any number of studies (Hamilton & Henley, 1982; Martyna, 1978) have shown, using "he" and "man" leads people to think about men rather than about both women and men (or some average of the two); and as we have seen in the present study, because of physical differences between women and men, it is not always sensible to ask people to judge the reasonableness of a woman's behavior on the basis of what a man would have done.

Further studies could be done to determine, one by one, the potential effects of using the words *man* and *he* and their variants in different legal settings. But the authors would argue that this should not be necessary. The verdict is in.

NOTES

1. Subjects also rated Wanrow on a series of adjective traits in an exploratory analysis. No significant differences were found for condition or sex of subject; therefore, this measure is not discussed here.

2. The description given to subjects was a shortened version of the case summary in *Criminal law and its processes: Cases and materials* (Kadish, Schulhofer, & Paulsen, 1983). Facts presented were faithful to the summary, with the exception that, in order to indicate Wanrow's feeling of being threatened in relatively few words, we stated that Wesler's hand was raised over his head as he approached her.

REFERENCES

Baron, D. (1986). *Grammar and gender*. New Haven, CT: Yale University Press.

Bem, S. L., & Bem, D. J. (1973). Does sex-biased job advertising "aid and abet" sex discrimination? *Journal of Applied Social Psychology, 3*(1), 6–18.

Calhoun, L. G., Selby, J. W., & Warring, L. J. (1976). Social perception of the victim's causal role in rape: An exploratory examination of four factors. *Human Relations, 29,* 517–526.

Conveyancer's notebook. (1985, May–June). *The Conveyancer and Property Lawyer*, pp. 157–236.

Cox, B. J., & Ray, M. B. (1986, June). Avoiding gender-biased language in legal writing. *Wisconsin Bar Bulletin*, pp. 23–25.

Hamilton, M. C. (1988a). Masculine generic terms and misperception of AIDS risk. *Journal of Applied Social Psychology, 18,* 1222–1240.

Hamilton, M. C. (1988b). Using masculine generics: Does generic "he" increase male bias in the user's imagery? *Sex Roles, 19,* 785–799.

Hamilton, M. C. (1989, March). *Does male-biased language in a state constitution really hurt?* Paper presented at the meeting of the Association for Women in Psychology, Newport, RI.

Hamilton, M. C., & Henley, N. M. (1982, April). *Detrimental consequences of generic masculine usage.* Paper presented at the meeting of the Western Psychological Association, Sacramento, CA.

Harrison, L., & Passero, R. N. (1975). Sexism in the language of elementary school textbooks. *Science and Children, 12*(4), 22–25.

Henley, N. M., Gruber, B., & Lerner, L. (1984, October). *Effects of sex-biased language on attitudes and self-esteem.* Paper presented at the Southern California Language and Gender Interest Group, Los Angeles, CA.

Keeton, W. P., Dobbs-Keeton, R. E., & Owen, D. G. (1984). *Presser and Keeton on the law of torts.* St. Paul, MN: West.

Kadish, S. H., Schulhofer, S. J., & Paulsen, M. G. (1983). *Criminal law and its processes: Cases and materials* (4th ed.). Boston: Little, Brown.

Kanowitz, L. (1973). *Sex roles in law and society.* Albuquerque: University of New Mexico Press.

MacKay, D. G., & Fulkerson, D. C. (1979). On the comprehension and production of pronouns. *Journal of Verbal Learning and Verbal Behavior, 18,* 661–673.

Martyna, W. (1978). Using and understanding the generic masculine: A social psychological approach to language and the sexes. *Dissertation Abstracts International, 39,* 3050B.

Prosser, W. L., Wade, J. W., & Schwartz, V. E. (1982). *Torts: Cases and materials* (7th ed.). Mineola, NY: Foundation Press.

Ritchie, M. (1975). Alice through the statutes. *McGill Law Journal, 21,* 685–707.

Schneider, J., & Hacker, S. (1973). Sex role imagery and the use of the generic "man" in introductory texts. *American Sociologist, 8,* 12–18.

Scott, J. A. (1985). Sexism in legal language. *Australian Law Journal, 59,* 163–173.

Silveira, J. (1980). Generic masculine words and thinking. In C. Kramarae (Ed.), *The voices and words of women and men* (pp. 165–178). Oxford: Pergamon Press.

Stericker, A. (1981). Does this "he or she" business really make a difference? The effect of masculine pronouns as generics on job attitudes. *Sex Roles, 7,* 637–641.

Towson, S. M. J., & Zanna, M. P. (1983). Retaliation against sexual assault: Self-defense or public duty? *Psychology of Women Quarterly, 8,* 89–99.

Washington, State of, v. Yvonne Wanrow. (1977). Supreme Court of Washington (559 Pacific Report, 2d series), 548–559.

■ 15
White Males' Bias Against Black Female Job Applicants

Eugenia Proctor Gerdes,
Rebecca S. Miner,
Marguerite A. Maynard Norchi,
Mary C. Dominguez Ranallo,
and Rosa Joshi

The labor market of the United States is still highly segregated by race and sex. For example, in 1982 the occupational category "managers and administrators" accounted for the following percentages of workers: 15.6% of white males, 8.0% of white females, 7.4% of nonwhite males, and 3.9% of nonwhite females (U. S. Department of Labor, 1983). Other high-status professions are similarly distributed. Underrepresentation of women in higher-status, traditionally male occupations is partly due to sex-role socialization, which reduces the number of women who are willing and able to assume these positions; but it is also due to discrimination, which limits the opportunities of able women who aspire to those positions (Terborg, 1977). Likewise, racial differences in occupational distribution do not derive solely from differences in preparation (Jones, 1986). Discrimination based on sex has been more thoroughly researched than has racial discrimination, but both appear to be based on stereotypical expectations (Dovidio & Gaertner, 1986).

179

To eliminate the possibility of real differences in qualifications, most psychological studies of discrimination present each subject with one of several hypothetical candidates, who differ only on the characteristics being tested. In such studies, equally qualified women often receive lower ratings than do male candidates for positions that are high-status or traditionally male and when some ambiguity remains about the fit of applicant qualifications with job requirements (Gerdes & Garber, 1983; Gerdes & Kelman, 1981; Heilman, 1984; Rosen & Jerdee, 1974). Much less is known about conditions fostering racial bias in hiring decisions. In one of the few studies that addresses hiring for a high-status, traditionally white occupation, Mc-Conahay (1983) manipulated the context in which white college students evaluated an average male candidate (white or black) for a management trainee program. Ambivalent subjects rated the black candidate lower than the white one in the negative (ambiguous) context that prevented comparison with other candidates and minimized the obtrusiveness of race; in the positive context, they rated the black candidate better than the white one.

Further information about racial bias in the hiring process is needed, especially given evidence that subtle racial bias still abounds in other decisions (Crosby, Bromley, & Saxe, 1980). Information about treatment of black women is particularly lacking. Are black women doubly disadvantaged, as suggested by Almquist (1979), or do the two stereotypes cancel each other out, as suggested by Epstein (1973)? The experiments presented here were designed to assess the interaction of candidate sex and race in hiring decisions. Both male and female evaluators were used because of the possibility of same-sex favoritism (Gerdes & Kelman, 1981). Evaluations of candidates for high-status, traditionally white-male jobs were compared to evaluations for jobs providing a clearer fit of candidate qualifications to job requirements.

METHOD

Subjects

The evaluators were white college students, volunteers from an introductory psychology course (32 females and 32 males) in Study 1 and second-semester senior volunteers (48 females and 48 males) in Study 2. Subjects were randomly assigned to conditions of job, candidate sex, and candidate race.

Procedure

In both studies, subjects read descriptions of one job and of one job applicant and then responded with a dichotomous hiring decision, an overall rating of qualifications for the job, more specific candidate evaluations, and

ratings of credibility and clarity of the experimental materials. Instructions
to the subjects emphasized the latter as the main purpose of the study; the
obtrusiveness of the race and sex manipulations was further reduced by indicating that their candidate was one of many. Actually, identical candidates
differed only on sex and race. Sex was manipulated by the first name of the
candidate, and race was manipulated by making the black candidate a member of a society for black students, in Study 1, or for black engineers, in
Study 2.

In Study 1, subjects read about one of two jobs, recreation manager or
recreation aide at a large resort. Each job was presented with a brief résumé of an appropriate candidate with average qualifications, college or
high school graduates, respectively. In Study 2, the same applicant was used
for both jobs, a technical engineering job and a position with the same technical responsibilities plus managerial responsibilities. Although the applicant had a detailed résumé, with a master's degree in engineering and
above-average grades, plus good recommendations, there was no evidence
of managerial experience (see Gerdes & Garber, 1983, for a description of
similar materials).

RESULTS

Study 1

In Study 1, candidates usually were accepted in the dichotomous hiring decision, with the striking exception of male subjects' rejection of the black
females (see Table 15.1). Male subjects' decisions concerning the black female candidates differed significantly from all other decisions, except those
concerning white females, at $p < .025$ by Fisher's exact test. In contrast, as
shown in the marginal three-way interaction in Table 15.2 ($F(1, 48) = 2.67$,
$p < .11$), the average "how qualified" rating given to black females by male
subjects was comparable to their rating of white females and white males.
Female subjects differentiated more, but the black female candidates received the most favorable ratings; the white females, the least favorable.

TABLE 15.1 Study 1: Dichotomous Hiring Decisions

	Candidate							
	White Female		White Male		Black Female		Black Male	
Subject Sex	Hire	No	Hire	No	Hire	No	Hire	No
Female	6	2	7	1	7	1	7	1
Male	5	3	7	1	2	6	8	0

TABLE 15.2 Study 1: Rating of How Qualified Candidate Is For Job on Scale from 1 (Very Unqualified) to 7 (Very Qualified)

	Candidate			
	White		Black	
Subject Sex	Female	Male	Female	Male
Female	4.13	5.13	5.38	4.63
Male	4.88	5.00	4.75	5.13

Tests of simple effects yielded a significant difference only for the race effect for female candidates evaluated by female subjects, $F(1, 48) = 4.17$, $p < .05$. The only other effect in this interaction that approached significance was the sex difference for white candidates evaluated by female subjects, $F(1, 48) = 2.67$, $p < .11$.

Candidate race did not interact with status of the job, but there was a significant three-way interaction on the candidate's qualifications involving job status, candidate sex, and subject sex, $F(1, 48) = 6.00$, $p < .02$. As can be seen in Table 15.3, each subject sex favored its own sex candidate in ratings for the high-status (managerial) job. Differences in ratings for the high and low status jobs were most pronounced for female subjects, who tended to prefer male candidates for the low-status job.

Study 2

In Study 2, candidates in all conditions usually were accepted on the dichotomous hiring decision; no combination of subject sex, candidate sex, and candidate race differed significantly from any other by chi-square tests (see Table 15.4). However, the three-way interaction, $F(1, 80) = 4.05$, $p < 0.5$, shown in Table 15.5 indicated downgrading of the black female candidate's overall potential for the job by male subjects. Tests of simple effects showed the only significant race effect to be male subjects rating black

TABLE 15.3 Study 1: Rating of How Qualified Candidate Is for High and Low Status Jobs on Scale from 1 (Very Unqualified) to 7 (Very Qualified)

	High-Status Job		Low-Status Job	
Subject Sex	Female Candidate	Male Candidate	Female Candidate	Male Candidate
Female	5.25	4.25	4.25	5.50
Male	4.63	5.25	5.00	4.88

TABLE 15.4   Study 2: Dichotomous Hiring Decisions

	Candidate							
	White Female		White Male		Black Female		Black Male	
Subject Sex	Hire	No	Hire	No	Hire	No	Hire	No
Female	11	1	11	1	11	1	11	1
Male	10	2	10	2	8	4	11	1

female candidates lower than white female candidates, $F(1, 48) = 4.05$, $p < .05$; the only significant candidate sex effect was male subjects rating black female candidates lower than black male candidates, $F(1, 48) = 6.69$, $p < .02$; and the only significant subject sex effect was male subjects rating black female candidates lower than female subjects rated black female candidates, $F(1, 48) = 10.00$, $p < .002$. Thus, the three-way interaction appears to have arisen primarily from the low rating given to black female applicants by male subjects. The sex difference in subjects' rating of the black female applicant also accounted for the marginal main effect for subject sex on the overall rating (see Table 15.6).

No other effects on the overall rating were significant, but there were effects on several specific evaluations that were significant or approached conventional levels of significance (see Table 15.6). On potential for technical aspects of the job, male subjects rated the female candidate lower than the male candidate and lower than both male and female candidates as rated by female subjects. The marginal interaction of subject sex and job resulted from women giving slightly higher ratings for technical aspects than did men for the technical engineering job but equivalent technical ratings for the technical-managerial job. The interaction of candidate and subject sex on administrative aspects paralleled that on technical aspects, with male subjects downgrading the potential of female candidates. The marginal interaction of candidate sex and job on administrative aspects resulted from

TABLE 15.5   Study 2: Overall Rating of Candidate's Potential for Job on Scale from 1 (Very Unfavorable) to 6 (Extremely Favorable)

	Candidate			
	White		Black	
Subject Sex	Female	Male	Female	Male
Female	4.83	5.08	5.25	5.08
Male	4.92	4.92	4.33	5.08

TABLE 15.6 Study 2: Analysis of Variance of Overall and Specific Ratings of Candidates

					Human	Long	Advance
Source	df	Overall	Technical	Administrative	Relations	Service	ment
Subject sex (SS)	1	2.98*	1.11	.25	4.57**	8.42***	.01
Candidate race (CR)	1	.00	.67	.01	1.14	.23	.68
Candidate sex (CS)	1	2.07	2.32	.09	2.24	4.74**	.13
Job (J)	1	.08	.01	.80	1.14	.94	.13
SS × CR	1	2.07	.67	.48	1.14	2.11	.01
SS × CS	1	1.32	3.96**	4.35**	3.70*	1.46	3.13*
SS × J	1	.00	3.08*	.09	.41	2.11	.01
CR × CS	1	.33	.12	.01	.73	7.08***	1.13
CR × J	1	.33	2.32	.25	.18	2.11	1.13
CS × J	1	.74	.34	3.56*	2.92*	.53	.35
SS × CR × CS	1	4.05**	.12	.09	.73	7.08***	2.35
SS × CR × J	1	.74	.01	.09	.00	.94	2.35
SS × CS × J	1	.33	.34	.09	2.92*	2.89*	1.69
CR × CS × J	1	1.32	.34	.25	.05	.06	.13
SS × CR × CS × J	1	2.07	1.11	.48	.41	.06	.35
Error	80						

*$p < .10$.
**$p < .05$.
***$p < .01$.

F ratios (column group header)

higher ratings for males for the technical job but equivalent ratings for female candidates for the two jobs. The two marginal two-way interactions on human relations aspects were qualified by the marginal three-way interaction; male and female subjects gave similar ratings to the male candidate, but male subjects rated female candidates low for both jobs, and female subjects rated female candidates low for the purely technical job but high for the technical-managerial job. Like the other interactions of subject sex and candidate sex, the marginal interaction on potential for advancement showed lower ratings of female candidates by male subjects.

The only effects on these specific evaluations involving candidate race occurred on potential for long service to the company. On that measure, the marginal three-way interaction of subject sex, candidate sex, and job resulted from male subjects rating the female candidates low for both jobs, whereas female subjects rated the female candidates lower than the male candidates only for the purely technical job. More important, the three-way interaction of subject sex, candidate sex, and candidate race paralleled the three-way interaction on the overall rating (see Table 15.7). The low rating by male subjects of the black female candidate's potential for long service

TABLE 15.7 Study 2: Rating of Candidate's Potential for Long Service on Scale from 1 (Extremely Unfavorable) to 6 (Extremely Favorable)

	Candidate			
	White		Black	
Subject Sex	Female	Male	Female	Male
Female	4.83	5.00	5.00	5.17
Male	4.83	4.50	3.58	5.08

fell between the "slightly unfavorable" and "slightly favorable" labels on the 6-point scale. Because of the similarity of the two interactions, an analysis of covariance was performed with the overall rating as the dependent variable and potential for long service as the covariate. The regression of the overall rating on potential for long service was highly significant, $F(1, 79) = 8.79$, $p < .001$. Statistically controlling for this regression eliminated the significant interaction on the overall rating, $F(1, 79) = 1.51$.

DISCUSSION

These two studies show white males' bias against black female job applicants in different ways, which may be due to the differences in experimental materials and subjects. In Study 2, white male subjects clearly considered black females as less suitable for the job than other candidates, whom they rated highly (about 5 on a 6-point scale). Although male subjects nevertheless reported willingness to hire black females for these engineering jobs, we must assume that comparable candidates from the other groups would be preferred. Real-world decisions require ranking candidates, so even a small bias can have a large effect on an applicant's chances. In Study 1, male subjects rated all types of candidates as somewhat "qualified" (about 5 on a 7-point scale); yet given the same moderate level of perceived qualifications, black women apparently were perceived as greater risks to hire. White female subjects in both studies saw black women more favorably—in fact, in Study 1, more favorably than they saw white women.

Although it was an important factor in previous studies of sex bias (Gerdes & Garber, 1983), type of job apparently did not affect the racial aspects of differential evaluations of black women. Same-sex favoritism, regardless of race, did appear to be especially associated with the jobs that included managerial duties. Same-sex favoritism was shown for the managerial job both on the qualifications rating in Study 1 and on evaluations of human relations potential in Study 2. Although management is a traditionally male profession, some of the requisite human relations skills coincide with interpersonal traits that are stereotypically feminine. The value of such characteristics might have been more salient for female subjects, whereas male subjects might have focused more on the requisite agentic skills. Where female subjects evaluated male and female candidates for the engineering jobs equivalently but male subjects favored male candidates (as on potential for long service for the technical managerial job and on technical aspects, administrative aspects, and potential for advancement for both jobs), the explanation might involve women's greater familiarity with diversity among women and consequent lesser reliance on stereotypes (Gerdes & Kelman, 1981).

A similar explanation could extend to white males' particular bias against black female job applicants in this study. White males are least able to individuate, identify with, or understand black women and thus are more likely to resort to stereotypes in judging them (Dovidio & Gaertner, 1986). The overall rating of the candidates' suitability for the engineering jobs apparently was related to judgments about their potential for long service. Although it is impossible to determine whether inferences about length of service preceded or followed the overall evaluation, it is interesting to consider what projected length of service might mean. Male managers in 1976 judged female candidates, whom they presumably perceived as white, to have less potential for long service than did male candidates (Gerdes & Garber, 1983). Because male subjects now seem to limit this concern to black female candidates, it seems unlikely to reflect concern about generically female matters such as childbearing. Potential for long service could instead reflect the extent to which the candidate "belongs" in this organization or how comfortably the candidate would "fit in" from the subject's perspective.

Our white female subjects probably had had more previous interaction with black women, and of course, they do have gender in common with black women, perhaps allowing them to make judgments with less reliance on stereotypes. Furthermore, differences in norms or stereotypes could account for female subjects rating black women higher than white women. For example, our female subjects might have considered black women to be more independent, more self-sufficient, or stronger than white women (Gump, 1980). Landrine (1988) found that the white-woman stereotype is closer than the black-woman stereotype to the "traditional" stereotype of women. Undergraduate women rated the stereotype of black women as more hostile and less competent but also less dependent, passive, and emotional than the stereotype of white women. The extent to which undergraduate men share these differentiated stereotypes is not known.

Regardless of the explanation for differences between white female and white male evaluators, the particular problem of white males' bias against black females requires further study. White men still do most of the hiring for high-status, traditionally male positions. That fact apparently puts women in general and especially black women at a serious disadvantage in the labor force.

REFERENCES

Almquist, E. M. (1979). Black women and the pursuit of equality. In J. Freeman (Ed.), *Women: A feminist perspective* (pp. 430–450). Palo Alto, CA: Mayfield.

Crosby, F., Bromley, S., & Saxe, L. (1980). Recent unobtrusive studies of black and white discrimination and prejudice: A literature review. *Psychological Bulletin, 87,* 546–563.

Dovidio, J. F., & Gaertner, S. L. (Eds.). (1986). *Prejudice, discrimination, and racism.* New York: Academic.

Epstein, C. F. (1973). Positive effects of the multiple negative: Explaining the success of black professional women. *American Journal of Sociology, 78,* 912–935.

Gerdes, E. P., & Garber, D. M. (1983). Sex bias in hiring: Effects of job demands and applicant competence. *Sex Roles, 9,* 307–319.

Gerdes, E. P., & Kelman, J. H. (1981). Sex discrimination: Effects of sex-role incongruence, evaluator sex, and stereotypes. *Basic and Applied Social Psychology, 2,* 219–226.

Gump, J. P. (1980). Reality and myth: Employment and sex role ideology in black women. In J. Sherman & F. L. Denmark (Eds.), *The psychology of women: Directions in research* (pp. 350–380). New York: Psychological Dimensions.

Heiman, M. (1984). Information as a deterrent against sex discrimination: The effects of applicant sex and information type on preliminary employment decisions. *Organizational Behavior and Human Performance, 33,* 174–186.

Jones, J. M. (1986). Racism: A cultural analysis of the problem. In J. F. Dovidio & S. L. Gaertner (Eds.), *Prejudice, discrimination, and racism* (pp. 279–314). New York: Academic.

Landrine, H. (1988). Race × Class stereotypes of women. *Sex Roles, 13,* 65–75.

McConahay, J. B. (1983). Modern racism and modern discrimination: The effects of race, racial attitudes, and context in simulated hiring decisions. *Personality and Social Psychology Bulletin, 9,* 551–558.

Rosen, B., & Jerdee, T. (1974). Effects of applicant's sex and difficulty of the job on evaluations of candidates for managerial positions. *Journal of Applied Psychology, 59,* 511–512.

Terborg, J. R. (1977). Women in management: A research review. *Journal of Applied Psychology, 62,* 647–664.

U. S. Department of Labor, Bureau of Labor Statistics. (1983). *Employment and earnings.* Washington, DC: U. S. Government Printing Office.

■ 16
How to Avoid Date Rape: College Students' Perceptions

Debra B. Hull,
Lisa Forrester,
John H. Hull, and
Marni-Lynne Gaines

All socially active women are at risk for date (or acquaintance) rape, regardless of personality characteristics (Koss, 1985). A relatively larger number of dating partners is the current life factor that contributes most to a woman's risk for date rape. Substance use, frequent exposure to pornography, and hostility toward women are current life factors that best predict the men who perpetrate date rape (Koss, 1987). Not surprisingly, then, college women are at great risk for date rape. In a nationwide sample of college women, Koss (1987) found that since age 14, 15% of the women had been raped, 12% had been victims of attempted rape, 12% had been psychologically coerced into intercourse, and 14% had been forcibly kissed or touched. Eighty-four percent knew the offender, the 57% of the attacks occurred on dates. In another study, Levin-MacCombie and Koss (1986) found that 12.7% of their sample of college women had been raped; an additional 24% were victims of attempted rape. Wilson and Durrenberger (1982) found that 15% of their sample of college women had been raped; an additional 18% were victims of attempted rape. A study of dating problems showed that 36% of the college women surveyed reported that pressure to engage in sexual behavior and sexual misunderstandings were significant dating problems for them (Knox & Wilson, 1983).

Despite increased attention to date rape in scholarly and popular media (e.g., Sweet, 1985), Koss (1985) found that 43% of college women who had had an experience that met the legal definition of rape did not view themselves as rape victims. The incidence of rape among college women, coupled with their hesitancy to see themselves as victims, makes this an important time to focus on effective prevention strategies. Until recently, prevention programs focused mainly on instructing women to identify and avoid presumably high-risk situations (e.g., traveling alone or at night). This approach places the responsibility for behavior control on the victim rather than on the perpetrator of the crime and requires women to limit their freedom to participate in a fully independent life.

Other programs, based on comparisons of attempted and completed rapes, focus on strategies that allow women to escape high-risk situations without being raped. In a study of college student victims and avoiders of acquaintance rape, Levine-MacCombie and Koss (1986) found that a low level of guilt and fear, combined with screaming and running away, was the most effective escape strategy. Crying and reasoning, generally not effective in stranger rape situations, were somewhat effective in avoiding acquaintance rape. The particular characteristics of the date rape situation (some degree of affection between the woman and man and the possibility of future contact) may account for the partial effectiveness of reasoning and crying in avoiding date rape.

The purpose of this chapter is to investigate in detail the expectations, attitudes, anticipated responses, and reactions of college students responding to simulated date rape situations where story details are constant. The ultimate goal is to help women and men understand their own and others' thoughts, feelings, and expectations in a potential date rape situation so that they can formulate effective strategies for avoiding date rape. Specifically, we investigated the following: the responses of women and men who were asked to complete a potential date rape story (Group 1), the understanding shown by women and men of the other sex's feelings in a potential date rape situation (Group 2), the effectiveness of women's anticipated responses when imagining a potential date rape situation happening to them (Group 3), and the responses of men imagining themselves the potential victims in a date rape situation (Group 4).

METHOD

Subjects

Subjects were 190 women and 136 men, 17–22 years old, who were residential students at one of three small liberal arts colleges in the mid-Atlantic region. The subjects volunteered to participate in a study on dating.

Procedure

All students were asked to complete a 260-word story in which two college students are described as being on a date. In the basic version of the story, reproduced below, the male (named Chuck) makes increasingly intimate sexual advances that the female (named Marsha) clearly does not want.

> Marsha, a college student, is out on a date with Chuck, a guy she had met and spoken with on other occasions with friends. He seemed like a nice guy, so when Chuck asked Marsha to go to a party with him at a friend's cottage, she said yes without much hesitation. The party was OK, but Marsha felt a little uncomfortable about the way Chuck was always touching her arm or putting his arm around her waist. Marsha figured that Chuck was just insecure or liked everyone to see that he had a date. In any case, she just quietly pulled away when Chuck got too close. Marsha wasn't really concerned about Chuck's behavior since she had known other guys to do the same thing. The evening progressed, and Chuck got tired of the party. He asked Marsha if she would like to go for a walk around the pond. This sounded like a good idea to Marsha since the cigarette smoke was really starting to bother her. Plus, she really had not got to talk to Chuck alone. They left the cottage and walked toward the pond. Chuck again put his arm around Marsha and pulled her close. She stiffened. Chuck stopped walking and began to kiss Marsha. She really didn't know if she wanted to be kissing this guy, so she tried to pull away and told Chuck to stop. But Chuck held her tight and started kissing her neck. He then put his hand up her sweater. Marsha struggled to get out of his grasp, but Chuck continued.

In one condition (Group 1), 63 women and 39 men were asked to finish the story, telling what happened to Chuck and Marsha. In the second condition, (Group 2), 53 women and 55 men were asked to finish the story, telling what happened to Chuck and Marsha but concentrating especially on what Chuck and Marsha were thinking and feeling. In the third condition (Group 3), 74 women read a modified version of the story. The characters were Chuck and "you." These subjects were asked to finish the story, describing what they thought would happen to them in this situation. In the fourth condition (Group 4), 42 men read another modified version of the story. In this version Marsha became Chuck (the sexual aggressor), and Marsha was replaced with "you." These subjects were asked to finish the story, describing what they thought would happen to them in this situation (i.e., as potential victims of sexual abuse).

After completing the story, subjects were asked for demographic information: sex, age, and year in college. Subjects then read the definitions of sexual abuse used in our state (any kind of unwanted sexual contact other than actual penetration) and of sexual assault (any unwanted sexual contact that includes penetration of any kind). They were asked if they had ever been the victim of sexual abuse or assault, if they knew the offender, their relationship to the offender (if any), and their age when the abuse or assault occurred. The word *rape* was never used. At the end of the procedure, students were given the names and phone numbers of two organizations to contact if they had any questions about sexual abuse or assault: their college counseling center and the community's Sexual Assault Help Center, where contacts could be made anonymously. The college counseling centers and the Help Center were aware that the study was taking place.

All subjects completed their stories in small, mixed-sex, mixed-condition groups, with ample space between subjects. They were instructed to place completed forms in an envelope and to return a blank form if they decided not to participate in the study. One of 327 subjects returned a blank form.

Following collection of the data, stories were coded for outcome (assault, no assault but further abuse, no further abuse, mutually desired intercourse), avoidance strategy used (no avoidance strategy used, screaming, running away, struggling, verbal protest, temporary bodily harm, permanent bodily harm), emotional content (anger, fear, shame, guilt, entitlement), evidence of a continuing relationship (yes or no), and overall story feeling (positive or negative). Interrater agreement of these factors ranged from 90% to 100%.

RESULTS AND DISCUSSION

Results showed that when asked to complete the standard story (Groups 1 and 2), 28 women (24%) and 26 men (28%) imagined that date rape (forced intercourse) was the outcome. This slight sex difference was not statistically significant, $\chi^2(1) = .94$, $p > .05$. An additional 44% of the women and 34% of the men thought the sexual abuse continued but did not end in forced intercourse. Thirty-two percent of the women and 38% of the men thought Marsha got away quickly, without further abuse or that Chuck stopped almost immediately.

Eighty-seven men (93%) and 103 women (89%) thought that Marsha actively resisted Chuck's advances, either physically or verbally. Again, this sex difference was not significant, $\chi^2(1) = .28$, $p > .05$. Physical resistance strategies predominated, both when further abuse/assault occurred and when it did not. Although less frequent in both abuse/assault situations, verbal resistance was more common in the no-abuse/assault than in the abuse/assault endings, $\chi^2(1) = 6.19$, $p < .05$.

Male subjects were more likely than females to offer excuses for Chuck's behavior (he was drunk, couldn't control his natural instincts, or she came on to him) $\chi^2(1) = 4.0$, $p < .05$ (see Appendix, Sample 1). Several men felt that Marsha deserved or wanted sexual intercourse, that despite her verbalizations to the contrary, she wouldn't have gone to the party, gone outside with Chuck, or allowed him to touch her unless she wanted sexual intercourse. These findings are consistent with those of Shotland and Goodstein (1983), who found that a woman is considered more to blame in a rape situation if she resists weakly or after some sexual contact has already occurred. Agreeing to or tolerating some degree of sexual activity is apparently seen by some men as agreeing to or tolerating all sexual activity.

The stories men wrote involved much more violence than the women's stories (she was beaten up, he ripped her clothes off, he stuffed a sock in her mouth, she was killed), $\chi^2(1) = 10.08$, $p < .01$. Indeed, one of the most disturbing results of this study for the researchers was seeing the degree of gratuitously violent imagery in the male story endings (see Appendix, Sample 2).

Significantly more men (18%) than women (4%) thought the relationship between Chuck and Marsha would continue even if forced intercourse occurred, $\chi^2(1) = 6.27$, $p < .05$. Subjects who ended the story with no further abuse thought the relationship between Chuck and Marsha was more likely to continue than did those who ended the story with further abuse or rape, $\chi^2(1) = 6.52$, $p < .05$. In contrast, in their study of actual and attempted rape victims among college students, Wilson and Durrenberger (1982) found that 39% of the rape victims and 12% of the abuse victims later dated their attackers. It may be that our subjects are not realistically anticipating their future behavior with respect to the attacker. Another possibility is that in the past 5 years women have become more confident of their right and ability to reject repeated exposure to abusive men.

In Group 2, the most frequently mentioned emotion for Chuck was anger; for Marsha, fear. Seventeen subjects (16%) thought Chuck was likely to feel angry in the situation, and 23 subjects (21%) thought Marsha would be frightened (see Appendix, Sample 3). There was no significant difference between men and women in their perceptions of the emotions of Chuck and Marsha (for the Anger × Sex comparison, $\chi^2(1) = 1.07$, $p > .05$; for the Fear × Sex comparison, $\chi^2(1) = 1.07$, $p > .05$: for the Fear × Sex comparison, $\chi^2(1) = .10$, $p > .05$). The expression of fear by Marsha in the story endings was not related to the outcome of the story, $\chi^2(1) = 2.32$, $p > .05$. However, stories that ended with no further abuse were more likely to attribute anger to Chuck than those that ended in further abuse or assault, $\chi^2(1) = 4.37$, $p < .05$.

Women who were asked what would happen to them in the situation (Group 3) were significantly less likely than the subjects in groups 1 and 2 to think that date rape was the result, $\chi^2(1) = 5.51$, $p < .05$. Only 3 women in this group (4%) completed the story in such a way that they were victims of date rape. On the one hand, this result suggests that although women may be aware of the general risk of date rape, they may not be realistically evaluating the chances that it will happen to them. On the other hand, the fact that our subjects were able to imagine vividly, and perhaps rehearse, effectively getting out of a potential date rape situation may make them less fearful and guilt-prone and more confident in an actual situation.

Women who were asked to imagine themselves in a potential date rape situation described two types of resistance strategies. One, favored by 41 subjects (55%), involved temporarily incapacitating the man (slapping him, kicking him in the groin, stomping on his instep), running back to the party, and going home with someone else (see Appendix, Sample 4). Eight of these women (11% of the total) mentioned using a specific self-defense strategy. They produced especially confident, nonfearful endings with no indication that they felt helpless (see Appendix, Sample 5).

A second type of strategy, favored by 12 women (16%), involved reasoning and was often designed to help the perpetrator save face ("I really like you. You're an interesting person, but I'm not ready for this yet"). Reasoners imagined a much less hostile response from the male, $\chi^2(1) = 14.25$, $p < .01$, and a much greater chance of continuing the relationship, $\chi^2(1) = 14.89$, $p < .01$, than did the physical resisters (see Appendix, Sample 6).

All but one woman in this group imagined some form of resistance; but because so few women imagined situations ending in date rape, the two strategies cannot be compared for effectiveness. On the basis of past research in actual date rape situations (Levine-MacCombie & Koss, 1986), though, one might argue that the verbal resisters are imagining a less effective strategy for themselves.

In the group of males who imagined themselves victims of sexual abuse, 19 (45%) thought the encounter ended in intercourse. But in no case was the intercourse described as forced or unpleasant. In over half of the stories (58%), the male took control of the situation and became the aggressor (see Appendix, Sample 7). About one-third of the males (32%) reported that they would just enjoy Marsha's aggressiveness (see Appendix, Sample 8). Ten percent described themselves and Marsha as mutually aggressive and willing partners (see Appendix, Samples 9 and 10). Whereas no female who imagined herself the victim of sexual assault saw the event as positive, all of the men did, $\chi^2(1) = 7.85$, $p < .01$.

Most of the men who resisted Marsha's advances described letting her continue for a while, then stopping her when they had had enough. There was no indication that these men felt fear, the most frequently reported female feeling. In fact, no resisting male reported any of the common female responses: running back to the party (38% of the females, no males), screaming (35% of the females, no males), getting another ride home (28% of the females, no males), telling parents or friends (12% of the females, no males). Further, there was no indication that men felt that there would come a point when they could no longer control Marsha's behavior (see Appendix, Sample 11). Clearly, men have more options in this situation. They are usually physically stronger so do not have to depend on others to hear their screams or struggles and respond. They generally drive their own cars so do not have to depend on others (usually other males) to take them home.

Among all women subjects, 36% reported having been a victim of actual sexual assault or abuse. This compares to Levine-MacCombie and Koss's (1986) finding of 36.7% among a much larger sample of college students. The mean age of our subjects when first abused or assaulted was 16 years (median age, 17 years; range, 7–22 years). Levine-MacCombie and Koss reported a mean age of about 18 years. None of our women subjects reported having been the victim of stranger rape. All were at least acquainted with the perpetrator; about 30% had a long-standing dating relationship with him. The story endings written by women who had been victims of sexual assault or abuse did not differ in any statistically significant way from those of nonabused women, nor were their story endings more likely to end in date rape than those written by nonabused/assaulted women, $\chi^2(1) = .14$, $p > .05$. However, their stories that did end in date rape were especially rich in heartrending detail (see Appendix, Samples 12 and 13).

Although our women subjects were much more likely than the men to have been victims of sexual assault or abuse, $\chi^2(1) = 8.24$, $p < .01$, 11% of our male subjects did report that they had been victims of sexual assault or abuse. Of the men who elaborated, one reported that a woman in a bar repeatedly "grabbed my crotch and ass." Another said, "It happens quite frequently that girls want more than I had planned, but I don't turn them down." One experience appeared to be homosexual in nature.

CONCLUSIONS

The conclusions drawn from this study are based on a simulated date rape study and are therefore subject to all of the limitations of analog research. On the other hand, simulated situations allow one to investigate a number of research questions in a controlled manner, without the limitations presented by the multiple differences in actual date rape situations. Our hope is that conclusions based on this work will be helpful to clinicians working in the area of data rape prevention among college students and to researchers who might glean new ideas for studies of actual date rape victims based on the results of this study. Our recommendations are directed toward those who work as college counselors, teachers, and researchers and to students themselves because of the need we see to work on this problem at a grass-roots level, with individual women and men.

With respect to the behavior of college women who find themselves in a potential date rape situation and are faced with an immediate need to resist, the results of this study lead to the following recommendations.

1. Believe that women have the inalienable right to stop a sexual encounter at any point, regardless of past verbal or physical behavior on this date or any previous dates. Women have the right to change their minds midway through a sexual encounter that they had previously anticipated completing. A woman need not take responsibility for the aggressive sexual behavior of a man by feeling guilty for leading him on or allowing him to go that far. Such guilt feelings are incapacitating and have been found to be related to completed date rape (Levine-MacCombie & Koss, 1986).

2. Actively dispute the common presumption among men that actions speak louder than words, by saying, "No matter what I've done in the past or what other women have done, I do not want to continue. I know you think I'm just saying this and that I really want/like it. But that's wrong. I want you to stop now."

3. Learn self-defense. Such skills make women more confident and less fearful in potential date rape situations, factors that have been found to be related to the avoidance of date rape. Self-defense skills also help women deal effectively with the greater physical power of men.

4. Be ready to respond to the needs of other women, freely offering protection and rides home in a nonjudgmental manner. Be sensitive to the verbal and physical efforts other women are making to avoid date rape and resist the urge not to get involved in another's problems. Form rescue parties to go and get women on single dates who need rides home.

With respect to the attitudes, expectations, and behavior of men, we have the following recommendations.

1. Believe, as she does, that she has the right to stop the sexual encounter at any point, regardless of what she has agreed to in the past. Understand that it is not the responsibility of women to provide sexual relief for men and that sexual behavior is not an appropriate expectation as a return on one's financial or time investment.

2. Believe the words she says. Men imagine themselves talking their way out of an unwanted sexual encounter and should allow women the same right. Understand that when a woman says no and then allows a man to continue, it is not because she likes it or wants to but because she is terrified that his anger will lead to violence.

3. Learn to control anger and, especially, to eliminate anger and violence from intimate relationships.

4. Realize that the chances are very good (96% in this study) that if sexual abuse or assault occurs, the relationship will not continue. One night of "pleasure" is very likely to result in the sacrificing of a long-term relationship.

In general, we believe that sexual behavior, particularly unwanted sexual behavior, occurs in part among college students for the following inappropriate reasons: it is an expectation among men, probably based more on bragging than on actual experiences of peers; it is the only alternative some people can think of, particularly those who have difficulty conversing; it is cheap entertainment. To begin to counter these inappropriate factors, men first need to see and deal with the contradiction between behavior and attitudes that are pleasing to the women they have affection for and that improve their status in the eyes of male comrades. An unfortunate part of the male bonding process in college involves "scoring" with women. The very behavior that is reinforced by male friends is harmful and degrading to women.

Those charged with the responsibility for planning activities for college students need to plan activities where group and private interaction is possible in a nonsexual setting. Privacy that occurs near the safety of the group (particularly if that group is responsive to the needs of its members) is ideal. Especially for men, sexual behavior may be a cover for shyness. Men need more training in the art of social intercourse than in the art of sexual intercourse. Events that involve well-defined activities (such as casino parties or game nights) should be easier for the socially shy than diffuse events (sitting around listening to music and drinking beer).

In dating situations, men and women must not rely on intuition but frequently and directly ask about the other's feelings and desires. One must not assume that all is well but actively check to see if the other person is comfortable with the activity. Women need to recognize and deal with their fear and men with their anger in intimate situations. It is indeed disheartening to imagine groups of college students who are angry and afraid in situations that should be trusting and pleasant and that certainly set the pattern of future intimate behavior.

Sexual encounters, like other human encounters, should be governed by an ethic of care rather than an ethic of conquest and resistance. An ethic of care means that one is able to recognize, appreciate and value the needs and desires of the other person. At the very least, one extends to the other person the same rights one claims for oneself. An ethic of care depends on experiencing the other person as an equivalent human being, with needs and rights as important and normative as one's own. Achieving this goal is inextricably linked to the efforts of feminism. When women are received as full and valuable partners in human life, date rape will not occur. Taking steps to control date rape until that point may hasten the arrival of these goals.

REFERENCES

Knox, D., & Wilson, K. (1983). Dating problems of university students. *College Student Journal, 71*, 225–228.

Koss, M. P. (1985). The hidden rape victim: Personality, attitudinal, and situational characteristics. *Psychology of Women Quarterly, 9*, 193–212.

Koss, M. P. (1987, March). *Rape vulnerability research: Pitfalls in the paradigm.* Paper presented at the annual meeting of the Association for Women in Psychology, Denver, CO.

Levine-MacCombie, J., & Koss, M. P. (1986). Acquaintance rape: Effective avoidance strategies. *Psychology of Women Quarterly, 10*, 311–320.

Shotland, R. L., & Goodstein, L. (1983). Just because she doesn't want to doesn't mean it's rape: An experimentally based causal model of the perception of rape in a dating situation. *Social Psychology Quarterly, 46*, 220–232.

Sweet, E. (1985, October). Date rape: The story of an epidemic and those who deny it. *MS.*, pp. 56–59.

Wilson, W., & Durrenberger, R. (1982). Comparison of rape and attempted rape. *Psychological Reports, 50*, 198.

APPENDIX

Sample Story Endings Written by Subjects

1. Marsha then proceeded to smack Chuck with immense force. Chuck then realized, even though he was completely wasted, that he was acting in a wrong way. He realized that he was drunk in the presence of an attractive girl, and when his natural instincts took over, he could not control himself until he was smacked in the face.

2. Chuck continued to pursue the issue, only to find Marsha was dating another guy at the time. Chuck, feeling dejected and used for a date, threw beer on her and called her a tease in front of his friends back at the party. Feeling embarrassed, Marsha ran from the cottage back to school. However, on her way she was hitchhiking and picked up by a total stranger. The stranger pulled down a dirt road, raped and killed Marsha, and Chuck was blamed for the murder later that night.

3. Chuck won't stop and Marsha will be very scared. He will get so angry with her saying no that he will end up hitting her repeatedly. She will try to get away but won't be able to see because of the blood in her eyes — from him beating on her. As she's running, she'll trip, she'll be unable to

move. He will rape her, saying she's a tease and she wanted it as much as he did. She won't say anything to anyone—she's too ashamed. She'll never speak to Chuck again or be able to look at him without being sick. He won't understand—he thinks she's still in love with him.

4. I scream and kick him in the balls. This stops him and I just walk back inside and find someone to give me a ride home.

5. I had this happen before so I knew what to do. I kicked him in the shins and grabbed his ankles and flipped him to the ground. I was not far from the cottage, so I ran all the way back and called my parents to come and get me.

6. I took Chuck's hand and held it firmly in mine and told him that I thought he was a nice guy, but I didn't want to get to know him that way. I would explain that it's not that I don't like him as a person, but rather that I don't prefer to get acquainted with someone in that way.

7. You lay her on the ground and give her the best sex she has ever had. If it is cold I'd take her back to the car and have sex with her.

8. If you are a normal male, you go along with it and see how far she'll go. Maybe she's just a tease, but maybe you really get lucky this time. You obviously wanted to be with her in the first place, so what's the problem. I live for stuff like this.

9. So I let Marsha go to see how far she will go. She pulls me down to the ground and begins feeling me all over. I'm thinking to myself, Wow, why can't I get girls like this more often? She rips my sweater off and starts to run her hands all over my well-developed chest. I can't take this much longer, so I rip all of her clothes off; she doesn't resist, she even helps me. Next we both hit the ground and go at it hard for an hour. I get up, get dressed, and go back to the party, which is almost over. I take Marsha home, then go home myself and have a very sound and pleasant sleep.

10. I decide what the hell, no one will know. My girlfriend is out of town and I'm free for the night. Marsha really is a hot smoker. So I gently lay her down on the ground. Slowly she takes off my sweater and shirt and I take hers off. We make a nice little blanket to lie on. We kiss for a while and then she starts taking off my pants. I'm getting really excited so I take her pants off also. She starts to moan and groan; I think she is really turned on. Then I insert my penis and have sex all night with her.

11. I back away, and try to initiate some sort of conversation, while keeping some sort of contact with Marsha (i.e., holding hands, hand on thigh). After talking for a while, I suggest we go back inside for a drink, and find a comfortable seat and talk. When I take her home, I give her a good-night kiss and arrange for another date.

12. Marsha tried to make him stop but Chuck overpowered her. The more that she struggled, the tighter his grasp got. Marsha started to panic and cry. Chuck delighted in this. He ripped her clothes to shreds and pro-

ceeded to get more violent. He told Marsha that if she didn't quit squirming that he would strangle her when he was finished. After Chuck took off his clothes in a hurry, he raped her. When he was finished, he put his clothes on and left, without a word. Marsha lay on the ground in a sobbing heap. She couldn't go anywhere because Chuck ripped her clothes. The pain and humiliation were hurting inside her. She wanted to die. She felt so unclean. She just wanted to take a shower. She didn't want anyone to see her because she felt that people would just know by looking at her (at any time) that she had been raped. She also felt hate and rage at Chuck. She most likely won't report this crime to the police because she's too embarrassed.

13. Chuck will continue to "feel her up" and Marsha will continue to struggle. She may or may not call for help, but they are far enough away from the cottage that no one will hear. The situation will end in date rape, with Chuck feeling (and perhaps bragging about) that he really had a hot date and Marsha feeling like she had lived through a nightmare. She won't tell anyone what happened and will explain away physical symptoms such as bruises, scrapes, etc., by saying she fell or walked into a door. To her friends, Marsha will seem very quiet and withdrawn, and she will kind of "disappear" from group gatherings, especially if Chuck is there. Marsha and Chuck will not go out again, even though Chuck will probably press for another date. "She was a lot of fun, and now she won't even talk to me; how come?" "I don't know, something's been bugging her lately, but she's a real clam about it. She'll get over it, I guess." Yes, but not for a long time.

■ 17
Attitudes toward
Pornography Control

Gloria Cowan and
Geraldine Butts Stahly

The issue of pornography, including the definition of pornography, its social message, its effect on attitudes and behavior, and what, if any, measures should be taken to control it, has been clouded by controversy. Despite the common concern expressed by many feminists regarding violent and degrading pornography, the issue of pornography control has resulted in a deep and often emotionally charged difference of opinion. Feminists can choose to align themselves with either the position taken by the Feminist Anticensorship Task Force (FACT), that censorship of pornography will endanger women's rights and freedom (Tong, 1987), or with the pro-ordinance civil rights violation position led by Catherine MacKinnon and Andrea Dworkin, who propose that pornography silences women, renders them powerless, and promotes inequality and violence against women.

From a *harm prospective*, attitudes toward pornography control should be based on the belief that pornography is harmful to viewers and targets of viewers. For feminists, the harm may be broadly defined as contributing to inequality and subordination of women or, more narrowly, in terms of pornography's effect on violence against women. For religious conservatives, the harm exists in the threat to traditional morality.

From a *free speech perspective*, the consequences of censorship are more serious than the effects of pornography. Regarding the direct and indirect harm of pornography, researchers in this area have been primarily interested in the impact of sexual material that includes violence and ideological support for rape. Social scientists have not as yet demonstrated that according to strict interpretations of causality, the viewing of violent pornography leads *directly* to acts of violence against women and are careful to note that laboratory-based data cannot provide such evidence. MacKinnon (1985) suggests, however, that "specific pornography directly causes some assaults" (p. 43). Parenthetically, it may be that the focus on sexual violence as the primary outcome of pornography is itself myopic.

Prominent pornography researchers such as Donnerstein, Linz, and Penrod (1987), in fact, argue that it is the violence, not the sexuality, in violent pornography that has harmful effects. However, the 1986 Attorney General's Commission on Pornography considered the evidence sufficient to conclude that violent pornography bears a causal relationship to violence against women. The belief that pornography causes violence may not be based on scientific evidence, and thus the relationship between attitudes toward pornography control and the belief that pornography causes violence may be more a reflection of other attitudes and values. Linz, Penrod, and Donnerstein (1986) suggest that even a clear demonstration of a relationship between pornography and violence would not substantially affect the courts' decisions regarding pornography, given the centrality of free speech in America.

We have been interested in understanding the bases of attitudes toward pornography control. At least for feminists, for whom the issue of conservative morality is not involved, the pornography control issue pits important values against each other: free speech versus harm. Gilligan's (1982) model of moral reasoning is helpful in understanding the split among feminists. Gilligan suggests that moral decisions emerge from two perspectives, one based on rights to noninterference and freedom and the other based on responsibility and caring. The ethic of care concerns itself with the preservation of personal ties and contextualized judgments, and the ethic of rights is based on an abstract system of general principles. According to Katzenstein and Laitkin (1987), the antipornography movement among feminists is built on a morality of caring and responsibility.

Using an intensive interview format, we (Cowan, Chase, & Stahly, 1989) investigated attitudes toward pornography control among feminist and fundamentalist women. Fifteen fundamentalist, 9 anticontrol feminists, and 20 procontrol feminists were interviewed. All respondents felt extremely negative toward pornography, and most believed that pornography causes violence against women; however, anticontrol feminists feared that censorship of pornography would lead to restriction of other basic rights. Though the procontrol feminists were concerned about censorship, they expressed greater concern about the harm done by pornography. When the sample was asked to prioritize individual rights and freedom versus responsibility to the welfare of others, a significant difference between procontrol and anticontrol feminists was found, with procontrol feminists choosing responsibility over freedom and anticontrol feminists choosing freedom over responsibility. These data suggest that procontrol feminists may use a responsibility and care model in deciding whether they believe in legal control of pornography, whereas anticontrol feminists may use the rights and freedom from noninterference orientation. Ranking of other values was also consistent with Gilligan's (1982) model. Additionally, procontrol feminists were more likely to have worked with victims of violence than were anticontrol feminists and tended to indicate spontaneously that they had been victims themselves.

The split in attitudes toward pornography control can be found in the population at large; the National Opinion Research Council survey of 1986 (Roper Center for Public Opinion Research, 1986), using a representative sample of English-speaking Americans over the age of 18 found that 42% of the 1,469 respondents responded yes to the question asking whether there should be laws against the distribution of pornography. An additional 53% believed that there should be laws against the viewing of pornography by people under the age of 18. Fifty-seven percent of the sample agreed that sexual materials lead people to commit rape; 36% disagreed, and the remaining respondents indicated that they did not know.

The present study is an extension of the Cowan, Chase, and Stahly (in press) study with a college student sample to investigate further the predictors of attitudes toward pornography control in an ideologically more diverse sample. We were interested in examining the relationship of attitudes toward pornography control to several sets of variables, including demographic information, broad attitudes and values, specific attitudes toward pornography, attitudes regarding harm and censorship, and personal experiences with victimization. We expected that demographics, general attitudes and values, experience with victimization, and attitudes toward pornography would predict attitudes toward pornography control; however, we further expected that attitudes toward the specific issues of harm done by pornography and repercussions of censorship would have the strongest relationship to attitudes toward pornography control. Compared to the analysis of the bases of differences among feminists, sexual and political conservatism should play an important role in a more broadly defined sample, such that a strong religious base and conservative values are related to procontrol attitudes.

METHOD

Participants

Participants were 339 undergraduates taking classes in psychology at a community college and a state university in Southern California (235 women and 104 men). The mean age of the sample was 24 years; 79% were white, and 70% were single.

Measures

A nine-page questionnaire was administered. Demographic questions assessed respondents' sex, age, ethnic background, marital status, whether they had children, personal and family income, religious preference and religious activity level, whether they considered themselves fundamentalist or born-again Christians, political affiliation, and political orientation.

The 15-item Attitudes Toward Women Scale (Spence & Helmreich, 1978) was used to measure profeminist attitudes, and the Rokeach Value Scale (Rokeach, 1973) assessed the prioritizing of 18 terminal and 18 instrumental values. A question pitting rights and responsibility asked, "In general, which is more important to you: Individual rights and freedom (or) responsibility for the welfare of others."

Six classes of possible pornography were defined for the respondents: (1) partial female nudity, (2) full female nudity, (3) male nudity, (4) nonviolent, noncoercive, nondegrading explicit sexual activity, (5) highly degrading or dehumanizing explicit sexual activity, and (6) violent sexually explicit activity such as rape, use of force, or threat of force. Respondents indicated whether they considered each of the six categories to be pornography, their feelings about each (on a 7-point scale), and their extent of exposure to each (on a 5-point scale). Scales based on these items included exposure, definitions, and feelings toward mild (1 through 4 above), extreme (5 and 6), and all pornography (1 through 6).

Regarding the effects of pornography, the respondents were asked to consider only degrading, dehumanizing, or exploitative material or sexually violent material in their responses. Questions followed that assessed the extent to which the respondents considered pornography to be a moral issue; the extent of direct, indirect, and personal harm caused by pornography; behavioral and attitudinal effects on the average male and on males they knew, and the extent of portrayal of women in pornography as sexual objects who enjoy pain and humiliation and as depersonalized or degraded (all 5-point scales).

Before responding to the items on attitudes toward pornography control, respondents were introduced to the issue. The written introduction to these items was as follows:

> People are divided on the issue of pornography. Some consider it a central issue connected with violence against women. They want to ban pornography on the grounds that it violates the civil rights of women by promoting violence against women, keeping them subordinate, and encouraging discrimination against women. They feel pornography supports the myth that women enjoy and incite sexual violence. Others believe that the first Amendment guarantee of freedom of speech, press, and expression is most important to protect. They

TABLE 17.1   Items in the Harm and Censorship Scales

Harm Scale
1. Pornography directly harms women (e.g., leads to rape, molestation, etc.).
2. Pornography indirectly harms women (e.g., creates negative social climate).
3. You have been personally harmed by pornography.
4. Pornography harms all women.
5. Feminists and fundamentalists should put aside their political differences in order to fight pornography.
6. Pornography violates the civil rights of women.
7. Pornography encourages discrimination against women.

Censorship Scale
1. First Amendment protection of free speech is more important than the control of pornography.
2. Censorship of pornography could lead to setbacks in women's progress toward equality.
3. Laws that restrict pornography would unfairly affect people's freedom to engage in alternative life-styles (e.g., lesbians).
4. Control of pornography could limit women's sexual freedom.
5. Enough laws already exist to control the harmful aspects of pornography.
6. The harm caused by pornography is greater than the harm caused by limiting free speech [scoring reversed].
7. Prohibiting pornography is not a violation of the First Amendment guarantee of free speech.

believe that as a free people it is impossible to censor speech we hate without imperiling the system of free expression in our society.

Again, respondents were asked to answer the control questions only with respect to degrading or violent pornography. The primary dependent variable was one item with a 7-point scale: "Laws should be passed to prohibit pornography." A set of items measured other actions besides legislative control, such as zoning ordinances, boycotts, and increased prosecution. A set of seven items measuring the harm done by pornography (alpha = .87) and a set of seven items measuring concern about censorship (alpha = .78) were derived by using factor analysis (see Table 17.1). Additional items focused on the extent to which pornography, pornography control, and free speech are moral issues; the conflict between the need to protect First Amendment rights and the need for legislative control; and if so, the extent to which respondents consider it a moral conflict.

Finally, a set of four items assessing experience with victims or victimization was included, asking whether respondents had worked with, known, or been victims of sexual violence and if their personal experiences with victims or as victims had been important in forming their attitudes about pornography control.

Procedure

Participants were given the questionnaires in their classrooms and were asked to return them to the instructor or to the investigator's office. Participation was voluntary and anonymous. All questionnaires were identical in format, with demographic information requested first; attitudes about pornography, second; pornography control, third; and experiences with victimization, last. Space was reserved at the end of the questionnaire for participant comments.

RESULTS

Correlational Analyses

Attitude toward legislative control of pornography was correlated with each predictor. The mean of the sample on the legislative control item was 4.8 on a 7-point scale, indicating "slightly agree," with a standard deviation of 2.05. Because many scales and items indicated sex differences, correlations are provided for men and women as well as for the total sample. Table 17.2 presents the correlational analyses. As the total number of predictors relative to the number of subjects was prohibitively large, regression equations were run for each set of predictors.

Demographic Predictors

Approximately one-third of the sample indicated that they were fundamentalist or born-again Christians ($n = 102$). Approximately equal numbers of respondents indicated that they considered themselves far left/liberal and far right/conservative in their political orientation. Sixty-nine percent of the sample was white; 9.7% black; 13.3% Hispanic, and 4.7%, Asian. Seventy percent of the sample was single, 80% had no children. Thirty-nine percent of the sample recorded Protestant, Catholic, or Jewish religions, with a large proportion indicating "other" (46%).

Female respondents, older respondents, those who were married, those who had children, those who were more religiously active and fundamentalist were more in favor of legislative control of pornography (see Table 17.2). Married, divorced, and separated respondents were more in favor of control than were single respondents, $F = 6.99$, $p = .001$. Although religious activity predicted procontrol attitudes for both males and females, fundamentalism predicted only for males. Political orientation was predictive only for males, with more liberal political ideology positively related to a procontrol attitude. Ethnicity, income, and political party affiliation were not related to attitude toward control.

TABLE 17.2 Correlations of Predictors with Attitude toward Legislative Control

Variables	Total Sample (N = 339)	Women (N = 235)	Men (N = 104)
Demographic variables			
Sex	−.28***	—	—
Age	.20***	.15**	.20*
Male children	.14**	.11*	.13
Female Children	.13**	.14**	.02
Personal income	.00	−.01	.12
Family income	−.06	−.01	−.15
Religion	.03	.00	.07
Religious activity	.20***	.23***	.14
Fundamentalist	−.11*	−.07	−.24**
Political orientation	−.02	.09	−.18*
Attitudes and values			
Attitudes toward women	.16**	.01	.24**
Freedom vs. responsibility	.42***	.41***	.40***
Terminal values			
Comfortable life	.14**	.10	.08
Exciting life	.19***	.17**	.08
Accomplishment	.08	.02	.24**
Peace	−.06	−.08	.08
Beauty	−.07	−.16**	.09
Equality	−.18***	−.09	−.29**
Family security	−.18***	−.18**	−.15
Freedom	.00	.03	.02
Happiness	.01	.06	−.10
Inner harmony	−.13**	.00	−.26**
Mature love	.14**	.18**	−.03
National security	.01	.02	−.03
Pleasure	.21***	.15**	.22**
Salvation	−.15**	−.18**	−.13
Self-respect	−.07	.02	−.08
Social recognition	.04	.00	.04
True friendship	−.07	−.11*	.04
Wisdom	.03	.08	−.10
Instrumental values			
Ambitious	.15**	.12*	.13
Broad-minded	.07	.10	.04
Capable	.03	.05	−.01
Cheerful	−.03	−.04	.05
Clean	.08	.04	.06
Courageous	−.15**	−.17**	−.08
Forgiving	−.09*	−.12*	.11
Helpful	−.16**	−.10	−.20*
Honest	−.14**	−.15*	−.05
Imaginative	.06	.09	.00
Independent	.13**	.12*	.19*

Continued

TABLE 17.2 Continued

Variables	Total Sample (N = 339)	Women (N = 235)	Men (N = 104)
Intellectual	.06	.08	.00
Logical	.08	.08	− .08
Loving	− .04	− .04	.03
Obedient	− .03	− .06	− .08
Polite	.02	− .11	.16*
Responsible	− .00	.01	.03
Self-control	− .01	− .02	− .06
Attitudes toward pornography			
Definition	.27***	.26***	.33***
Definition, extreme pornography	.14**	.07	.23**
Feelings	− .40***	− .35***	− .36***
Feelings, extreme pornography	− .08	− .07	− .01
Exposure	− .27***	− .19**	− .32***
Exposure, extreme pornography	− .16**	− .05	− .29**
Moral issue	.39***	.37***	.31***
Average male affected	.37***	.30***	.39***
Known males affected	.19***	.14*	.23**
Portrayal of women	.40***	.38***	.20*
Control-related attitudes			
Harm Scale	.68***	.67***	.61***
Censorship Scale	− .66***	− .67***	− .56***
Control a moral issue	.28***	.22***	.26**
Free speech a moral issue	− .03	− .02	− .02
Other forms of control	.87***	.86***	.86***
Conflict on control	− .02	− .04	.06
Moral conflict on control	.07	− .00	.21*
Experiences with victims			
Worked with victims	− .06	.02	− .20*
Known victims	.04	− .06	.15
Self as victim	− .02	.08	− .06
Experience affects attitudes	− .23***	− .19**	− .39***

*p < .05.
**p < .01.
***p < .001.
Note. Lower numbers on value scales indicate more important values; thus, a negative correlation indicates a positive relation between importance of that value and a procontrol attitude.

For the demographic variables, including sex, age, religious activity, having female and male children, fundamentalism, and marital status, significant prediction was obtained. $F(7, 301) = 8.06$, $p < .001$, $r^2 = .16$, with sex, religious activity, and marital status significant individual predictors (p's $< .01$).

Attitudes and Values

Table 17.2 also presents the correlations of procontrol attitude with other attitudes and values. Profeminist attitudes significantly predicted procontrol attitudes only for men. Overall, and for both men and women separately, prioritizing of individual rights and freedom versus responsibility for the welfare of others showed a strong relationship with attitude toward control. Those respondents who prioritized responsibility over freedom were more in support of legislative control of pornography. For the entire sample, rankings of terminal values indicated that importance of equality, family security, inner harmony, and salvation were positively related to procontrol attitudes, whereas the importance of a comfortable life, an exciting life, mature love, and pleasure were negatively related to procontrol attitudes. (Negative correlations indicate a positive relationship between that value and procontrol; more important values are ranked lower than less important values). For females, but not for males, the importance of an exciting life, a world of beauty, family security, love, salvation, and friendship were related to attitude toward pornography control; whereas for males, but not for females, a sense of accomplishment, equality, and inner harmony were significant predictors of attitude toward pornography control.

The regression analysis showed that terminal values significantly predicted attitude toward pornography control, $F(18, 305) = 3.07$, $p < .001$, $r^2 = .15$, with family security ($p < .001$), mature love ($p < .03$), and salvation ($p < .01$) significant predictors and friendship and equality marginally significant predictors (p's $< .10$).

Overall, for the instrumental values, courageous, forgiving, helpful, and honest were positively related, and ambitious and independent were negatively related to procontrol attitudes. For the females, but not the males, courageous, forgiving, and honest were related to procontrol; and for the males, but not the females, helpful was positively related to procontrol and polite negatively related to procontrol attitudes.

Although less than terminal values, instrumental values predicted a significant amount of variation in attitude toward pornography control, $F(17, 303) = 1.81$, $p = .027$, $r^2 = .09$, with courageous ($p < .03$) and helpful ($p < .05$) significant individual predictors and ambitious and independent marginally significant predictors (p's $< .10$). When the prioritizing of freedom versus responsibility was added to the regression equation of both terminal and instrumental values, it accounted for a larger proportion of the variance than did the other values (F's > 39.00, $p < .001$).

Attitudes toward Pornography

The definition of pornography, feelings about pornography, and the extent of exposure to pornography all significantly predicted procontrol attitudes (see

Table 17.2). Definition of and exposure to extreme pornography (degrading and violent) predicted attitudes toward control only for males (the tendency to define degrading and violent sexually explicit material as pornographic and the less exposure to this type of material, the more procontrol), probably because of the truncation of response to those items among women. In general, a broad definition of pornography was related to procontrol attitudes. Positive feelings toward pornography and increased exposure to all types of sexual material were negatively related to procontrol attitudes. That is, respondents who were more likely to include nudity in their definition of pornography were more in favor of control. Respondents who viewed more pornography and felt more positively about pornography were less likely to want it controlled with legislation. The extent to which pornography was regarded as a moral issue was positively related to procontrol, as was the judged impact—both behavioral and attitudinal—on the average male and males known by the respondents. The belief that pornography portrays women as degraded and abused also was significantly related to procontrol attitudes.

Regression analyses indicated that attitudes toward pornography significantly predicted the control item $F(10, 220) = 16.17$, $p < .001$, $r^2 = .42$, with portrayal of females, exposure to pornography, viewing pornography as a moral issue, effects on the average male, and feelings toward all forms of pornography making significant contributions (p's $< .05$).

Attitudes toward Harm and Censorship

The relationship between belief in legislative control and other forms of action was high and positive ($r = .87$). The attitudinal scales measuring the harm of pornography and the consequences of censorship both strongly predicted the control item, with the greater harm and the lesser consequences of censorship independently predicting procontrol attitudes. Interestingly, the belief that control of pornography is a moral issue was related to procontrol, whereas the belief that the protection of free speech is a moral issue showed no relationship to the control item. Neither the extent of conflict or whether the conflict was seen as a moral conflict was related to attitude toward control, with the exception of the male sample, for whom a moral conflict regarding control was positively related to procontrol attitudes.

Regression analysis of the control measures showed a large and significant effect $F(6, 166) = 35.64$, $p = .001$, $r^2 = .56$, with the harm and censorship scales showing large individual effects on the regression equation

Experiences with Victimization

Although 22.8% of the sample indicated that they had been victims themselves, experiences with victims or reports of their own victimization did not predict attitude toward pornography control; however, those respondents who felt their personal experiences with victims or their own victimization have been important in forming their attitudes about pornography control were more in favor of control. Surprisingly, having worked with victims predicted males' attitudes toward pornography control but not those of females.

A regression equation using the four items regarding victimization showed an overall effect on procontrol, $F(4, 301) = 4.22$, $p = .002$, $r^2 = .05$, but only the item measuring their perceptions of the importance of victimization on their attitudes was significant.

Conflict and Moral Conflict

To better understand the conflict about pornography control and whether conflict can best be represented as a moral conflict, regression analyses were performed using both the extent of conflict between the need to protect free speech versus the need for legislative control of pornography and the extent to which this conflict is seen as a moral conflict as criteria. Predictors included sex of respondent and pornography, control of pornography, and protection of free speech as moral issues. Regarding the conflict between the need to protect free speech versus the need for legislative control, the regression equation was not significant $F(4, 178) = 2.26$, $p = .06$, with none of the variables individually contributing to the equation. Prediction of a moral conflict, however, was high, $F(5, 177) = 13.53$, $p < .001$, $r^2 = .28$, with items measuring the extent to which pornography, pornography control, and free speech are seen as moral issues and the conflict between free speech and legislative control each contributing significant unique variance to the equation. The conflict between free speech and legislative control made the largest contribution. Sex of respondent was not significant.

Sex Differences

Table 17.3 presents the variables, means and F-values for which significant gender differences were found. On the instrumental values, males, more than females, significantly valued ambitious, clean, logical, obedient, and polite. Females, significantly more than males, valued forgiving, helpful, and honest. On the terminal values, males, significantly more than females, valued a comfortable life, an exciting life, pleasure, and social recognition. Females, significantly more than males, valued peace, equality, inner harmony, and responsibility. Females chose responsibility to others over freedom significantly more often than males ($\chi^2 = 4.06$, $p = .04$), with 47.1% of the females and 34.3% of the males choosing responsibility. Females scored significantly higher in the profeminist direction on the Attitudes towards

TABLE 17.3 Significant Sex Differences in Attitudes and Values

Variable	Women (Means)	Men (Means)	F-Value
Instrumental Values			
Ambitious	9.05	7.45	6.57**
Clean	12.31	10.97	4.49*
Forgiving	7.89	9.84	10.94***
Helpful	8.61	10.10	6.28**
Honest	5.36	6.38	4.47*
Logical	11.46	9.44	12.23***
Obedient	14.71	13.56	4.04*
Polite	11.57	10.04	8.21**
Terminal Values			
Comfortable life	7.59	9.64	12.21***
Exciting life	9.66	11.93	13.59***
Pleasure	12.25	10.59	10.21***
Social recognition	13.60	12.60	3.89*
Peace	9.19	10.46	3.95*
Equality	10.02	11.21	4.30*
Inner harmony	7.96	20.26	14.30***
Responsibility	5.89	7.57	13.18***
Attitudes toward women	35.60	30.44	40.97***
Pornography			
Feelings toward pornography	17.29	21.06	22.26***
Feelings, extreme pornography	3.12	4.10	11.99***
Feelings, mild pornography	14.00	17.34	22.65***
Exposure, pornography	17.93	19.84	22.87***
Exposure, mild pornography	28.58	29.53	8.69**
Pornography as moral issue	3.97	3.33	19.08***
Harm Scale	29.06	22.16	42.71***
Free Speech Scale	21.49	26.74	32.05***
Average male	6.30	5.56	5.63**
Portrayal of women	8.03	6.30	50.85***
Legislative control	5.20	3.96	21.47***
All control	20.51	17.10	15.67***
Control as moral issue	5.71	5.06	7.22***

*p < .05.
**p < .01.
***p < .001.
Note. Smaller numbers on value scales indicate more important values.

Women Scale. Males felt significantly more positive toward pornography, including degrading and violent pornography; had more exposure to all forms of pornography and to only violent and degrading pornography; and believed more strongly in the negative consequences of censorship. Females, significantly more than males, believed that both pornography and the control of pornography are moral issues, saw the harm in pornography, believed that the average male is more affected by pornography, and believed that females are portrayed more negatively in pornography. Finally, females, more than males, favored legislative control as well as other forms of pornography control.

DISCUSSION

Demographic indicators and broad sets of values were related to attitudes toward pornography control. Attitudes toward pornography itself predicted control attitudes to a greater extent than did demographic variables, and attitudes related to issues of harm and free speech predicted procontrol attitudes more strongly than did feelings and attitudes toward pornography itself. In general, this supports the reasoned action model of attitudes proposed by Ajzen and Fishbein (1980); to predict behavior from attitudes, knowledge of the individual's beliefs about the consequences of that behavior and his or her evaluation of those possible outcomes is critical. Hence, the importance of harm and free speech and the consequences of pornography control for harm and free speech are key issues in understanding attitudes toward pornography control. Individuals who regard pornography as harmful and are not as concerned about the implications of censorship favor legislative control.

Support is also evident for the applicability of Gilligan's (1982) model to decisions regarding pornography control. Those individuals who prioritized responsibility for the welfare of others over freedom and individual rights were more likely to favor pornography control. The overall importance of the censorship and harm scales in understanding attitudes toward pornography control also strongly supports Gilligan's model.

The rankings of terminal and instrumental values provided some additional support for an interpretation that relates attitudes toward pornography control to moral reasoning. Gilligan (1982) has suggested that responsibility and freedom bases of moral reasoning are gender-differentiated. Some of the values that related to procontrol attitudes were also those on which sex differences were found. For example, the terminal values of equality and inner harmony were ranked as more important and pleasure, an exciting life, and a comfortable life as less important by females than by males. Respondents who favored pornography control also rated equality and inner harmony as more important and pleasure, an exciting life, and a comfortable life as less important than did those who did not favor pornography control. Interestingly, it was the men in the sample for whom equality and inner harmony most strongly predicted procontrol attitudes and the women in the sample who favored a comfortable or exciting life who most opposed pornography control. Likewise, the instrumental values of forgiving, helpful, and honest were more important and ambitious was less important to those who favored pornography control; forgiving, helpful, and honest were seen as more important and ambitious as less important by females in the sample. Similar to terminal values, some of these values were found to predict procontrol attitudes most strongly among the sex lower on the value (e.g., ambitious and helpful). A related finding that fits this pattern was that although women scored significantly higher on profeminist attitudes, these attitudes were related to control of pornography only for men. This suggests that gender-differentiated values predict attitude toward pornography control in such a direction that values and attitudes on which females score higher than males predict males' attitudes toward pornography control and values, and attitudes on which males score higher than females predict females' attitudes toward pornography control.

Regarding values, it is also clear that some of the values related to pornography control reflect conventional religious morality. Respondents who value family security and salvation highly also support pornography control. A fundamentalist orientation and extent of religious activity also predict procontrol attitudes. Given the relatively large percentage of fundamentalists in our sample, it is not surprising that religious conservatism plays a role in understanding attitudes toward pornography control.

In general, the findings themselves are not surprising. It is reasonable to expect that older, married, more religiously active and fundamentalist people, and women support pornography control. Nor is it particularly startling to learn that those who feel positive about pornography and are less willing to label all sexually explicit material pornography are less in favor of control, that people who watch more pornography would not want it controlled, or that those who want to control pornography more strongly believe that it portrays women negatively and believe that it has more impact on the average man and men they know.

More interesting, at least theoretically, is that the attitude toward control appears to be related to basic values—values reflecting pleasure and hedonism, values reflecting care and concern about others, religiously conservative values, and most important, freedom versus responsibility to others. The pitting of basic values against each other becomes more difficult when we realize that the values of responsibility to others and freedom are not independent: equality and justice are related to both freedom (rights) and protection from harm. Freedom is empty without caring for others, and protection of others is paternalism without freedom. Resolution of the pornography control issue is particularly difficult because of the value base differences underlying arguments for and against control.

214 :: *Research*

REFERENCES

Ajzen, I., & Fishbein, M. (1980). *Understanding attitudes and predicting social behavior.* Englewood Cliffs, NJ: Prentice-Hall.

Attorney General's Commission on Pornography. (1986). *Final report* (Vol. 1). Washington, DC: U.S. Department of Justice.

Cowan, G., Chase, C. J., & Stahly, G. B. (1989). Feminist and fundamentalist women's attitudes toward pornography control. *Psychology of Women Quarterly, 13,* 97–112.

Donnerstein, E., Linz, D., & Penrod, S. (1987). *The question of pornography: Research findings and policy implications.* New York: The Free Press.

Gilligan, C. (1982). *In a different voice.* Cambridge, MA: Harvard University Press.

Katzenstein, M. F., & Laitkin, D. D. (1987). Politics, feminism, and the ethics of care. In E. F. Kittay & D. T. Meyers (Eds.), *Women and moral theory* (pp. 261–281). Totowa, NJ: Rowman & Littlefield.

Linz, D., Penrod, S., & Donnerstein, E. (1986). Issues bearing on the legal regulation of violent and sexually violent media. *Journal of Social Issues, 42*(3), 171–193.

MacKinnon, C. A. (1985). Pornography, civil rights, and speech. *Harvard Civil Rights–Civil Liberties Law Review, 20,* 1–70.

Rokeach, M. (1973). *The nature of human values.* New York: The Free Press.

Roper Center for Public Opinion Research. (1986). *General social survey, 1872–1986: Cumulative codebook July, 1986.* Storrs, CT: University of Connecticut Press.

Spence, J., & Helmreich, R. (1978). *Masculinity and femininity: Their psychological dimensions, correlates, and antecedents.* Austin: University of Texas Press.

Tong, R. (1987, September–October). Women, pornography, and the law. *Academe,* pp. 14–22.

■ 18
Courtship in the 1980s: Female and Male Responses to a Personals Ad

Karen Keljo Tracy

Because of the rising divorce rate and a trend toward later marriage, many individuals find themselves involved in the courtship process at midlife. Few empirical studies exist regarding midlife courtship patterns. One promising source of data in this area is in personals columns, which are rapidly increasing in popularity. In many cities, personals ads are used by middle-aged single professionals who are seeking relationships with others at similar levels of education and professional standing. The ads offer a means of reaching a wider range of individuals than might be available at traditional singles meeting places and also reach more professionals who are single than are found in traditional professional networks.

Although no studies have been done using personals ad data specifically targeted toward middle-aged professionals, general ad content has been analyzed, with specific attention to sex differences. Results generally have supported a social exchange model of courtship: women offer beauty and seek financial security, and men offer financial security and seek youth and beauty (Deaux & Hanna, 1984; Harrison & Saeed, 1977).

The author would like to thank Paul Stenborg for his help in collecting the data, Kathleen Hennigan for her assistance in coding the data, and Dale Hietanen for his help in data analysis, editing, and manuscript preparation.

Murstein (1986) states that the social exchange model applies especially well to the "open field encounter," a situation where men and women are unknown to each other, such as a mixer, a singles' organization meeting, or a bar. Seasoned participants, according to Murstein, use a "minimax strategy," in which they seek the greatest reward at the lowest cost within a range where physical attractiveness is approximately equal. Physical attractiveness is the most important determinant of initial attraction and satisfaction with a new acquaintance for both men and women (Reis, 1985) and thus is the salient dimension for choice in open-field situations. Only when attractiveness level is mutually satisfactory do individuals explore other dimensions important to relationships—personality factors, interests, education, prestige, and finances.

Personal ads present an interesting situation; they are definitely in the open-field category; however, they do not allow initial screening by attractiveness. Therefore, the typically later valued dimensions of personality, interests, education, prestige, and finances, as represented by advertisers and their respondents, act as the initial screening mechanisms. Of course, most individuals also do mention their physical appearance, but appearance is only weakly conveyed in a few brief words.

Because individuals who place personal ads must capture the interest of a potential dating partner in a highly public medium, it is perhaps understandable that they would often resort to sex-stereotypic clichés. They must seek not to offend yet must present their assets and stipulations in a fashion that will be clearly understood by readers in a society with sex-stereotypic ideals. Thus, perhaps the demand characteristics of the situation rather than the personality of the advertiser evoke the sex-stereotypic descriptors and stipulations.

Previous research has explored only the ads themselves and has used samples from a heterogeneous population of ads. This study was designed to analyze *responses* to a particular stimulus ad that was aimed at a specialized population, that of highly educated professionals.

The major goal of this research was to try to ascertain whether an advanced degree, high intelligence, and professional status have differential value for the two sexes in the dating arena. Marriage and divorce literature indicates that with respect to getting and staying married, these qualities are an asset for men but a liability for women (Jacobson, 1983). It was thus hypothesized that a personals ad describing a professional with a PhD would evoke more responses from women than from men.

A second goal was to discover whether respondents would be as sex-stereotypic in their replies as advertisers have been found to be in previous personals ad research (Deaux & Hanna, 1984; Harrison & Saeed, 1977). It was anticipated that, for several reasons, respondents would be less sex-stereotypic than previous research on personals ads would indicate. First, it was assumed that respondents to an ad portraying a person with a PhD degree would, on average, be similarly intelligent because individuals prefer partners comparable to themselves intellectually (Murstein, 1986). Because much research (Haan, 1974; Noble, 1987; Russo, 1985) has indicated that intelligence is negatively correlated with sex-stereotyping, these respondents should be low in sex-stereotyping. In addition, the respondents would probably not feel as constrained to "sell themselves," using brief, sex-stereotypic descriptors, as would the advertisers. Finally, the ad presented a high level of attractiveness, education, and occupational status and thus lessened the probability that respondents would feel the necessity to stipulate these traits in their letters.

No specific hypothesis was made with respect to whether the responses would support Murstein's (1986) social exchange model, with its minimax strategy, because of the lack of experimental control, impossible in a field study of this type. However, it was hoped that some of the descriptive information derived from the study would furnish some hypotheses that could be tested in the future.

METHOD

An ad with gender-neutral wording was composed; it presented a PhD who is a divorced, 38-year-old with intellectual and cultural interests, seeking heterosexual friendship. The same ad was placed in each of the two major newspapers in a large midwestern city, one addressed to men and one to women. Two weeks later the ads were reversed. To minimize the possibility that the gender manipulation would be detected, the ad began: "Ladies" or "Men," with the expectation that only individuals of the stated sex would read further. The text of the ad was as follows:

> Ladies [Men], tired of mindless bodies? Put intellectual and cultural excitement in your life. Attractive, professional divorced male [female], 38, Ph.D., seeks friendship with nonsmoker. Interests: active sports, art, theater, movies, nature, and concerts. Please send letter and phone number to Box—.

Letters were received through newspaper box numbers and were retyped with all identifying information omitted to protect the anonymity of the respondents.

RESULTS

Sample

Thirty letters were received from women and 59 from men; thus, the ratio of women to men was 1:2. This result is typical according to statistics com-

TABLE 18.1   Percentage of Respondents Giving Information

	Sex of Respondent	
Category	Female	Male
Nonsmoking	47%	41%
Marital status	40%	56%
Education	53%	66%
Age	73%	76%
Occupation	80%	71%
Appearance	87%	73%
Interests	100%	90%

piled by the newspapers where the ads were placed. Because it was important to know that respondents had replied to the stimulus ad specifically, all of the letters that did not directly address some aspect of the stimulus ad were discarded, as were all duplicate responses. In addition, two angry, threatening, obscene letters, written by men who had detected the gender manipulation, were excluded from analysis. Fifteen (50%) of the women's responses were excluded, and 18 (33%) of the men's were excluded, leaving a usable sample of 15 women and 41 men.

Among those replies discarded from males were photocopied letters, business cards with a brief note scrawled on the back, and in one case a poster advertising the respondent's appearance in a nightclub with a written invitation to meet him there. No woman responded in any of these ways. Women were more likely than men to make their replies look personal. Double replies were often handwritten, and computer-generated form letters were often printed in blue script lettering that was hard to distinguish from very neat handwriting.

Reciprocal Provision of Information

The advertiser disclosed age, marital status, level of education, occupational status, attractiveness, and interests in intellectual-cultural activities and sought friendship with a nonsmoker. Thus, data was inspected by sex to ascertain how many respondents provided reciprocal information about themselves, as shown in Table 18.1.

Similarity

The advertiser's self-portrait included an age of 38, divorced marital status, professional status, a PhD degree, attractiveness, and cultural–intellectual interests, including active sports, movies, theater, nature, art, and concerts. Congruent with general cultural patterns (Murstein, 1986), women were younger (median age = 35) and men older (median age = 42) than the age

TABLE 18.2 Percentage of Respondents with Similar Interests

	Sex of Respondent	
Category	Female	Male
Any cultural	100%	73%
Any intellectual	66%	34%
Active sports	80%	68%
Theater	73%	24%
Movies	67%	27%
Concerts	67%	49%
Art	67%	22%
Nature	33%	20%

of the advertiser (38). However, there was a much greater range for men (23–66) than for women (26–41); about one-quarter of each sex did not mention their age at all. Whereas 73% of the women were within 4 years of the advertiser's age, only 27% of the men were within this range.

Of those mentioning marital status, 33% of the women and 52% of the men were divorced; 50% of the women and 22% of the men had never been married; 17% of the women and 9% of the men were single, unspecified; and 9% of the men were separated or widowed. Interestingly, half of the respondents did not disclose their marital status. The other low category of reciprocal information was smoking status. Perhaps many respondents who failed to disclose these categories of information assumed that the advertiser would assume that they were also nonsmokers and divorced because they had answered an ad in which nonsmoking status was stipulated and divorced status mentioned.

Regarding occupation, 58% of the women and 90% of the men who specified occupational status were in professional, technical, or managerial positions. Of those giving their educational status, 25% of the women had attained some college education: 25%, a BA; 37%, an MA; and one had a professional degree (JD). Forty-one percent of the men reported a BA; 26%, an MA; and 33%, a professional degree (7 PhDs, 3 EdDs).

Of the total sample, 47% of the women and 34% of the men described themselves as attractive. Although a few of the men admitted that attractiveness was not their strong suit, none of the women did so. All respondents, however, mentioned similarity in interests. Table 18.2 shows the percentage of respondents who stated specific interests similar to the advertiser's.

Identification

Respondents differed in terms of how much identifying information they gave for the purpose of allowing the advertiser to contact them. All but two men gave their first names, and all but two women and two men gave their home phone numbers; the stimulus ad had requested only a phone number. Half of each group provided last names. All four of the women who included their home addresses lived outside the metropolitan area in which the newspapers were located; by contrast, almost half of the men gave their home addresses, and only one of these lived out of town. A business phone number was offered by only one woman and four men; only one man offered his business address.

Personality

Although the only direct reference to personality made by the advertiser was intelligence, many respondents offered and sought specific personality traits. Sixty percent of the women and 37% of the men explicitly described themselves as intelligent; one woman and one man even mentioned their IQs. Additional personality characteristics were also furnished by 87% of the women and 68% of the men. The researcher listed each trait and categorized those that were unambiguously instrumental and expressive. About one-third of the traits offered by each sex were clearly expressive adjectives such as nurturant, loving, compassionate, and affectionate; only about one-tenth were clearly instrumental, such as aggressive, adventuresome, and ambitious.

Just under half of each sex described traits they desired in a partner. Here women were slightly more likely than men (60% vs. 39%) to request expressive traits and not to request instrumental traits (4% vs. 15%).

Self-presentation

About one-half of the women but only one-quarter of the men wrote on stationery or a note card; about one-fifth of each sex sent photographs of themselves. Most letters were well written in terms of style, grammar, and spelling. Most were also socially graceful, with about half of the respondents complimenting the ad writer and about a third using humor in their letters. One-third of the respondents included material obviously designed to impress the reader, such as the importance of their jobs, their outstanding physical attractiveness, or their expensive possessions. Fewer than one-quarter of each sex mentioned interest in marriage, financial security, or sexual tastes. Although the same proportion of both sexes, one-third, mentioned weaknesses, men were significantly more likely than women to offer defenses for these weaknesses (0% for females, 22% for males, $\chi^2 = 3.92$, 1 df, $n = 56$, $p < .05$). Men disclosed rather serious limitations as well as trivial ones; women were more likely to admit to minor weaknesses or pseudo-weaknesses. Evidence of poor social skills was rare; negativism, criticism, self-pity, self-derogation, and instances of sheer bad taste were unusual and were no more common in one sex than the other.

Stated Interest in Ad

Most respondents indicated what had drawn them to the ad. Nearly every respondent (100% of the women, 90% of the men) mentioned similar interests. The catch phrase used to attract attention in the ad was "tired of mindless bodies?"; this drew comments from two-thirds of the respondents, men and women alike. Attractiveness was mentioned as eye-catching by few (7% of the women and 13% of the men). Only 13% of the women mentioned that they found a PhD degree desirable, whereas 41% of the men stated that they were drawn by this. This sex difference was significant $\chi^2 = 3.88$, 1 *df*, $n = 56$, $p < .05$). One man who had a BA explicitly stated that although he was "intimidated" by the PhD, he was also attracted by it; two who had PhDs specifically stated that they were "not intimidated" by it.

DISCUSSION

The first hypothesis that the ad would draw proportionately more letters from women than from men, was not supported. The typical response ratio obtained — number of the replies from men double those from women — was similar to that found by the newspapers publishing these ads. However, when responses not directly pertaining to the stimulus ads were removed, the female–male ratio became nearly 1 to 3, which was in the opposite direction of what had been predicted. Thus, it would seem that an intelligent professional with a PhD was more attractive as a potential companion to men than to women. Further support for this premise was furnished by the fact that male respondents were significantly more likely than female respondents to state explicitly that they found the PhD appealing.

The fact that the doctorate seemed to hold more appeal for men than for women in a potential romantic relationship is surprising if one looks at the literature on divorce and remarriage. A man with a high level of education has less risk of divorce and better chances for remarriage; the opposite is true for women (Jacobson, 1983).

There is, however, a critical difference between being attractive to men and marrying them. As Simeone (1987) writes in her book on academic women, "For women who have attained high levels of achievement within their professional spheres, it may be . . . difficult to play a subordinate role in their relationships" (p. 128). And Hochschild (1983) emphasizes that the problem is not with individual men but rather is inherent in the structure of a sexist society. Societal inequality between the sexes "is filtered into the intimate daily exchanges between wife and husband" (p. 169).

The second hypothesis, that respondents to this ad would be less sex-stereotypic in their replies than had been found in studies of personals ads themselves was generally supported. Because many of the most highly valued qualities for both sexes were promised in the stimulus ad, it is no surprise that respondents did not engage in redundancy and stipulate these qualities. However, it is interesting that there was no sex difference in the presentation of personality traits, both sexes promoting more of their expressive than their instrumental traits. This would seem functional in the context of trying to establish a personal relationship.

Previous research on personals ads has indicated that men seek youth and beauty in exchange for prestige and financial security, and women do the opposite (Deaux & Hanna, 1984; Harrison & Saeed, 1977); however, this study indicated that the two sexes did not differ significantly in what they offered or sought. Women rarely alluded to financial security or prestige, nor did men allude to beauty. In addition, both sexes expressed a similar variety of interests, showed sophisticated interpersonal and writing skills, and displayed a keen sense of humor. According to Noble (1987), these traits are typical of the intellectually gifted. As indeed most respondents described themselves as intelligent and accomplished, the results support the contention that gifted individuals tend to be less sex-stereotyped in their personalities, interests, and professional pursuits than are the less gifted.

Some subtle sex differences did exist with respect to age and descriptions of physical attractiveness. Because attractiveness is relatively more important to men seeking women than to women seeking men (Murstein, 1986), it is no surprise that the majority of female respondents described themselves as attractive and that none admitted to flaws in beauty. However, as Reis (1985) notes, men are less apt than women to believe that their attractiveness is critical in establishing relationships with the other sex and less apt to believe that their attractiveness diminishes with age; thus, it was no surprise that they were less likely to mention their appearance and did sometimes admit to a less than perfect face or physique. The sole woman who admitted to being older than the advertiser (by 3 years) stated that people told her she didn't look her age, but the only man who apologized for his age was more than 25 years older than the advertiser. Interestingly, two men who were 7 years younger wrote that they hoped their youth was not a problem; one stated that though only 31, he "thought of much older stuff."

Murstein (1986) states that in the initial stage of courtship, the social exchange model fits best and that each party uses the "minimax" strategy to attract the most qualified partner at the least personal cost. Personals ads, therefore, would seem to present a situation ideal for initiating courtship in that there is little risk of social embarrassment for being refused and that financial, privacy, and time costs are minimal. Individuals who have had experience in answering and placing such ads and who have subsequently met the advertiser or respondent state the individuals are typically very truthful in describing themselves. However, often only one person in 15 or 20 who respond is geographically close enough and otherwise compatible enough to date more than one or two times. Therefore, it may be costlier in time and effort than is immediately apparent.

What type of strategy tended to underlie the persuasive attempts by ad respondents? In the current experiment, the minimax strategy posited by Murstein (1986) was more evident in males than in females. This tendency was exemplified by the fact that men tended to admit to more serious liabilities than did women, but they usually explicitly defended these liabilities, often suggesting compensatory traits that offset them. For example, one man stated that he was missing a limb but was in good physical shape, owned a large estate, and was found very attractive by "quality" women. Another said he had no college education or professional job but looked like a movie star, was 15 years younger than the advertiser, and knew how to please older women sexually. Men were also more likely to be much older or younger than the advertiser and to argue that the age difference was inconsequential.

Women were more apt to seek equality, except in level of education and occupational status, where they were slightly less qualified than male respondents. Overall, women reported more similarity to the advertiser in age, attractiveness, intelligence, and every category of interest, including active sports. The only woman who explicitly mentioned that a man's income was important specified her own income and stipulated that the man match that as well as her interests, personality traits, attractiveness, and sensuality. This example was extreme and perhaps illustrates that a very literal emphasis on relationship equality is not always positive.

In summary, then, men were less likely than women to offer directly comparable qualities and showed more of a tendency to take risks in pursuing a possibly unattainable advertiser. Fewer women's letters were usable for the study because they were less apt to address the stimulus ad specifically. Those who did respond were less likely than men to provide their addresses for would-be correspondents, and of those who did, all lived out of town, thereby demonstrating more caution, which may indeed be functional in a society in which date rape is sometimes inflicted on women by men but rarely the reverse. The author's experience in receiving the two irate, threatening letters from men who noticed the experimental manipulation would lend support to the exercise of caution by women in general in the personals ads arena. Thus, this study supported Murstein's (1986) contention that more societal constraints exist on a woman's ability to initiate courtship than on a man's.

Although this study is limited from a statistical sense because of its small sample size and the lack of control available in a field study, it is a start in exploring the dating process at midlife for intelligent professional people. Intellectual giftedness is a rare quality in the population; it makes sense that similarly gifted people would be attracted to each other and that their similarity in personality and interests would transcend their differences in gender. However, attraction and friendship may not necessarily imply marital intentions, as discussed above.

Finally, this study is socially sensitive (Sieber & Stanley, 1988), as the class of people who make use of the personals ads are vulnerable to ridicule by society in general and by social science in particular. Some of the research (Harrison & Saeed, 1977) refers to these people, for example, as "lonely hearts" trying "to make a deal." As many authors (Jones, 1982; Shaver, 1986) have pointed out, lonely people in general are stigmatized in social science research, being blamed for their unpleasant emotion as being deficient in social skills and personality inadequacies.

Emotional loneliness probably is the chief motivation to advertise and respond to personals ads. However, I believe that the respondents in this study were suffering from temporary, situationally induced loneliness rather than the more dispositional chronic loneliness. The deficient social skills outlined by Jones (1982), which are characteristic of the chronically lonely, were rarely observed in the responses for this study. Indeed, the majority of the letters were notable for their wit, charm, humor, warmth, and display of interest in the ad writer.

Shaver (1986) points out that temporary emotional loneliness due to loss of an intimate relationship can be adaptive and is possibly biologically based. It has the function of motivating us to find a new close attachment when we have suffered a primary loss and is therefore potentially growth-inducing. Most respondents to these ads seemed to be using an active, problem-solving style of coping with their lonely feelings by genuinely reaching out to the personals ad writer. With sources of situational loneliness increasingly common in our society, it seems that further exploration into the personals ads medium would also enrich our understanding of and respect for people who are trying to deal with this strong, subjectively unpleasant but potentially adaptive emotion.

REFERENCES

Deaux, K., & Hanna, R. (1984). Courtship in the personals column: The evidence of gender and sexual orientation. *Sex Roles, 11*, 363–375.

Haan, N. (1974). Changes in young adults after Peace Corps experiences: Political-social views, moral reasoning, and perceptions of self and parents. *Journal of Youth and Adolescence, 3,* 177–194.

Harrison, A. A., & Saeed, L. (1977). Let's make a deal: An analysis of revelations and stipulations in lonely hearts advertisements. *Journal of Personality and Social Psychology, 35,* 257–264.

Hochschild, A. R. (1983). *The managed heart.* Berkeley, CA: University of California Press.

Jacobson, G. F. (1983). *The multiple crises of marital separation and divorce.* New York: Grune & Stratton.

Jones, W. H. (1982). Loneliness and social behavior. In L. A. Peplau & D. Perlman (Eds.), *Loneliness: A sourcebook of current theory, research, and therapy* (pp. 238–254). New York: Wiley-Interscience.

Murstein, B. I. (1986). *Paths to marriage.* Beverly Hills, CA: Sage.

Noble, K. D. (1987). The dilemma of the gifted women. *Psychology of Women Quarterly, 11,* 367–378.

Reis, H. T. (1985). The role of the self in the initiation and course of social interaction. In W. Ickes (Ed.), *Compatible and incompatible relationships* (pp. 210–226). New York: Springer-Verlag.

Russo, N. F. (1985). Sex-role stereotyping, socialization, and sexism. In A. G. Sargent (Ed.), *Beyond sex roles* (pp. 150–167). New York: West.

Shaver, P. (1986, August). *Being lonely, falling in love: Perspectives from attachment theory.* Paper presented at the Annual Convention of the American Psychological Association, Washington, DC.

Sieber, J. E., & Stanley, B. (1988). Ethical and professional dimensions of socially sensitive research. *American Psychologist, 43,* 49–55.

Simeone, A. (1987). *Academic women.* South Hadley, MA: Bergin & Garvey.

The Effects of Gender-Role Salience on Women's Causal Attributions for Success and Failure

Beverly Ayers-Nachamkin

Attribution theory maintains that individuals generate explanations for behavioral events in their world. By means of such causal attributions, the individual is able to develop and maintain an orderly, understandable world (Heider, 1958).

Many investigations have focused on self-attributions for success and failure: the explanations that people generate to explain their performance on a given task. Four factors have been identified to account for the different kinds of self-attributions people typically use: (1) ability or skill, (2) motivation or effort, (3) task difficulty, (4) luck or fate (Frieze, 1976; Weiner, 1972, 1974; Weiner et al., 1971). The ability and effort factors are regarded as internal causes (a quality or factor within the individual), whereas task difficulty and luck are considered external causes (a quality or factor inherent in the particular situation). These four factors are further distinguished in terms of their stability. Ability and task difficulty are considered to be stable and enduring, characteristics that remain unchanged across time; effort and luck are considered to be temporary factors, conditions that are relevant only to the current situation.

factors (personal ability or effort), but external factors (difficulty of the task or bad luck) are blamed for failure (cf. Bradley, 1978; Miller & Ross, 1975). Initial interpretations of this phenomenon focused on self-esteem (e.g., Bowerman, 1978; Covington & Omelich, 1979). It seemed logical that individuals would try to bolster their self-esteem by taking personal credit for success and blaming failure on something or someone else; logical, that is, until cumulative research made it clear that this attributional pattern, the "self-serving bias," is more common among men that it is among women. In fact, research indicates that it is not unusual for women to attribute success to external factors and failure to internal ones (e.g., Deaux & Farris, 1977; Gould & Slone, 1982; Hackett & Campbell, 1987; Zuckerman, 1979).

In the effort to discover a comprehensive explanation of the "self-serving bias," one that could emphasize the behavior of women as well as men, three general approaches emerged: (1) task relevance or ego involvement, (2) information-processing based on expectations, and (3) self-presentation.

The ego-involvement approach proposed that the self-serving bias would be exhibited only to the extent that the individual regarded the task in question as relevant to self, specifically to gender identity.[1] It was pointed out that most of the tasks used in this research could be regarded as primarily relevant to stereotypically masculine domains such as intelligence, competition, and spatial ability (cf. Zuckerman, 1979). The idea was that women had less ego involvement in such tasks and therefore experienced no need to protect or enhance self-esteem in terms of their attributions for performance on tasks less relevant to the woman's self-image. Studies designed to test this hypothesis found that in general men more reliably exhibited the self-serving bias than did women even when the task was described as one on which women typically perform better than men do (e.g., Deaux, 1976a; Deaux & Emswiller, 1974; Deaux & Farris, 1977).

The second line of research focused on individuals' prior expectations for their performance on a given task. The hypothesis was that when actual performance matched previous expectations for that performance, individuals would be more likely to make internal stable attributions for their performance because their expectations had been confirmed. Conversely, when actual performance did not match initial expectations, individuals would be more likely to make external, temporary attributions because their expectations had been disconfirmed; their performance had surprised them. From this perspective, individuals who expect to succeed on a task and do so will attribute that success to their own ability, for instance; individuals who expect to perform poorly on a task and, in fact, succeed at it are surprised and attribute this unexpected success to good luck (e.g., Frieze, Whitley, Hanusa, & McHugh, 1982; Simon & Feather, 1973). This information-processing approach is less a solution than an extension of the dilemma because women typically report lower expectations for their performance than men do on most tasks (cf. Deaux, 1976a). An adequate explanation for the observed gender differences in use of the self-serving bias must also include an explanation of the preceding gender differences in level of expectations for performance.

In her review article, Bradley (1978) identified strategic self-presentations as a potential explanatory model for self-serving biases. She suggested that people are keenly interested in presenting themselves to others in the most positive way possible. Most of the time the result would be taking personal credit for success so that others will see us as competent and blaming situational factors for failure so that others will at least not view us as incompetent. She suggested, although not specifically in terms of gender differences, that there are times when it might be to one's advantage to appear modest and to cite good luck as an influential factor in one's success.

A fourth approach to understanding observed gender differences in attributions for success and failure has been suggested by a number of researchers, all of whom call attention in one way or another to the differential gender-role expectations that critically influence the behaviors of women and men (e.g., Ayers-Nachamkin, 1982; Deaux, 1976b; Deaux & Major, 1987; Eagly, 1987).

The classic studies of Rosenkrantz, Vogel, Bee, Broverman, and Broverman (1968) and Broverman, Vogel, Broverman, Clarkson, and Rosenkrantz (1972) demonstrated that people expect and perceive women to be less competitive, intelligent, and self-confident and more dependent, subjective, and passive than men. Although these characteristics may be viewed as stereotypes or even as reflections of reality, they may be more importantly viewed as gender-role expectations, shared cognitive conceptions of the manner in which individuals *ought to* conduct themselves depending upon whether they are male or female. It is worth noting that in spite of the fact that these studies were conducted two decades ago, there is no evidence of substantial change in the content of these gender-role expectations (e.g., Deaux & Lewis, 1983; Eagly & Steffen, 1984; Poppen, 1987; Ruble, 1983; Stangor, 1988; Werner & LaRussa, 1985).

Most people fill a number of roles even on a daily basis, for example, mother, daughter, homeowner, commuter, business manager, supervisor, subordinate, restaurant patron. What is less obvious is that each individual is always involved in at least one other role concurrently by virtue of sex. Linton (1945) termed the social positions we occupy as a result of biological/physiological characteristics (e.g., race, age, sex) ascribed roles,[2] and these ascribed roles "are probably always active, with the role expectations of other achieved roles superimposed upon them" (Sarbin & Allen, 1968, p. 538). The success/failure setting involves role expectations that are incompatible with feminine gender-role expectations, but nearly identical to masculine gender role expectations (Ayers-Nachamkin, 1982). When a woman is asked to explain her performance in such a setting, she must at some level decide whether her attributions will be compatible with the expectations surrounding the role of "achiever" (competent, competitive, assertive, confident) or with those surrounding her ever-present, ascribed gender role (mediocre, cooperative, submissive, uncertain). Rather than run the risk of incurring the negative sanctions associated with failure to conform to gender-role expectations (e.g., Costrich, Feinstein, Kidder, Maracek, & Pascale, 1975; Davidson, 1981; Tilby & Kalen, 1980). It is suggested that women more often choose to attribute success or failure in a way that is compatible with their gender role, hence incompatible with the expectations surrounding the role of achiever. In other words, women are less likely to exhibit the self-serving bias.

The present study examined a simple prediction based on the above model. If a woman is put in a success/failure setting where the expectations surrounding the role of achiever are compatible with her gender-role expectations, she should explain her performance in such a way that she appears to exhibit this self-serving bias; that is, she will attribute success internally and failure externally. Second, if gender-role expectations are made salient, this attributional pattern should be even more pronounced. To test these predictions, salience of gender-role expectations (high or normal) and outcome of task performance (success or failure) were varied factorially in a 2 × 2 design.

METHOD

Subjects

Sixty female students enrolled in the introductory psychology class at a large university participated in this study in partial fulfillment of class requirements. Subjects were randomly assigned to one of the four conditions resulting from the two grouping factors, salience (high, normal) and performance outcome (success, failure).

Procedure

Subjects were tested individually. Upon arriving for the study they were invited to be seated at a desk in a small room and asked to read and sign the consent statement, which informed them that the purpose of the experiment was to learn additional information about certain psychological inventories. Subjects for whom feminine gender role was to be salient were asked to fill out a questionnaire as a favor to another researcher "since we have some extra time." The questionnaire was actually the Personality Attributes Questionnaire (PAQ; Spence & Helmreich, 1978), a measure of gender typing with relatively high face validity. All subjects, regardless of salience condition were given instructions to read about the "Feminine Design Coordination Task" they were to perform. Those instructions included information intended to convince subjects that this was a task designed to yield information about the feminine personality:

> . . . Many studies have shown that this task is a reliable measure of sensitivity, and also that it gives a good indication of a person's success in sensing other people's subtle feelings — or more generally, their capacity for sympathizing with the wants and needs of other people. As you can see, this task was basically designed to yield information about the feminine personality.

The subjects were then told about the more specific aspects of the task. They were given a series of multicolored, geometric designs (referred to as figuregrams). For each figuregram they were asked to select which of three control figuregrams the stimulus best matched. They were given a sample figuregram to match to the first set of control figuregrams. This sample figuregram, unlike those that followed, was designed to match just one of the controls. The experimenter (female) pointed out the correct match to the subject and explained that in the course of the experiment they would be given three different groups of figuregrams, five figuregrams to a group. With each group they would be given three different control figuregrams from which to choose a match. As a result, they were making a total of 15 matches. Subjects were informed that the average number of correct matches on the task was 8.

At this point, subjects were given a short questionnaire that asked them to predict the total number of correct matches they would make (a measure of their expectancy of success) and asked them to rate on 11-point scales the extent to which they valued in themselves the characteristics involved in doing this task and how important it was to them to score as high as possible (measures of ego-involvement in the task).

Upon completion of the questionnaire, the experimenter left the room, telling the subject to begin the task and saying that the experimenter would notify her every 20 seconds to go on to the next figuregram.

Each time the experimenter returned to tell the subject to go on to the next figuregram, the match the subject had just selected was surreptitiously noted and then marked on a score "key" in such a way as to give the subject the appropriate feedback for the condition to which she had been randomly assigned. Feedback on their performance was given to the subjects after each set of five figuregrams. The experimenter presented them with a fictitious score key and showed the subjects how well they had done on that set. Subjects in the failure condition were given feedback indicating that they had matched only one of the first set of five matches correctly, two of the second set correctly, and one of the third set. For subjects in the success condition, the feedback was four of five correct on the first set, five of five on the second set, and four of five on the third set. After each subject had completed all 15 matches, the experimenter gave her a computer printout showing various statistics about the task, including the "average score" on the task (8). Subjects in the failure condition had it pointed out to them that they matched only four figuregrams correctly, placing them in the bottom 20% of our sample. Subjects in the success condition were told that they had matched 13 of 15 figuregrams correctly, placing them easily in the top 10% of our sample.

At this point the subjects were asked to answer a short posttask questionnaire to measure their perceptions of success/failure ("What was your score on the task?") and of gender-role linkage of the task. For the latter, they were presented with an 11-point scale anchored at one end with "men definitely higher" and at the other end with "women definitely higher" and asked to rate the extent to which they thought men or women score higher on this task. They were asked to evaluate their performance in terms of the four major attributional factors of ability, effort, task difficulty, and luck. For each of these attributional factors the subjects rated the extent to which that factor hindered, helped, or had no effect on their performance, using scales ranging from -11 to $+11$. Finally, they were asked to predict how well they thought they would perform on such a task in future.

RESULTS

Factorial analyses of variance were performed on the various measures taken in this study. The independent variables were gender-role salience (high, normal) and performance outcome (success, failure).

All subjects, regardless of gender-role salience, reported that they expected to make slightly more than 50% correct matches ($M = 9.32$). The difference between the two groups was negligible. In other words, their expectations for success were not low, but neither were they much above the reported average (8).

There were no differences among the subjects' ratings of how much they valued the characteristics supposedly measured by this task ($M = 7.27$) or of how important it was to them to score as high as possible ($M = 7.18$). These ratings suggest just slightly above average ego involvement in this task (the median rating on the 11-point scale would be 6).

The subjects reported that they thought women were more likely to receive higher scores on the Design Coordination Task than men were ($M = 7.77$), and all subjects reported their own scores accurately, 13 correct in the success condition and 4 correct in the failure condition. It appears

TABLE 19.1   Mean Attributions to Internal Factors as a Function of Gender-Role Salience and Performance Outcome

	Gender-Role Salience	
Outcome	High	Normal
Success	5.81[a]	3.07[b]
Failure	−0.63[c]	0.16[c]

Note. The higher the score, the more internal the attribution. Means with different superscripts differ significantly at $p < .05$, one-tailed.

($M = 7.77$), and all subjects reported their own scores accurately, 13 correct in the success condition and 4 correct in the failure condition. It appears that the subjects believed this to be a measure of the "feminine personality" and that they correctly understood the feedback concerning their own performances.

Subjects had also been asked to assess the degree to which ability, effort, task difficulty, and luck affected their outcome on the task. Response scales ranged from −11 to +11. When a rating indicated that the subject felt her outcome, success or failure, was helped by a given factor, the rating was scored positively. If a factor was felt to hinder their performance, that factor was scored negatively. Thus, in the success condition, all factors that the subjects believed to be helping them were scored positively and all hindering factors were scored negatively. In the failure condition, however, all factors subjects believed to be hindering performance were scored positively because they were perceived as contributing to the failure. Factors believed to be helping performance were scored negatively because they were perceived as working against the subjects' ultimate outcome, failure (Stephan, Rosenfeld, & Stephan, 1976). Based on these transformed scores, a composite attribution score was calculated: the average of the ratings for external attributions (task and luck) were subtracted from the average of the ratings for internal attributions (ability and effort).

As predicted, the subjects who succeeded on a task they believed to be a measure of feminine personality attributed that success to their own ability and effort to a much greater degree than did the subjects who failed, $F(1, 56) = 17.37$, $p < .0001$. Although the predicted main effect for gender-role salience was not significant, this was primarily due to the similarity of attributional ratings in the failure condition. As may be seen in Table 19.1, successful subjects for whom gender role was highly salient made significantly higher internal attributions than did successful subjects for whom gender role was not unusually salient.

There was a main effect for performance outcome in terms of how well subjects thought they would perform on such a task in the future, $F(1,$

in the future ($M = 12.86$), whereas the subjects who had failed on the present task expected to make an average of about 7 correct matches in the future ($M = 6.60$).

There were no significant interactions observed among the remaining three attributional factors; however, subjects who experienced success credited their own efforts to a significantly higher degree than those who experienced failure, $F(1, 53) = 37.23$, $p < .0001$. On the other hand, those who experienced failure blamed that failure on the difficulty of the task to a significantly greater degree than did those who experienced success, $F(1, 53) = 8.34$, $p < .006$.

DISCUSSION

The data with regard to subjects' attributions for their performance are a reasonably clear demonstration of the classic self-serving pattern, remarkable because it is so seldom observed among women. This result supports the hypothesis that women choose to make attributions for performance that are compatible with the expectations that accompany their gender role. When the latter expectations are compatible with those for the role of an achiever (a relatively rare occurrence outside the domestic domain), women will appear to engage in much the same self-serving bias that men do. Unlike men, women more often have to choose which self to serve, the feminine or the competent.

Even when the expectations relating to gender role are compatible with the expectations relating to achievement, however, a woman must still weigh the cultural expectation that she should present herself modestly (Gould & Slone, 1982). It's interesting to note that the women in the failure condition in this study still did not forcefully blame external circumstances, as evidenced by the fact that their average attribution scores were not profoundly negative. Then, too, although their internal attribution scores were significantly elevated in the success condition, they are still modest in view of a ceiling of $+ 11$. To some extent it may be reasonable to suggest that these data do lend support to strategic self-presentation as a partial explanation of the self-serving bias.

The subjects in this study indicated moderate levels of ego involvement in the task: the values supposedly measured by the inventory were of slightly more than average importance to them, as was their score. On the basis of the task relevance or ego involvement explanation of the self-serving bias, the exhibition of such midrange scores would lead one to predict that subjects would have little need to use a self-serving bias to enhance or protect their self-esteem. Such a prediction would not be supported by these data.

The information-processing explanation of the self-serving bias would predict that subjects whose expectations regarding their anticipated performance were confirmed would make more internal attributions for that performance, whereas subjects whose initial expectations were disconfirmed would make more external attributions for their performance. In either case, according to this model, subjects should make predictions for future performance that were very similar to their originally expected performances. Again, these data do not support this explanation. All of the subjects in this study reported that they expected to perform in a sightly better than average manner. All of the subjects therefore could be said to have had their original expectations disconfirmed, half by virtue of surprising success and half by virtue of surprising failure. The half who experienced disconfirming success attributed it more to internal causes (ability and effort) and revised their expectations for future performance upward. The half who experienced disconfirming failure attributed it significantly less to internal causes and revised their expectations for future performance downward. In other words, these subjects not only evidenced the self-serving bias, they appeared to adopt a logical approach to future prediction as opposed to the approach proposed by the information-processing model.

The laboratory experiment used in this study, as in so many others, addresses only average differences, in this case in the attribution patterns of women in achievement settings. Often the researcher who adopts a "role theoretical approach" has been led to conclude that socialization is the causal agent—a global explanation for global phenomena. Recently, Eagly (1987) has directed attention to a more specific aspect of the differential socialization of women and men: division of labor. She has suggested that parents tend to place their children in different kinds of settings depending on their sex. Girls are more likely than boys to be asked to assist with food gathering (grocery shopping), preparation, and presentation; with washing dishes, dusting, and cleaning the bathroom. Boys are more likely than girls to be asked to assist with taking out the garbage, shoveling the snow, mowing the lawn, and washing and waxing the car. Boys are more likely than girls to be given "action" toys: cars and trucks, model trains, baseball gloves and bats, basketballs and backboards, and footballs. Girls are more likely than boys to be given "passive" toys: dolls, crayons and paints, and stuffed animals. Before long we are giving girls gifts that are not toys at all, such as perfume, jewelry, and clothes, the literal trappings of femininity. Meanwhile, boys are receiving chemistry and Erector sets and watches that incorporate stopwatch or calculator functions and relate time to the movement of planets in space. These settings we create for our children carry very definite messages about what we expect boys and girls to be interested in and capable of doing. Within this organizing structure (division of labor) causal factors that in isolation seemed weak and simplistic realize the power of drops of water etching stone over time: Henning & Jardim (1977) pointed to women's lack of participation in team sports as a factor important in explaining the small numbers of women in managerial positions; other researchers (e.g., Fagot & Littman, 1976; Sprafkin, Serbin, Denier, & Connor, 1983) claimed that differential experience with toys helped explain women's lower average performance at visual-spatial tasks relative to men's; differential evaluative feedback promoted learned helplessness in girls (e.g., Dweck, Davidson, Nelson, & Enna, 1978), and so on.

To be sure, differential socialization of girls and boys is not an inflexible dichotomy. Nevertheless, Eagly (1987) maintains that on the average this relative division of labor leads to (1) differential gender-role expectations and (2) sex-typed skills and beliefs, both of which contribute to observed "sex" differences in social behavior. She goes on to suggest that a variety of such differences may be attributed in part to the proximal environmental cues that exist in any given situation.

Focusing in large part on this aspect, the immediate environmental situation, Deaux and Major (1987) use a greatly expanded version of the self-fulfilling prophecy to aid in understanding and predicting the occurrence of observed gender differences (see also Darley & Fazio, 1980). This "expectancy confirmation" model points to a variety of potential mediators or environmental cues that can be expected to influence the actual display of gender-linked social behaviors:

> The behavior of women and men, we have argued, is influenced by several sets of factors: the target's own goals and self-schemata, the expectancies and goals of other people with whom the target interacts, and the context in which that interaction takes place. In our view, the weights of these factors are not stable, but fluctuate. This pattern of fluctuation, we suggest, depends on two major modifying conditions: (a) characteristics of the expectancy, such as the degree to which it is perceived as socially desirable, the degree to which it is held with high certainty by the perceiver or the self, and the degree to which it is clearly conveyed by situational cues; and (b) the degree to which concerns with self-presentation or self-verification are aroused in the target (Deaux & Major, 1987, pp. 377–378).

Within the context of these two models, especially the latter, it is possible to view the present study as having initially created two slightly different environmental situations to which we assume the subjects have brought similar (Caucasian, middle-class) gender-role socialization histories. In one situation (high salience) subjects were gently reminded of the centrality of gender-role expectations, thus increasing their weight relative to the second situation (normal salience). In both sets of circumstances subjects were made aware of the desirability of feminine personality characteristics as promoters of higher performance levels. In both cases subjects displayed self-serving biases compatible with the cues provided and weighted in accordance with the initial manipulation. It is actually rather impressive that such a comparatively weak manipulation (administration of the PAQ) was sufficient to produce significant gender role–related differences in the attributional behavior of these women. Clearly this study supports the prediction that in those environments in which gender role is even minimally salient, one may expect to observe greater apparent adherence to gender-stereotyped behavior.

Taken in combination, the theoretical propositions of Deaux and Major (1987) and Eagly (1987) should provide researchers interested in gender differences in social behavior with a wealth of testable hypotheses and a dynamic framework in which to place their results for some time to come.

NOTES

1. As suggested by Unger (1979) and Sheriff (1982), the term *gender* is used to refer to a social categorization connoting psychological attributes considered characteristic of members of each sexual (anatomical) category.

2. Sociologists working within the framework of expectation states theory (e.g., Berger, Cohen, & Zelditch, 1972; Berger, Fisek, Norman, & Zelditch, 1977; Berger, Rosenholtz, & Zelditch, 1980) use the term *diffuse status characteristics* in somewhat the same way.

REFERENCES

Ayers-Nachamkin, B. (1982). Sex differences in self-serving biases: Success expectancies or role expectations? *Dissertation Abstracts International, 43*, 4193–B.

Berger, J. H., Cohen, B. P., & Zelditch, M., Jr. (1972). Status characteristics and social interaction. *American Sociological Review, 37*, 241–255.

Berger, J. H., Fisek, M. H., Norman, R. A., & Zelditch, M., Jr. (1977). *Status characteristics and social interaction: An expectation states approach.* New York: American Elsevier.

Berger, J. H., Rosenholtz, S. J., & Zelditch, M., Jr. (1980). Status organizing processes. In A. Inkeles, N. J. Smelser, & R. H. Turner (Eds.), *Annual review of sociology* (Vol. 6, pp. 479–508). Palo Alto, CA: Annual Reviews.

Bowerman, W. R. (1978). Subjective competence: The structure, process, and function of self-reference causal attributions. *Journal for the Theory of Social Behavior, 8*, 45–75.

Bradley, G. W. (1978). Self-serving biases in the attribution process: A reexamination of the fact or fiction question. *Journal of Personality and Social Psychology, 36*, 56–71.

Broverman, I. K., Vogel, S. R., Broverman, D. M., Clarkson, F. E., & Rosenkrantz, P. S. (1972). Sex-role stereotypes: A current appraisal. *Journal of Social Issues, 28*(2), 59–78.

Costrich, N., Feinstein, J., Kidder, L., Maracek, J., & Pascale, L. (1975). When stereotypes hurt: Three studies of penalties for sex-role reversals. *Journal of Experimental Social Psychology, 11,* 520–530.

Covington, M. V., & Omelich, C. L. (1979). Are causal attributions causal? A path analysis of the cognitive model of achievement motivation. *Journal of Personality and Social Psychology, 37,* 1487–1504.

Darley, J. M., & Fazio, R. H. (1980). Expectancy confirmation processes arising in the social interaction sequence. *American Psychologist, 35,* 867–881.

Davidson, L. R. (1981). Pressures and pretense: Living with gender stereotypes. *Sex Roles, 7,* 331–347.

Deaux, K. (1976a). *The behavior of women and men.* Monterey, CA: Brooks/Cole.

Deaux, K. (1976b). Sex: A perspective on the attribution process. In J. H. Harvey, J. I. Ickes, & R. E. Kidd (Eds.), *New dimensions in attribution research* (Vol. 1). Hillsdale, NJ: Erlbaum.

Deaux, K., & Emswiller, T. (1974). Explanations of successful performance on sex-linked tasks: What is skill for the male is luck for the female. *Journal of Personality and Social Psychology, 29,* 80–85.

Deaux, K., & Farris, E. (1977). Attributing causes for one's own performance: The effects of sex, norms, and outcomes. *Journal of Research in Personality, 11,* 59–72.

Deaux, K., & Lewis L. L. (1983). Components of gender stereotypes. *Psychological Documents, 13*(25, No. 2583).

Deaux, K., & Major, B. (1987). Putting gender into context: An interactive model of gender-related behavior. *Psychological Review, 94,* 369–389.

Dweck, C. S., Davidson, W., Nelson, S., & Enna, B. (1978). Sex differences in learned helplessness: 2. The contingencies of evaluative feedback in the classroom; 3. An experimental analysis. *Developmental Psychology, 14,* 268–276.

Eagly, A. H. (1987). *Sex differences in social behavior: A social-role interpretation.* Hillsdale, NJ: Erlbaum.

Eagly, A. H., & Steffen, V. J. (1984). Gender stereotypes stem from the distribution of women and men into social roles. *Journal of Personality and Social Psychology, 46,* 735–754.

Fagot, B., & Littman, I. (1976). Relation of pre-school sex-typing to intellectual performance in elementary school. *Psychological Reports, 39,* 699–704.

Frieze, I. H. (1976). Causal attributions and information seeking to explain success and failure. *Journal of Research in Personality, 10,* 293–305.

Frieze, I. H., Whitley, B. E., Jr., Hanusa, B. H., & McHugh, M. C. (1982). Assessing the theoretical models for sex differences in causal attributions for success and failure. *Sex Roles, 8,* 333–344.

Gould, R. J., & Slone, C. G. (1982). The "feminine modesty" effect: A self-presentational interpretation of sex differences in causal attribution. *Personality and Social Psychology Bulletin, 8,* 477–485.

Hackett, G., & Campbell, N. K. (1987). Task self-efficacy and task interest as a function of performance on a gender neutral task. *Journal of Vocational Behavior, 30,* 203–215.

Heider, F. (1958). *The psychology of interpersonal relations.* New York: Wiley.

Henning, M., & Jardim, A. (1977). *The managerial woman.* Garden City, NY: Anchor Press/Doubleday.

Linton, R. (1945). *The cultural background of personality.* New York: Appleton-Century-Crofts.

Miller, D. T., & Ross, M. (1975). Self-serving biases in the attribution of causality: Fact or fiction? *Psychological Bulletin, 82,* 213–225.

Poppen, P. J. (1987, August). *Male and female sexist beliefs: Persistence and change over ten years.* Paper presented at the annual meeting of the American Psychological Association, New York.

Rosenkrantz, P. S., Vogel, S. R., Bee, H., Broverman, I. K., & Broverman, D. M. (1968). Sex role stereotypes and self-concepts in college students. *Journal of Consulting and Clinical Psychology, 32,* 287–295.

Ruble, T. L. (1983). Sex stereotypes: Issues of change in the 1970s. *Sex Roles, 9,* 397–402.

Sarbin, T. R., & Allen, V. L. (1968). Role theory. In G. Lindzey & E. Aronson (Eds.), *Handbook of social psychology* (Vol. 1) (pp. 488–567). Reading, MA: Addison-Wesley.

Sherif, C. W. (1982). Needed concepts in the study of gender identity. *Psychology of Women Quarterly, 16,* 375–398.

Simon, J. G., & Feather, N. T. (1973). Causal attributions for success and failure at university examinations. *Journal of Educational Psychology, 64,* 46–56.

Spence, J. T., & Helmreich, R. L. (1978). *Masculinity and femininity: Their psychological dimensions, correlates, and antecedents.* Austin: University of Texas Press.

Sprafkin, C., Serbin, L. A., Denier, C., & Connor, J. M. (1983). Sex-differentiated play: Cognitive consequences and early interventions. In M. B. Liss (Ed.), *Social and cognitive skills* (pp. 167–192). New York: Academic Press.

Stangor, C. (1988). Stereotype accessibility and information processing. *Personality and Social Psychology Bulletin, 14,* 694–708.

Stephan, W. G., Rosenfield, D., & Stephan, C. (1976). Egotism in males and females. *Journal of Personality and Social Psychology, 34,* 1161–1167.

Tilby, P. J., & Kalin, R. (1980). Effects of sex-role deviant lifestyles in otherwise normal persons on the perception of maladjustment. *Sex Roles, 6,* 581–592.

Unger, R. K. (1979). Toward a redefinition of sex and gender. *American Psychologist, 34,* 1085–1094.

Weiner, B. (1972). *Theories of motivation: From mechanism to cognition.* Chicago: Markham Publishing.

Weiner, B. (Ed.). (1974). *Achievement motivation and attribution theory.* Morristown, NJ: General Learning Press.

Weiner, B., Frieze, I., Kukla, A., Reed, L., Rest, S., & Rosenbaum, R. M. (1971). *Perceiving the causes of success and failure.* Morristown, NJ: General Learning Press.

Werner, P. D., & LaRussa, G. W. (1985). Persistence and change in sex-role stereotypes. *Sex Roles, 12,* 1089–1100.

Zuckerman, M. (1979). Attribution of success and failure revisited, or: The motivational bias is alive and well in attribution theory. *Journal of Personality, 47,* 245–287.

■ 20
Stereotypes and Desirability Ratings for Female and Male Roles

Michele F. Larrow and Morton Wiener

There has been much controversy over the use of the terms *stereotype* and *prejudice* (Allport, 1954; Ashmore & Del Boca, 1981; Katz & Braly, 1933). We would distinguish three terms: categorization, stereotypes, and prejudice. *Categorization* will be used when classification of a person into a category is based on the necessary defining attributes of class membership. *Stereotype* is the classification based on nondefinitional attributes. Finally, *prejudice* is classified when social evaluation is explicitly included with the stereotype. Although stereotypes and prejudice may not be separated in everyday usage, we hold that they are at least capable of being assessed separately. In the field of sex/gender research, we would like to make a distinction between using the term *sex* to refer to categorizations of males and females based on biological attributes, such as chromosomes, genitalia, reproductive function, and so on, and *gender* to refer to stereotypes of women and men based on nonbiological attributes such as clothing, hairstyle, behaviors, and the like. Most of our beliefs about men and women are based on gender stereotypes.

The purpose of this study was to examine gender and sex stereotypes by eliciting ratings of women and men in a variety of different roles. When gender is held constant, we will be examining the effect of roles; and when role is held constant, we will be examining the effects of gender (because we are investigating stereotypes, we can make no claims about sex differences). Researchers (Broverman, Vogel, Broverman, Clarkson, & Rosenkrantz, 1972; Sherriffs & McKee, 1957; Williams & Bennett, 1975) have investigated stereotypes of men and women as if each group were homogeneous, that is, independent of different gender roles within each sex. Later researchers (Clifton, McGrath, & Wick, 1976; Deaux, Winton, Crowley, & Lewis, 1985; England & Hyland 1986) proposed that men and women may fill different roles and that the stereotype in terms of instrumental and expressive traits will vary with the role (e.g., housewife, professional woman, athletic woman, macho man, businessman, family man). These researchers typically examined a range of roles but did not examine the social desirability associated with the traits typical of each of the roles, nor did they (except England and Hyland [1986]) explicitly contrast men and women in comparable roles. Also, the methods used for measuring stereotypes did not always permit detailed comparisons to be made within gender and within roles. The Rasch latent trait method (Wright & Stone, 1979), which was used in this study, produces a scale distribution of the 30 traits for each of the stereotypes. General comparisons can be made between the scales, using correlational coefficients, and more detailed comparisons of single traits across roles or gender can be made using a Tukey t-test.

For this study, the distribution of the typicality and social desirability of the trait ratings for gender subtypes was assessed. This study compared the ratings of "equivalent" man–woman role subtypes: Typical Man and Typical Women, Wife-Mother and Husband-Father, Jock and Dumb Blond–Airhead, Feminist and Macho Man, Gay Man and Lesbian, Career Woman––Professional Woman and Professional Man–Businessman, Wimp-Nerd and Wallflower-Brain, and Sensual Women–"Cosmo" Type and Playboy. Comparisons were made within gender to examine role effects and within role to examine gender effects. Comparisons were also made between the social desirability and the typicality ratings.

METHOD

Subjects

Participants were 74 men and 83 women, aged 17–58 years; mean age, 21 years. They were undergraduates and continuing-education student volunteers recruited from a liberal arts university and an engineering college in Massachusetts.

Procedure and Materials

Ten graduate students (four male and six female) were asked to list "types" of women and men. From this list, the most popular responses were chosen and modified by the authors so that there was an "equivalent" male and female in each role. The 16 gender stereotypes selected were Typical Man and Typical Woman, Wife-Mother and Husband-Father, Jock and Dumb Blond–Airhead, Feminist and Macho Man, Gay Man and Lesbian, Career Woman–Professional Woman and Professional Man–Businessman, Wimp-Nerd and Wallflower-Brain, and Sensual Women–"Cosmo" Type and Playboy. Participants rated 4 of the 16 stereotypes on 30 personality traits. Ten of the traits had been identified in the literature as connoting expressive-"feminine" behaviors: appreciative, dependent, emotional, gentle, sensitive to others, sociable, sympathetic/tender/kind, tactful, understanding, and warm/affectionate. Ten were identified as instrument-"masculine": active/adventurous, aggressive, ambitious, assertive-outspoken, competitive, dominant, independent, individualistic, logical/analytical, and skillful-competent. Finally, 10 were ostensibly gender-neutral: adaptable, conventional, even-tempered, good sense of humor, happy, honest, intelligent, interesting, likable, and sincere. The participants rated the typicality on a 3-point scale (not typical, typical, and very typical), as well as the social desirability (positive, negative, or neutral) of each of the 30 traits for each subtype they were rating. They also rated themselves on the 30 traits and rated how similar they were to the 16 stereotypes (on a 3-point scale).

RESULTS

Stereotypes

The data were analyzed using a Rasch latent trait analysis, which produced a scale that showed how typical or desirable the traits were for each role. For each trait, a value is derived (in "logits," or the natural log odds) that represents how easy it is to endorse that trait for that particular role. Correlations of the values for the traits across roles were calculated to determine what commonalities existed among the roles.

Three distinct female stereotype clusters were discriminated—one identified by instrumental traits, with feminist, career woman, lesbian, and sensual woman. Feminist was characterized as assertive-outspoken, independent, and ambitious; lesbian was rated as individualistic, independent, and assertive-outspoken; career woman was described as ambitious, intelligent, and independent; and sensual woman was characterized as ambitious, sociable, and competitive. A second cluster had predominantly expressive traits, with typical woman, wife-mother, and dumb blond. Typical woman was described as emotional, sensitive to others, and sociable; wife-mother was rated understanding, sensitive to others, and warm-affectionate; and dumb blond was characterized as sociable, emotional, dependent. A third cluster with masculine, feminine, and gender-neutral trait constellations was wallflower-brain, who was characterized as intelligent, logical-analytical, and skillful-competent.

Only two distinct male clusters were found—one predominantly defined by instrumental traits, with typical man, husband-father, professional man, jock, macho man, and plaboy. The first three in this group seemed to form a subcluster. Typical man was characterized as competitive, ambitious, and independent; husband-father was described as ambitious, dominant, and skillful-competent; and professional man was rated as competitive, ambitious, independent, aggressive, and assertive-outspoken. In the second subcluster, jock was described as competitive, active-adventurous, and aggressive; macho man was rated as aggressive, dominant, and competitive; and playboy was characterized as active-adventurous, sociable, and competitive. The second cluster had a mixed pattern of traits, with gay man and wimp-nerd. Gay man was described with "feminine" descriptors: understanding, gentle, sympathetic/tender/kind, emotional, and sensitive to others; and wimp-nerd was most characterized by "masculine" and gender-neutral traits such as intelligent, logical-analytical, and honest. (Because of space limitations, only the tables for career woman, professional man, feminist, macho man, and typical woman and typical man are included. Other tables are available on request from the first author).

Within the man–woman pairs, different patterns of traits were identified. Typical man and typical woman and husband-father and wife-mother were both negatively correlated (see Table 20.1). In each case, the man was characterized as masculine, and the woman was characterized as feminine. Jock (masculine) and dumb blond (feminine) and lesbian (masculine) and gay man (feminine) were not significantly correlated. The rest of the pairs were positively correlated: macho man and feminist, career woman and professional man, wimp-nerd and wallflower-brain, and playboy and sensual woman. For those pairs that were both characterized by instrumental traits, there were indications that gender stereotypes are still more prevalent for men. For career woman and professional man, the professional man was rated more extremely on "hard" masculine traits such as dominant, assertive-outspoken, competitive, logical-analytical, and aggressive than was career woman. Career woman was rated more ambitious, and intelligent than professional man (see Table 20.2). Macho man is rated more aggressive, dominant, competitive, active-adventurous, and sociable than is feminist, who in turn is rated more assertive-outspoken, independent, ambitious and intelligent than macho man (see Table 20.3). Playboy is rated more active-adventurous, sociable, competitive, dominant, aggressive, assertive-outspoken, independent, and with a better sense of humor than is sensual woman. Sensual woman is rated more warm-affectionate, gentle, and emotional than is playboy.

TABLE 20.1 Comparison of Rasch Scale Typicality Ratings for Typical Woman and Typical Man

Typical Woman Typicality Ratings (*N* = 40)		Typical Man Typicality Ratings (*N* = 39)	
Least typical:	3.08 Dominant	Least typical:	2.66 Emotional
	2.49 Aggressive		1.73 Dependent,
	2.10 Independent		sympathetic/
	2.01 Assertive/outspoken		tender/kind
	1.75 Competitive		1.53 Sensitive to others
	1.58 Logical/analytical		1.43 Warm/affectionate
	1.42 Individualistic		1.24 Gentle,
	1.19 Active/adventurous		understanding
	1.04 Ambitious		0.95 Appreciative, tactful
	0.43 Even-tempered		0.76 Even-tempered
	0.21 Skillful/competent		0.66 Sincere
	0.05 Conventional, happy		0.08 Happy
	0.05 Good sense of humor		− 0.02 Intelligent, honest
	− 0.17 Adaptable, interesting		− 0.31 Conventional
	− 0.33 Intelligent, honest		interesting
	− 0.41 Dependent		− 0.31 Logical/analytical
	− 0.57 Sincere		− 0.41 Individualistic
	− 0.90 Tactful		− 0.60 Assertive/outspoken,
	− 0.99 Likable		sociable, likable
	− 1.16 Appreciative		− 0.79 Skillful/competent,
	− 1.55 Warm/affectionate		adaptable
	− 1.65 Gentle, sympathetic/		− 0.89 Good sense of humor
	tender/kind		− 1.08 Aggressive
	− 1.76 Understanding		− 1.27 Dominant
	− 1.88 Sociable		− 1.36 Active/adventurous
Most typical:	− 2.00 Emotional, sensitive		− 1.74 Independent,
	to others	Most typical:	ambitious
			− 2.13 Competitive

Note. Scale values, in logits, are based on the probability that subjects would endorse each item for that role. Negative values are most typical, and positive values are least typical. The correlation between these two scales is $r = .76$, $p < .001$.

Social Desirability

The social desirability ratings indicated, for the most part, that there is a positive correlation between what is deemed typical and what is socially desirable or appropriate for both women and men. For all stereotypes except macho man and husband-father, there was a positive correlation between the typicality ratings and the social desirability ratings. Interestingly, many of the masculine traits such as dominant, aggressive, competitive, and assertive-outspoken and feminine traits such as emotional and dependent were viewed as negative or neutral for most of the subtypes. There were fewer distinct clusters when the desirability ratings

TABLE 20.2 Comparison of Rasch Scale Typicality Ratings for Career Woman and Professional Man

Career Woman/Executive/ Professional Woman Typicality Ratings (N = 37)		Professional Man/Executive/ Businessman Typicality Ratings (N = 41)	
Least typical:	2.97 Dependent	Least typical:	2.49 Dependent, sympathetic/tender/kind
	2.33 Emotional		2.37 Emotional, warm/affectionate
	1.79 Warm/affectionate		
	1.79 Sympathetic/tender/kind		2.26 Gentle
	1.62 Gentle		1.94 Sensitive to others
	1.23 Conventional		1.58 Appreciative
	1.15 Understanding, sensitive to others		1.50 Even-tempered, sincere
	0.99 Good sense of humor		1.42 Understanding, honest
	0.92 Likable		0.97 Happy
	0.84 Appreciative		0.63 Likable
	0.69 Even-tempered		0.43 Good sense of humor
	0.61 Happy		0.30 Tactful, interesting
	0.45 Sincere		−0.22 Adaptable
	0.30 Tactful		−0.35 Conventional, active/adventurous
	−0.02 Sociable		−0.62 Individualistic
	−0.10 Honest		−0.75 Sociable
	−0.27 Dominant		−1.70 Skillful/competent, intelligent
	−0.62 Active/adventurous, interesting		−1.70 Logical/analytical
	−0.71 Adaptable		−2.35 Dominant
	−0.81 Individualistic, logical/analytical		−2.63 Aggressive, assertive/outspoken
	−1.34 Aggressive, assertive/outspoken		−2.63 Independent
	−1.59 Competitive		−2.97 Ambitious
	−2.03 Skillful/competent	Most	
	−2.33 Intelligent	typical:	−3.43 Competitive
	−2.62 Independent		
Most			
typical:	−3.66 Ambitious		

Note. Scale values, in logits, are based on the probability that subjects would endorse each item for that role. Negative values are most typical, and positive values are least typical. The correlation between these two scales is $r = -.79$, $p < .001$.

were correlated because all of the correlations were positive or not significant, but the clusters generally were similar to the typicality clusters. Within pairs (same role, male vs. female), the different traits associated with the female subtypes were generally rated as more positive than those for the male, in part because the extreme instrumental traits (e.g., dominant, aggressive), more typical of males, were viewed as undesirable. This was especially noticeable in the pairs of

TABLE 20.3   Comparison of Rasch Scale Typicality Ratings for Macho Man and Feminist

Feminist Typicality Ratings (*N* = 39)		Machoman Typicality Ratings (*N* = 36)	
Least typical:	2.26 Dependent	Least typical:	3.52 Gentle, sympathetic/tender/kind
	2.02 Conventional		2.40 Sensitive to others
	1.81 Warm/affectionate		2.10 Understanding, warm/affectionate
	1.54 Even-tempered		
	1.29 Tactful, good sense of humor		1.85 Appreciative, logical/analytical
	1.21 Gentle		1.47 Intelligent
	0.99 Understanding, likable		1.31 Sincere
	0.99 Sympathetic/tender/kind		1.04 Tactful
	0.92 Happy		0.81 Emotional
	0.79 Logical/analytical		0.70 Even-tempered, happy
	0.65 Appreciative, sensitive to others		0.60 Interesting
			0.51 Likable
	0.40 Sociable		0.17 Adaptable
	0.21 Emotional, interesting		−0.06 Dependent
	0.09 Adaptable		−0.27 Conventional, skillful/competent
	−0.40 Sincere, honest		
	−0.46 Intelligent		−0.40 Good sense of humor
	−0.65 Skillful/competent		−0.96 Happy
	−1.21 Individualistic		−1.26 Sociable, ambitious
	−1.45 Dominant		−1.38 Individualistic
	−1.71 Active/adventurous		−1.70 Independent
	−1.81 Competitive		−2.45 Active/adventurous
	−2.14 Aggressive		−2.74 Assertive/outspoken
	−2.27 Ambitious		−3.43 Competitive
	−2.41 Independent		−3.85 Dominant
Most typical:	−3.48 Assertive/outspoken	Most typical:	−4.56 Aggressive

Note. Scale values, in logits, are based on the probability that subjects would endorse each item for that role. Negative values are most typical, and positive values are least typical. The correlation between these two scales is r = .69, p < .001.

typical man and typical woman, wife-mother and husband-father, feminist and macho man, and career woman and professional man. The social desirability ratings for typical man clearly show that many of the typical masculine traits are not rated as highly positive, whereas many of the typical traits for typical woman are rated as positive (see Table 20.4). In comparing the social desirability ratings for career woman and professional man, career woman was rated more positively on the traits skillful-competent, individualistic, and gentle. Professional man was rated more positively on intelligent, sociable, logical-analytical, and good sense of

TABLE 20.4 Comparison of Rasch Scale Desirability Ratings for Typical Woman and Typical Man

Typical Woman Desirability Ratings (N = 40)		Typical Man Desirability Ratings (N = 38)	
Negative:	2.97 Dependent	Negative:	2.12 Dependent
	1.99 Dominant		1.15 Emotional,
	1.87 Aggressive		aggressive,
	1.64 Conventional		conventional
	1.51 Competitive,		1.03 Dominant
	emotional		0.47 Competitive
	1.39 Assertive/outspoken		0.34 Gentle
	0.94 Logical/analytical		warm/affectionate,
	0.81 Active/adventurous		tactful
	0.59 Independent		0.21 Sensitive to others
	0.26 Individualistic		0.07 Appreciative,
	0.18 Even-tempered		individualistic,
Neutral:	0.08 Ambitious		sincere
	−0.12 Tactful		0.07 Sympathetic/tender
	−0.34 Adaptable		/kind, even-tempered
	−0.46 Happy, honest,	Neutral:	0.00 Assertive/outspoken
	appreciative		−0.30 Likable, interesting
	−0.59 Good sense of		−0.38 Understanding
	humor		−0.47 Logical/analytical,
	−0.73 Skillful/competent		ambitious
	−0.89 Likable		−0.56 Active/adventurous
	−1.07 Gentle, warm/		−0.56 Independent, honest
	affectionate,		−0.75 Happy, adaptable
	intelligent		−0.75 Good sense of
	−1.07 Sincere, interesting		humor
	−1.26 Sensitive to others		−0.85 Intelligent, sociable
	−1.49 Sociable,	Positive:	−1.20 Skillful/competent
	sympathetic/		
	tender/kind		
Positive:	−2.09 Understanding		

Note. Scale values, in logits, are based on the probability that subjects would endorse each item for that role. Negative values are most socially desirable, and positive values are least socially desirable. The correlation between these two scales is $r = .66$, $p < .001$.

humor. The masculine traits such as competitive, aggressive, dominant, and assertive-outspoken were rated neutrally, but ambitious and independent were rated positively (see Table 20.5).

DISCUSSION

The findings support the thesis that there are different roles within gender and that there are also some underlying gender stereotypes still prevalent.

TABLE 20.5 Comparison of Rasch Scale Desirability Ratings for Career Woman and Professional Man

Career Woman/Executive/ Professional Woman Desirability Ratings (*N* = 36)		Professional Man/Executive/ Businessman Desirability Ratings (*N* = 41)	
Negative:	2.06 Dependent	Negative:	2.29 Dependent
	1.81 Emotional		1.94 Emotional
	1.16 Conventional		1.23 Gentle, conventional
	1.10 Warm/affectionate		0.92 Warm/affectionate
	0.79 Sympathetic/tender/kind		0.60 Sensitive to others
	0.53 Likable		0.60 Sympathetic/tender
	0.38 Dominant, aggressive, gentle		/kind
	0.38 Understanding, sensitive to others		0.43 Individualistic, aggressive
	0.23 Good sense of humor		0.31 Even-tempered
			0.24 Sincere, appreciative
	0.06 Appreciative, active/adventurous		0.11 Dominant, assertive/outspoken, tactful
Neutral:	−0.03 Sociable	Neutral:	0.04 Understanding, happy
	−0.12 Even-tempered, sincere, honest		−0.11 Honest, competitive
	−0.12 Assertive/outspoken, competitive		−0.19 Active/adventurous, interesting
	−0.12 Logical/analytical		−0.36 Likable
	−0.22 Tactful		−0.55 Good sense of humor
	−0.32 Happy		−0.77 Independent
	−0.44 Interesting		−0.89 Logical/analytical
	−0.56 Adaptable		−1.03 Sociable
	−0.69 Individualistic		−1.18 Adaptable
	−1.01 Independent		−1.35 Ambitious
	−1.44 Ambitious intelligent		−1.79 Skillful/competent
Positive:	−2.84 Skillful/competent		
		Positive:	−2.09 Intelligent

Note. Scale values, in logits, are based on the probability that subjects would endorse each item for that role. Negative values are most socially desirable, and positive values are least socially desirable. The correlation between these two scales is *r* = .85, *p* < .001.

It is important to note that the "typical" woman and man were stereotyped in a traditional way, although the social desirability ratings of these traits seem to have changed. The masculine traits tended to be viewed as negative or neutral, for both men and women, even in "masculine" roles. Such findings are in clear contrast to the "traditional" stereotype of men, in which instrumental traits are supposed to be highly valued (Broverman et al., 1972). Another important issue is whether the stereotype of the "typical" man or woman is more pervasive than the role stereotypes. We would argue that in most interactions with others, the role and gender stereotypes are combined, as our data tend to show. It is very rare that we know only people's gender with no knowledge of other aspects of them, such as role. When we do have role information, our stereotypes of men and women become much more differentiated, and even our preponderance of masculine stereotypes for male roles show subtle distinctions.

In comparing men and women in "masculine" roles, especially businessperson, we found that the men were rated with the more extreme "masculine" traits, such as dominant, aggressive, competitive, and assertive-outspoken. Thus, there is some evidence that men and women performing the same masculine role may not be perceived the same way. From these findings, we would predict that people might expect different behaviors from, and interact differently with, male and female businesspeople. For example, people who might expect female businesspeople not to be as aggressive and competitive as male businesspeople may be less likely to interact with the women in a way that elicits aggressiveness. However, people may also be more likely to react negatively to aggression from women than from men in the field of business (although the trait aggression was rated equally neutral for each role on the social desirability scale).

It is also interesting to note that intelligence is rated as highly typical of career woman, more typical than for professional man or typical woman. It may be that intelligence is a more salient trait in our perceptions of career woman than professional man or that people believe a woman has to be more intelligent and ambitious to excel in a traditionally male field.

Our study did not allow us to conclude whether these stereotypes are a result of "real" differences in behavior of men and of women in these roles or whether we assign some old stereotypes for the equivalent behaviors of men and women in similar roles. Future research aimed at controlled behavioral studies is needed to assess this distinction. Given that women in masculine roles are not rated as possessing the "extreme masculine" traits to the same degree as the men in those masculine roles, it would also be worthwhile to investigate whether women are more negatively valued for such behaviors when they do exhibit them, especially using people performing in "real life" situations. In addition, the implications of the belief that career women are more intelligent than professional men for our interactions with businesswomen and businessmen needs further exploration.

REFERENCES

Allport, G. W. (1954). *The nature of prejudice*. Reading, MA: Addison-Wesley.

Ashmore, R. D., & Del Boca, F. K. (1981). Conceptual approaches to stereotypes and stereotyping. In D. L. Hamilton (Ed.), *Cognitive processes in stereotyping and intergroup behavior* (pp. 1–36). Hillsdale, NJ: Erlbaum.

Broverman, I. K., Vogel, S. R., Broverman, D. M., Clarkson, F. E., & Rosenkrantz, P. S. (1972). Sex-role stereotypes: A current appraisal. *Journal of Social Issues, 28,* 59–78.

Clifton, A. K., McGrath, D., & Wick, B. (1976). Stereotypes of women: A single category? *Sex Roles, 2,* 135–148.

Deaux, K., Winton, W., Crowley, M., & Lewis, L. L. (1985). Level of categorization and content of gender stereotypes. *Social Cognition, 3,* 145–167.

England, E. M., & Hyland, D. T. (1986, April). *Role based subcategories of females and males.* Paper presented at the 57th Annual Meeting of the Eastern Psychological Association, New York.

Katz, D., & Braly, K. (1933). Racial stereotypes of one hundred college students. *Journal of Abnormal and Social Psychology, 28,* 280–290.

Sherriffs, A. C., & McKee, J. P. (1957). Qualitative aspects of beliefs about men and women. *Journal of Personality, 25,* 451–464.

Williams, J. E., & Bennett, S. M. (1975). The definition of sex stereotypes via the Adjective Check List. *Sex Roles, 1,* 327–337.

Wright, B. D., & Stone, M. H. (1979). *Best test design.* Chicago: MESA Press.

Conclusion

This collection of chapters brings to mind two opposing constellations of observations. On the one hand, we are reminded of the institutionalized, integrated, and internalized sexism, racism, and other "isms" that continue to affect women's lives. On the other hand, we read in these pages of increasingly sophisticated theory, research, and techniques of psychotherapy that have evolved from the study of the psychology of women. Many of these chapters address changes over time. Some analyze different theoretical formulations and their current and historical pertinence and value. Others identify new models to empower women to take control of their lives.

The chapters on the practice of therapy focus on the fundamental daily problems of women in general, women of color, and women as victims and describe the ways in which feminist therapy can help to resolve those problems. The gender theory chapters bring into focus ways women can assert our place in the history of psychology and produce changes in educational systems, societal paradigms, and our roles in the discipline of psychology. The chapters in the research section acquaint us with new findings and demonstrate ways to broaden and demasculinize psychological research. These chapters leave us thinking, as feminist analyses always do: what else is there to explore and reveal, what new directions lie ahead for feminist psychology?

In a time when many walls have been breached, when new opportunities have opened up to new generations of women, it is more urgent than ever to maintain forward movement and to avoid complacency. Many positive changes have occurred in women's lives as a result of feminist psychology. The psychology of women, both within our discipline and in the larger society, is still overshadowed by sexist and racist compromises and rationalizations. The authors and editors who produced this book set their sights higher—toward a truly nonsexist, nonracist society. We hope that our work answers some questions and raises others.

Index